Siwa Oasis

Ahmed Fakhry

Siwa Oasis

The American University in Cairo Press

113 Sharia Kasr el Aini, Cairo, Egypt
420 Fifth Avenue, New York NY, 10018
www.aucpress.com

Originally published in 1973 and reprinted in 1982 as *The Oases of Egypt, Volume One: Siwa Oasis*. Reprinted as *Siwa Oasis* in 1990, 1993, 1997, 2001 by arrangement with Ali Fakhry.

Dar el Kutub No. 4338/85
ISBN 977 424 123 1

Printed in Egypt by the American University in Cairo Press

Contents

Illustrations

Preface

From the beginning of my archeological researches in the deserts in 1937 until 1973. I was assisted, in most of my trips, by some of the officials of the Antiquities Department of Egypt. I am much indebted to them all, and express to them my thanks.

A simple form of the universally recognized system of transliteration was followed in this book to acquaint the reader with the exact pronunciation of Arabic names, except in two cases :

1) where English forms of Arabic names are common, such as Alexandria, Suez, Luxor, etc.

2) where Arabic names are quoted from European references.

However, this system was not literally applied to ancient non-Arabic names, such as Hieroglephic and Berber, which were presented in the nearest forms to their actual pronunciation.

My greatest gratitude is to the late Mr. Etienne Drioton, the eminent Director General of the Antiquities Department from 1936 to 1952. It was his constant encouragement, sympathy and honest understanding which made me continue my interest in the desert researches besides my other duties in the Antiquities Department, and to overcome all the obstacles, especially during the difficult years of the Second World War.

Since 1968, Dr. Gamal Mukhtar, the Under-Secretary of State for Egyptian Antiquities, and the late Dr. Gamal Mehrez, the Director-General of the Antiquities Department did all within their power to enable me to resume and continue my work in the Oases ; I am grateful to both of them.

It gives me also a great pleasure to mention with gratitude my indebtedness to the German Archeological Institute, to Dr. Endre Ungar of Mexico City and to the University of Chicago Press for their encouragement and financial help. Without their assistance I could never have accomplished some of my trips in the desert or prepared many of the drawings or the photographs published in these three volumes.

I wish to thank also the American University in Cairo Press for their full cooperation. I am particularly indebted to Dr. Ahmad Al-Sawi, Assistant Director, for his fruitful efforts and useful suggestions which were always of great help to me. The introduction and the first two chapters were edited by Mrs. Marsden Jones and the balance by Mason Rossiter Smith, Director of AUC Press.

Ahmed Fakhry

Cairo, March 8, 1973

Introduction

The Three Deserts and the Five Oases

The Desert

This book is not concerned simply with the antiquities of Siwa, as the reader might expect. Nor is it a book of anthropology dealing with man, his customs and the like, nor a book of travel that deals with certain things seen or experienced by an author. Yet it includes these, in addition to many other topics.

The desert is like the sea; the word gives the hearer a certain undefined thrill and fills his heart with a feeling of mystery, although not everyone reacts to it in the same way. For one person, the desert is simply a waste, an endless sea of sand, full of danger, which may be haunted also by invisible and mysterious powers. For another, it is the setting of the ancient Arab romances of love. Someone else might think of the desert as the home of that wise and patient animal, the camel, and its owners in their dark tents. The imagination of another might dwell upon church history, meditating upon those great fathers who had fled into the desert and withstood all its hardships because of their faith. Yet another might call to mind a shady, cool corner beside one of the springs of an oasis, surrounded by groves of palm trees and plantations. In the flight of his fancy, he may steal a glance at the young girls heading for the spring. They appear wrapped up in colourful attire and with silver ornaments, filling the air with their habitual gossip and giggling.

As for the archeologist, the desert is the home of many surface flint finds, temples, tombs, ancient towns, fortresses and monasteries, which are now in ruins and still not properly studied or excavated. The desert is a fruitful field for future work, but how can the archeologist develop it without support and subsidy and a well-organised expedition ? He always faces one question : "Who is going to sponsor such work ?" Nowadays, everybody seems to be interested in other fields. Government staff, in particular, are reluctant to take up duties in the desert, mechanically discharging their tasks there. They tend to conform to a certain type, who while away spend their leisure time in brooding over a city life of gaiety and amusement, and the imaginary comfort of their homes there. The word "desert" irritates them and makes them grumble resentfully. However, it is unfair to be cruel to them ; one has either to like the desert or dislike it, if one lives there for a long time. It depends on the person himself and his disposition towards it. I must confess that I love the desert and its people and I love all that belongs to it. It is true that I am an archeologist and that my main interest lies in ancient history and antiquities, but whenever I hear the word "oases" or the word "desert", many pictures float through my mind. It is true that all these pictures have monuments in the background, but the scenes in the foreground differ.

Sometimes I see myself travelling in an old car which breaks down from time to time and I have to help in pushing it through the sandy spots. At times, I recollect the thirst which has brought me to the point of perishing more than once. All these difficulties I dismiss with a shrug of the shoulder, as my fancy returns to pleasant recollections and memories. However, such reveries do not last long. I look back to the success of my work and the enjoyable times I have spent in this enchanting desert, not to mention its inhabitants whom I met over so many years. Life there, as I knew it, was not easy. Many of my journeys were made by camel and I lived either in tents or in the houses of the oases ; occasionally, I stayed in one of the government rest-houses. The beauty of the desert lay in its simplicity and its being far from modern material comforts. I loved it that way and enjoyed the so-called difficulties of desert life. In fact, there was nothing difficult or unbearable ; it is an interesting experience to test yourself, in order to see whether you can do the things which the men and women of the desert can do (Fig. 1).

My First Trip

My first trip to the interior of the desert for the study of its antiquities was in December 1933, when I was Inspector of Antiquities at Luxor. I travelled by car from Luxor to Wādī Daghbaj in the Eastern Desert and returned to the Nile Valley at Idfū, passing by the famous temple of Bīr al-Kanāyis (Temple of al-Radīsīyah). However, my keen interest in the monuments of the oases began in the year 1937. Before making my first trip to the Kharga (Khārijah) and Dakhla (Dākhilah) oases in October of that year, I spent a few months collecting all the data relative to the monuments known to be there. This was the beginning of a long and fruitful attachment, which has lasted for more than thirty-five years. In this respect, I dare say that there was a mutual love which developed between me and the antiquities of the desert and its people.

When I say "my first trip to the desert", I do not mean my first treading on sand or venturing a few miles into its wastes. All my life I have done so, because Egypt is a land bordered on both sides by deserts. Most of its monuments exist on the edge of the desert, and some of them are now three or four miles distant from cultivation. Moreover, my original home in Egypt was al-Fayyūm, which is more or less an oasis surrounded by the desert. I also had relatives who lived at its edge, and, as a schoolboy I loved to go there and live with them and ride a few miles in the Ḥamrāyah, i.e. the open desert. For the first time in my life, I became fascinated by its beauty and I learned something about the life on its fringes ; not only the life of men and women, but also the lives of animals, birds, plants and insects. I heard many exaggerated stories about the Bedouin. I do not recollect many of the details of these early visits, but I do remember the stories and the man who was first to tell me tales about the oases and made me, in later years, try to fathom the mysterious nature of the desert (Fig. 2).

Fig. 1. A mid-way rest in the open desert.

Uncle Sa'īd

I was eight years old when I first saw 'Amm (uncle) Sa'īd, an old negro in the family house at al-Fayyūm. He had been kidnapped from his home, somewhere in Africa, when he was a child and had been sold as a slave in Siwa (Sīwah) Oasis, where he was brought up. He lived there until the age of twenty-five, when he had to run for his life after one of his many romantic involvements. In those days there was a regular caravan route between Siwa and al-Fayyūm, and so he accompanied some Bedouin on their return to the Nile Valley. Slavery was abolished and he became a free man. As a free labourer he lived with some of my relatives for more than fifteen years, and after that he decided to go back to the scene of his youth and his first love. From time to time he used to come back to al-Fayyūm with one of the caravans, bringing some loads of dates as a present. He would spend a few weeks among us, then turn up again after several years.

It was in the year 1913 that I first saw 'Amm Sa'īd. He was stricken by his years ; the women used to say that he was over ninety, but really this was much exaggerated ; for he was certainly not more than seventy. To me, he looked very ancient and time-worn. I could not fully understand his broken Arabic, mixed as it was with the Siwan language, which is not Arabic but a Berber dialect. He was short, broad-shouldered and well-built, with a close-cut head of hair and a very light beard, not white but half grey. His features were typically negroid and his skin was as black as a crow. He had returned to al-Fayyūm after a five-year's absence. On his arrival it was already dark, about two hours after sunset, and nearly everybody rushed to the yard of the house to welcome him. Some of the men hastened to relieve the camel of its burden of dates and the children dashed in, as swift as lightning, to see what was going on. In less than half an hour Uncle Sa'īd was heartily eating his meal amidst the fussing children. The boys were bold enough to come nearer to him, but the girls kept afar. I cannot tell now whether they were shy or afraid. I was taken aback by his almost toothless mouth and kept watching him while he was munching and eating his fill. When he was informed of my identity, he stopped eating and tears filled his eyes, for he remembered my father who had died when I was two and a half years old. He got up and carrying me in his arms began to perform some kind of rhythmic dance, calling out, in memory of my father whom he loved, in sweetly chosen phrases. I remember that evening clearly ; I recall how I felt so close to him and how I sat on the wooden sofa beside him and gladly accepted his invitation to eat with him. My first request was to ask him to tell me all about my father. On the other days of that one-month visit, as well as on his other visit two years later, I always insisted on hearing his stories. Uncle

Fig. 2. Wind erosion — on the caravan route between Baḥrīyah Oasis and Wādī al-Rayyān south of al-Fayyūm.

Sa'īd did not return after 1915 ; there was the First World War and the Western Desert, particularly Siwa, began to be the scene of activities of the Sanūsī order. When the war was over, he did not return. When I visited Siwa in 1938, I made many inquiries about him but nobody could help me. I did not expect to find him alive after all those years ; however, if he was dead I was eager to visit his grave, if he had actually died in this oasis, but all my inquiries were without avail.

I loved his stories and he repeated most of them to me many times. It was he who made me acquainted with the oasis and the customs of its dwellers. Uncle Sa'īd was also the one who introduced me to the life of the Bedouin near the coast, and the stories of the caravans. I was too young and inexperienced to appreciate his adventures in love and his little romances, but I was thrilled by the stories of his quarrels and fights. I liked to hear from him the Siwan folksongs, and in spite of his advanced years, he was always ready to dance — especially the dance of the **zaggālah** (unmarried garden labourers) of Siwa. One day, while he was imitating a young Bedouin girl dance, he was taken by surprise by the entry of one of my uncles, arrayed, as far as he could, to look like a girl. The story which I loved to hear repeatedly described how, when Uncle Sa'īd was about twenty years old, his master wanted to kill him and he had to hide in a certain garden in Siwa for a whole month. At nightfall, when the oasis was hushed in slumber, he used to go out naked as a newborn baby, smeared all over with olive oil, so as to slip away if anybody tried to catch him. The inhabitants believed that this garden was haunted by a black ghost swinging to and fro among the palm trees. This rumour frightened most people and made them keep away from the place, save for a young woman who knew what was going on. She used to dress as a boy and meet him at night and give him food. She was his first love and the cause of all his early troubles, and it goes without saying that it was she who inspired in him the fighting spirit and the feeling of independence which were deeply rooted in his soul throughout his life.

In my childish imagination, I thought of myself doing the same thing in the gardens at Siwa, swinging in the trees, smearing my body with olive oil and frightening the people, but I left out the love element in his story.

I saw Siwa a quarter of a century later and I remembered the stories of my old friend, but my trip was for another purpose — the study of its antiquities. I realized how brave the girl was who took the risk of going out in the dead of night to meet him. She must have had a most unusual character, because the Siwans are very superstitious. It is also strictly forbidden for any woman to leave her house after sunset, or even go alone to the gardens in daylight.

In later years, there were other things in the desert which called me, rather than the stories of Uncle Sa'īd. These were the ancient monuments and the people who lived around them.

It was a new field for me as an Egyptian archeologist. I love pioneer work and here was a challenging and difficult job. I have given my heart to the exploration of our oases and over many years have excavated many of their monuments and travelled along the ancient caravan routes. From time to time, I have managed to find a few months to spend there — and still do when my other duties and obligations permit. Most of the results of my excavations were published in due course, but there are still many archeological discoveries which have not been disclosed. However, all my books dealt with the monuments, rather than the inhabitants of the oases and their customs.

The introduction of the motor car has changed the life of the desert dwellers in a fundamental sense. Moreover, Egypt had started many new projects for reclaiming more land. More than thirty-four million Egyptians live on the product of less than six million acres; an alarming fact. The High Dam will solve a part of the problem, but more land is needed. It means a fight between the people and the desert, and there can be no doubt that many of the pioneer projects of the Egyptian General Desert Development Authority (EGDDA) have met with great success. They will add several hundreds of thousands of acres to the cultivated areas in the oases and near the coast in a few years. Inevitably, this will endanger local cultures, because many dwellers in the new villages will be immigrants from the Nile Valley.

The Deserts of Egypt

The deserts of Egypt are a part of the desert belt which begins at the Atlantic coast of North Africa and extends to the Red Sea, Sinai, Arabia, Iraq and continues eastward to Central Asia. The Nile Valley itself is, in fact, nothing but an oasis in this desert. The total area of Egypt is about one million square kilometres, from which less than four per cent is cultivated land.(1) Egypt measures 1,073 kms. at its greatest length from north to south, and 1,226 kms. at its greatest breadth from east to west. It embraces a total area of almost a million square kilometres.(2)

More than 99 per cent of the total population of the country (30,076,000 in 1966 and estimated in 1971 to be over 34 millions) are settled within the 35,000 square kilometres comprising the Nile Valley and the Delta, al-Fayyūm Province and the settlements along the Suez Canal ; less than one per cent of the population inhabit the remaining 965,000 square kilometres of the country.(3)

---

(1) About 36 per cent of the area of the land surface of the earth can be classified as desert. The area of the arid zone in North Africa is 17,750,000 sq. kms. (See Peveril Meigs, **Arid Zone Hydrology**, UNESCO, 1953).

(2) Ball, **Contributions to the Geography of Egypt** (Cairo, 1953), p. 1.

(3) **Ibid.**, p. 2.

In that great sea of sand, we find the fertile lands of the Delta and Upper Egypt along the Nile and a number of oases scattered in the Western Desert. The best known amongst them are Siwa, Baḥrīyah, Farafra, Kharga and Dakhla, besides other smaller oases which have a few inhabitants or are nowadays uninhabited.(1)

We can divide the deserts of Egypt into three : Sinai, the Eastern (or Arabian) Desert, and the Western (or Libyan) Desert (Fig. 3).

The Desert of Sinai is a peninsula with the Mediterranean sea to its north, Palestine to the east and the Suez Canal in the west ; its southern triangle lies between the Gulf of Suez and the Gulf of 'Aqabah (Aqaba). It has a total area of 61,000 square kilometres. The southern part has several high mountains, and its Bedouin inhabitants live scattered along its different valleys. Only at the village of al-Ṭūr in the south, at al-'Arīsh and Shaykh Zuwayd in the north, do we find settlements of any considerable size. According to the census of 1966, the number of inhabitants of the Sinai Governorate was 130,849.

al-'Arīsh	50,675
al-Shaykh Zuwayd	28,591
al-Qanṭarah east	15,840
Abū Zinaymah	8,616
al-Ṭūr	2,230
Bīr al-'Abd	12,567
al-Shaṭṭ	5,238
al-Ḥassānah	4,789
Nikhil	2,303

The inhabitants do not live in one village, but are scattered along the valleys and near the different wells. Sinai is rich in minerals, some of which were exploited by the ancient Egyptians from the dawn of their civilization, and they have left many inscriptions and temples in the districts of al-Maghārah and Sarabīṭ al-Khādim. There are also the remains of ancient monuments near the northern coast along the great military road between Egypt and Palestine. There are also many remains in the

(1) The total population of the four frontier governorates (in 1966) was 251,858. This figure included the Palestinians who settled after 1948 in Rafaḥ, Shaykh Zuwayd and al-'Arīsh districts, and labourers who work in the oil fields and the mines of Sinai.

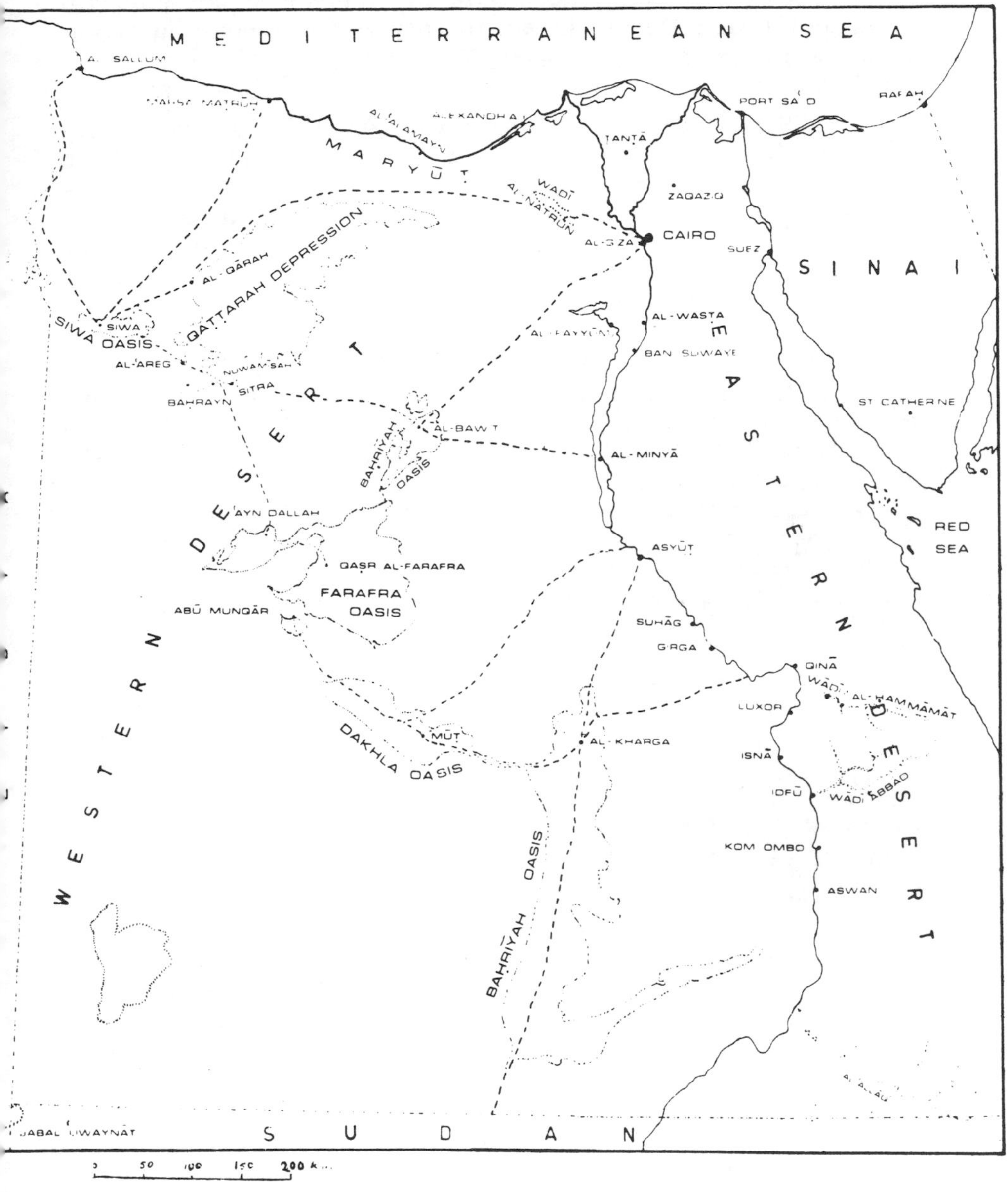

Fig. 3. Map of Egypt : The three deserts (Sinai, the Eastern Desert and the Western Desert) and the five Oases.

south, dating from Christian times, especially near the beautiful oasis of Fīrān, the most important being the famous Saint Catherine's Monastery.

The Eastern Desert has an area of about 223,000 square kilometres. It extends eastward from the Nile Valley to the Suez Canal and the Red Sea. It has several mountains, particularly near the Red Sea, whose peaks rise to a considerable height, the two highest among them being Jabal al-Shāyib (2,181 metres) and Jabal Ḥamāṭah (1,978 metres). Its water sources are barely sufficient for the maintenance of the nomad population and their animals. These sources consist of springs, wells and rock-pools in the mountains, but nowhere do we find any important springs such as those in the oases of the Western Desert. Besides the Bedouin, who live in tents, there are a few other places populated by settlers. The total number of inhabitants in the Eastern Desert (generally called the Governorate of the Red Sea) was 37,818 according to the census of 1966. The densely populated spots are near the coast of the Red Sea, where phosphates and other minerals are mined and petroleum extracted. The largest concentrations are at Quṣayr (13,695 persons) and Hurghādah (4,087 in the village itself and 2,082 near the harbour), and 2,274 at Safājah, where the inhabitants depend upon distilled sea water. Gold and other minerals were mined by the ancient Egyptians in the different regions of the desert. Many inscriptions were recorded by early expeditions on the rocks of the valleys and on stelae ; examples can be seen at Wādī al-Ḥammāmāt and Wādī al-Hūdī. The remains of ancient monuments lie scattered near the ancient mines and some of the ancient harbours of the Red Sea. The Christian period is well represented by the two monasteries of Saint Paul and Saint Anthony.

The Western Desert embraces an area of 681,000 square kilometres, or more than two-thirds of the whole area of Egypt. It is one of the most arid regions in the world, the sources of water within it being in many places hundreds of kilometres apart.(1)

There is a high plateau of Nubian sandstone in the south, extending from the mountains of 'Uwaynāt (over 1,800 metres) which descends slowly till it reaches the depression containing the oases of Kharga and Dakhla. To the north of the depression, a limestone plateau (500 metres above sea level) extends to the depressions of Farafra and Baḥrīyah. The surface of this plateau slopes northward and ends in a great depression, some parts of

---

(1) Ball, **Contributions...**, pp. 9 - 10.

which are below sea level, such as the depressions of Siwa and Qaṭṭārah.(1) To the north of the last depression rises a third plateau, averaging 200 metres above sea level, which slopes northward toward the coast of the Mediterranean between Alexandria and Sallūm. The main depressions are those of :

Dakhla	33,780
Kharga	25,605
Farafra	1,010
Baḥrīyah	9,601
Siwa	5,169

There are other depressions containing only salt lakes and salt marshes and consequently uninhabitable. The largest and deepest of these is the Qaṭṭārah, the floor of which descends at its lowest point to 134 metres below sea level.

At different places in the depressions of the Western Desert, we find long parallel lines of high sand dunes, which extend in a north-south direction, sometimes for great distances ; they are almost impassable for cars. Many of these, at Kharga and Baḥrīyah, already cover parts of the existing villages. The most famous is the series of sand dunes which are to be found east of the line of the oases, extending to the south of Kharga. They are about 700 kilometres in length.

Each oasis has a culture which differs in many respects from the others ; but we can say in general that Kharga and Dakhla constitute one cultural group, and the two oases of Baḥrīyah and Farafra also form one group.

The coastal regions, as well as all the oases, contain monuments which date from different periods of Egyptian history. The monuments of the five oases will be discussed in some detail in the following chapters. Temples, painted tombs, the remains of towns, fortresses and Christian monuments exist in all the oases and point to a flourishing past at certain periods of their long history.

The Present Day Inhabitants

Before concluding this general survey, a few remarks are essential. It is wrong to think that all the desert dwellers live in houses or tents, or speak the Arabic language, or have the same customs. Those who live on the coast in Sinai reside in villages,

---

(1) The total number of inhabitants of the five oases was 75,165 according to the 1966 census ; along the coast there were 97,477 and, at Wādī al-Naṭrūn, 10,480. The total number living in the Western Desert, along the coast and in Wādī al-Naṭrūn was 183,065 in 1966.

but the nomads in the interior live in tents and belong to many tribes with different traditions. However, they are closely related to the Bedouin of Jordan and the northern parts of Saudi Arabia and of Palestine. Although they have different dialects, Arabic is their mother tongue. Those who live in the northern part of the Eastern Desert are also Arab Bedouin, but further south are the 'Abābdah, who belong to the Hamitic group. A few hundred years ago, they had their own language, but nowadays they speak Arabic only ; many are still nomads. Further south, there live the Bishārīn nomads, who have their own language. Among them we find a number who speak Arabic as a second language. These Bishārīn are closely related to the Hamitic groups, living along the southern coast of the Red Sea and have a culture of their own. Their territory is south of the latitude of Aswan.

The inhabitants of the Western Desert are different. Near the coast live some branches of Arab tribes, having their relatives in Libya and on the west side of the Nile (in Biḥīrah, al-Fayyūm and al-Minyā Governorates). Many of them now live in villages or settlements, but there are still a few who lead a nomad life in their tents. They speak Arabic, but they have their own dialects, customs and laws, which differ considerably from those of the inhabitants of Sinai.

The Five Oases of the Western Desert

All of the oases dwellers live in villages. If the visitor to the oases sees tents there, these belong either to the Bedouin from the coast, coming for pasture or trade, or to officials and their labourers who happen to be doing some temporary work there.

Every one of the oases has its own traditions and has a dialect which differs from those of the others. Anyone who knows the desert can distinguish between a native of Kharga and an inhabitant of Dakhla. There are even differences between the dialects of the villages of each oasis. All four oases have Arabic as a mother tongue, but Siwa is different ; Siwan is one of the dialects of Berber. The men, and a number of the women, understand Arabic quite well, but they speak it as a second language. Many of the older people, and especially the women, do not understand Arabic at all. Young people who have been to school, or have lived in Alexandria or on the coast, speak Arabic fluently.

1

The Oasis of Siwa A General Survey

Four of the oases of the Western Desert have much in common. All their inhabitants use the Arabic language as their mother tongue and most of their customs and traditions are not unknown to many of those who live in villages at certain points in the Nile Valley.

Baḥrīyah and Farafra can be compared with the villages of the governorates of al-Fayyūm, al-Minyā and Asyūṭ; Kharga and Dakhla have something in common with the villages of the governorates of Sūhāg and Qinā, with which they have been connected for thousands of years. But Siwa is different. Its general outlook, the architecture of the houses, the clothes and features of its inhabitants, their language, their attitude toward strangers and their way of life inside and outside their houses all remind us that we are no longer in the Nile Valley. This was my feeling when I set foot in the oasis in August 1938, and it has not much changed in subsequent years. On my last visit, in May 1972, I felt that a change had occurred which narrowed the gap between Siwa and villages in the other oases and in the Nile Valley. The children, girls and boys, have deserted their traditional clothes and are now dressed in hideous school uniforms. New, modern buildings which spoil the landscape have come into existence in some districts and more strangers, especially labourers from Cairo and Upper Egypt, appear in the marketplace. But many of the changes are only on the surface. They have been forced on the people, and I wonder if they will ever have any serious impact on the life of the Siwans until twenty or thirty years have elapsed. Siwa is still the most interesting of all the oases, not only for its place in history, but because of its beauty and its people's peculiar ways of life (Fig. 4).

In very ancient times, donkeys were used for transportation between Siwa and other places. But since the introduction of the camel into the Egyptian Desert, and its use for transportation in Ptolemaic times, it has become the most serviceable friend for the Bedouin.

The camel provided the principal means of transportation prior to the introduction of the motor-car ; the first automobile entered Siwa in 1917. Nowadays, the Siwans use the bus which runs twice a week between Marsā Maṭrūḥ and the oasis, but before the bus service began, they depended entirely in travelling to the coast, on the trucks which since the late twenties have been used to transport crops. The camels seen occasionally nowadays in Siwa, belong to the Bedouin, who come to buy dates or for pasturing.

The Routes between Siwa and the Outside

Visitors to Siwa use the principal main route connecting Siwa with Marsā Maṭrūḥ. It is quite safe for cars and is substantially the same ancient caravan route which connected the two places from time immemorial. This was the route used by all who came to Siwa from the other side of the Mediterranean to consult its oracle ; Paraetonium (Marsā Maṭrūḥ) was the harbour at which they landed and from there they took this desert route. It was used by Alexander the Great when he visited the oasis in the year 331 B.C. and by the great majority of visitors before and after him. It is called on the maps "Masrab al-Isṭabl", but is known to the Bedouin under the name of Darb al-Maḥashas ; it is some 300 kilometres in length. The present-day telephone line is built along it and travellers can be guided by it from the time they leave Marsā Maṭrūh until they enter the town of Siwa. There was a plan for building a good road to Siwa after the visit of King Fu'ād to the oasis in 1928 ; but after a part of it was completed the project was abandoned. The first 125 kilometres after Marsā Maṭrūḥ and the last 25 kilometres before reaching Siwa were macadamized, but the intervening distance is still a desert track. Cars need some seven to nine hours to cover this route (including time for one or two stops), because it is rather rough going over most of the unpaved section. However, it is free of sand dunes, and the traveller will be quite safe if he bears in mind that he must never lose sight of the telephone poles. At kilometre 160 from Marsā Maṭrūḥ, the traveller reaches Bīr al-Nuṣṣ, where there is a water cistern and a wooden hut occupied by a policeman; from here, telephone messages can be conveyed to Siwa or Marsā Maṭrūḥ. Until 1939, there stood near al-Buwayb, before reaching Bīr al-Nuṣṣ, a large, wooden house erected originally in 1928 for King Fu'ād to spend the night. Thereafter it was convenient for travellers, but it was removed at the outbreak of the Second World War, since it was a well-known landmark along the route.

There are several caravan routes connecting Siwa with the coast, besides Masrab al-Isṭabl already mentioned; the most important are those between al-Garawlah (on the coast east of Marsā Maṭrūḥ) and Siwa, passing the Qaṭṭārah Spring and the small oasis of Qāret Umm al-Ṣughayyar (sometimes called "al-Qārah" only), and about 350 kms. long; and Masrab Diqnāsh, which connects Siwa with Sallūm, a distance of about 310 kms.

There are three other routes; one going west to Jaghbūb, which was Egyptian until 1926 and then given to Libya. Another route connects Siwa with Baḥrīyah Oasis, passing al-Zaytūn and the small uninhabited oases of al-'Areg, Sitra, and al-Baḥrayn. The third connects Siwa with the Nile Valley; it reaches Qāret Umm al-Ṣughayyar and then continues through the Qaṭṭārah Depression until it reaches the spring of al-Mughrah(1). From al-Mughrah it goes on to Wādī al-Naṭrūn, a branch reaching to al-Fayyūm, while the main caravan route continues to the village of Kirdāsah, near the Pyramids of Giza. This route connected Siwa with the ancient Egyptian capital of Memphis; it was used by Alexander cn his return to the Nile Valley after his visit to Siwa.

Cars can be used on all these routes, but such trips should only be undertaken with strong cars fitted with balloon tyres and with the help of desert guides recommended by the Frontier Administration. Neglecting this rule can have unhappy consequences and some adventurous but incautions motorists have lost their lives.

The Town of Siwa

After leaving the coast at Marsā Maṭrūḥ, the traveller to Siwa observes no trees or fields until he reaches the oasis. He might see some small green shrubs at the side of the road within the first fifty or sixty kilometres, which are within the Mediterranean rain belt; but after climbing the plateau approximately seventy kilometres from the shore, there is nothing but barren desert until the traveller finds himself descending the escarpment and the palm groves of Siwa greet his eyes.

The caravans used to cover this route in eight or nine days. We can imagine how pleased the travellers were when they found themselves near the flowing springs, palm groves and other trees, in whose shade they could rest after more than a week of continuous travel.

The highest parts of the plateau are a little over 240 metres above sea level (the average is 200 metres), but the floor of the

---

(1) Before reaching al-Mughrah, at Maṭ'an Frayn, there is a route which goes northwards to al-'Alamayn on the coast.

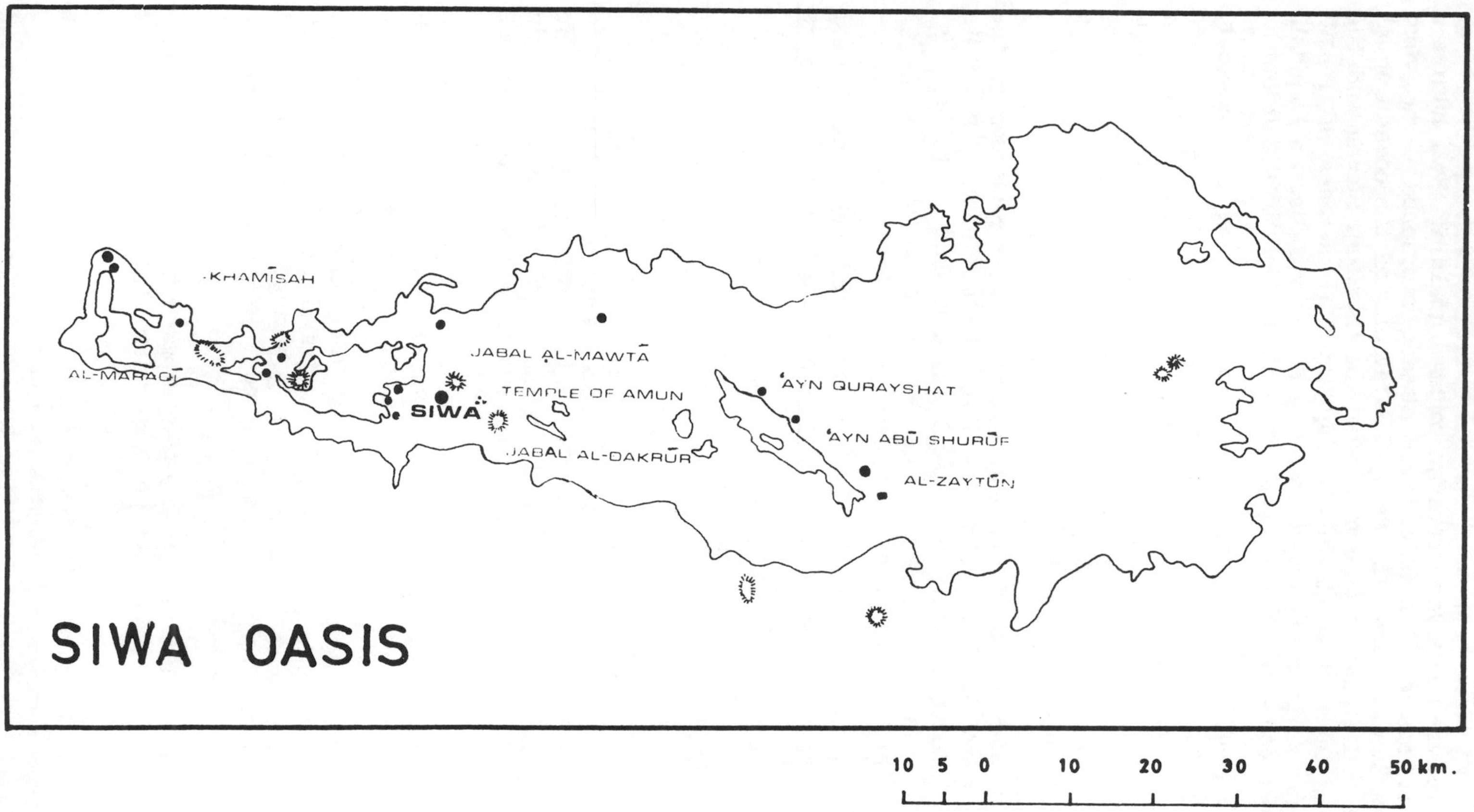

Fig. 4. Map of Siwa.

oasis averages 18 metres below sea level. (R.L.: 11 — 22 metres). The depression of Siwa is some 82 kms. long from east to west — between 25° 16' and 26° 7' east, and 29° 7' and 29° 21' north. Its western boundary begins at al-Marāqī and its eastern at al-Zaytūn; the town of Siwa is roughly at the centre. The breadth of the depression is about 9 kilometres at the west and reaches about 28 kilometres in the east, but is narrow in the middle. In addition to the town of Siwa, in which live the majority of the inhabitants, there are a few villages scattered through the depression, each having a small population: al-Marāqī, Khamīsah, Abū Shurūf and al-Zaytūn are the more important. There are several salt lakes at Siwa; the largest is the famous lake of al-Zaytūn which begins near Jabal al-Dakrūr and extends for more than twenty-five kilometres, with an average width of five kilometres.(1)

The ancient city of Siwa was originally at Aghūrmī, where the remains of the two principal temples of the oasis still stand, the Temple of the Oracle which stood on a huge rock in the middle of the plain, and the Temple of Umm 'Ubaydah which is at a distance of about one kilometre to the east (Fig. 5).

During the middle ages, the ancient town suffered greatly from the attacks of the Berber and Arab Bedouin; many of the latter lived in their tents in the oasis where they found good pasture, plenty of water and abundant palm groves.

In the local history of Siwa (generally called the Siwan Manuscript) which is kept by one of the families of the oasis, we find interesting details concerning the origin of the different families and some of their ancient laws and customs. The number of men of the original inhabitants of the oasis diminished to forty, belonging to seven families. They decided to leave their ancient village and choose a new settlement; there they built a new fortified village on a hill, for greater security. The new settlement is the present-day town of Siwa, founded, according to the Siwan Manuscript, in the year 600 A.H. (A.D. 1203); they called it "Shālī", which means in the Siwan language "the town". They built their new houses inside a strong girdle wall, which for purpose of defence, had only one entrance. This entrance still exists; it is called al-Bāb Inshāl, a mixture of two Arabic and Berber words, "The entrance to the town"; it stands at the northern side of the old girdle wall, near the ancient mosque, and leads by an ascending narrow street to the interior of the town.

A century later, another entrance, al-Bāb Atrāt "the new entrance", was made in the south side of the wall near the oil press; it was useful for those who wanted to avoid passing in

(1) The other larger lakes are those of Khamīsah and al-Marāqī in the eastern part of the oasis.

front of the **agwād,** heads of the families, who held their daily meetings near the main entrance. It also afforded advantages whenever the town was threatened or attacked by strangers, since it was known only to the inhabitants and no one could detect its position from outside.

Fig. 5. A part of the town of Siwa.

As the number of Siwans increased, they planted more gardens and many of them were forced to come and go more often. Moreover, it was their custom to forbid the women to go outside the walls of the town ; and so they decided, a century later, to open a third entrance in the wall. The women were given the right to go out into the gardens through this third entrance only, thus to avoid the main gate, near which the **agwād** used to sit, and the second gate, not far from the oil press where many men were accustomed to loiter. This third gate was called "Bāb Qaddūmah" because it was built on the site of a house belonging to a man of that name.

The Siwan population increased greatly over the centuries. Each family would add one floor on top of the other for the accommodation of its members; nobody was allowed by the **agwād** to build a house outside the walls. The walls of the houses were built with **karshīf;** the mud taken from salt-impregnated soil; after drying, it becomes almost like cement; some of the houses rose to seven and eight storeys. The great drawback of building with **karshīf** was the fact that it suffered badly from prolonged rains. Fortunately, rain is rare in Siwa; it occurs always in small showers and for very short durations. Once in every few years it rains heavily(1) and always with disastrous results, since the salt in the **karshīf** dissolves.

In the year 1820, Siwa was conquered by the troops of Muḥammad 'Alī, and from that time onwards the Siwans felt secure and were not threatened by Bedouin assaults. After the year 1826, the council of **al-agwād** gave permission to the people to build outside the walls, if they wanted to do so.

It is interesting to note that Mūsā Būbash, the head of the oasis at that time, laid down very strict rules to be followed by the builders of new houses near the foot of the fortress. The main streets were twenty ells (approximately fourteen metres), the side streets were twelve ells and the small cul-de-sacs were eight ells. There were also open squares; nobody was allowed to build a house of more than two storeys. The enlightened head of Siwa, who used to travel every year to Cairo, found it necessary to impose such regulations to ensure that the people lived a healthier life and obtained enough air and light. The streets of the old fortified town were so narrow that it was impossible for more than one loaded donkey to pass at a time. If two of them chanced to meet, one had to retreat, or enter one of the houses.

The travellers who visited Siwa toward the end of the 18th and during the first half of the 19th centuries have left us descriptions of the ancient monuments in the oasis and have given us important information about certain aspects of Siwan life. Some of them, such as Cailliaud, who went there in 1819 before the conquest of Muḥammad 'Alī, and Von Minutoli in 1820, have left us valuable sketches which show how Shālī and Aghūrmī looked in those days (Fig. 6).

Since 1826, the Siwans have built new settlements outside Shālī, the largest of them being at the foot of the medieval fortress; others were sited further away near the gardens.

Some families have continued to live in the houses at the foot of the ancient town; all the houses at the top of the hill had by then fallen down. Comparing my photographs taken in 1938 with those taken in 1968 and 1969, we find a great change. According to what I was told in 1938, many of the families were very reluctant to leave their old homes prior to 1926, when an unusually heavy rain, which continued for three successive days, caused the collapse of many houses and rendered many others

---

(1) The heaviest one-day rain recorded in recent years at Siwa is 28 millimetres ; this was on December 28, 1930. In January 1970 there was a heavy fall which continued for more than a day.

unsafe. Since that time, most of the house owners in Shālī, as well as the inhabitants of Aghūrmī, have abandoned their ancient houses and built new ones at the foot of the hills, taking with them all doors, windows and wooden rafters from the ceilings, whenever this was possible.

In spite of the ruinous condition of the ancient town of Siwa, the visitor enjoys the view. It commands the landscape in this part of the oasis, and its ancient minarets with their typical architecture and conical shapes, add to the beauty of the scene. The visitor can also view the ancient gate, al-Bāb Inshāl (Fig. 7), which leads to a small corridor in which we find a mud seat, a **maṣṭabah** on which the gate keeper used to sit; nearby was a fire kept alight day and night, to which the inhabitants came if their own fires or torches went out. Since matches were not available in ancient days, the Siwans used to make fire by rubbing together pieces of the husk of the date bunches and palm ribs; this method of making fire is still in use in some of the distant areas in the oasis, in cases of necessity (Fig. 8).

The narrow street remains and we can still see the small door of the dungeon; shortly afterwards, we reach a wider place in which there still exist the mud benches on which the **agwād** used to sit, under an open shed. Near this meeting place is the door of the ancient mosque which was constructed of **karshīf**-mud like the houses. The mosque itself is built outside the girdle wall; in its north-eastern side it has two large rooms, one for each of the two rival factions of the city — the Sharqīyīn, the Easterners (called also al-Takhṣīb), and the Gharbīyīn, the Westerners (called by their rivals al-Lafāyah). The mosque is still in use. Inside the fortified town there were four wells.

Nowadays, the centre of the town is not far from the government buildings and the modern mosque. Here are the small shops and the market place, where we find Siwans and strangers sitting in front of the shops and two or three small coffee-houses. The visitor who walks or drives through the streets may come across children playing, but if he ever gets a glimpse of a woman walking or sitting in a cart drawn by a donkey, he sees only a figure wrapped in dark clothes, her face always covered with a part of her **milāyah**. The Siwans are generally a conservative people, although it is not too difficult to see more of their life and visit their houses and gardens — especially if arrangements are made by influential local government officials, or one of the heads of the families.

Undoubtedly, a great change has taken place in the life of the Siwans. It is no longer the romantic medieval fortress which still existed up to the beginning of this century. The place is also very different from the town of Siwa which I had known twenty years ago. But in spite of all the changes which have taken place,

Fig. 6. Town of Siwa in 1820 (After Von Minutoli, Atlas, Pl. V).

it is still one of the most romantic and interesting of places — not only in our deserts, but in all of Egypt. It will always be a bright spot in the memory of the visitor.

Springs, Gardens and Crops

According to the census of 1966, the total population of Siwa Oasis was 5,169 persons (2,702 males and 2,467 females); those living in the town of Siwa totalled 3,569; those in its near suburbs numbered 289. Nearby Aghūrmī had 537 inhabitants. In other words, out of a total number of 5,169 persons, 4,935 lived in the town of Siwa and its vicinity, within a circle whose diameter was not more than ten kilometres. The remaining 974 lived in villages scattered through the depression. Al-Marāqī counted 558 persons, Abū Shurūf 53, and al-Zaytūn 21. The number includes also the inhabitants of the small oasis of Qāret Umm al-Ṣughayyar (142 persons) which is on the edge of the Qaṭṭārah depression, at a distance of 130 kms. northeast of Siwa (Fig. 9).

These figures show very clearly that, nowadays, the densely populated part of the oasis is near the main town, where the most important springs and gardens lie. The situation was somewhat different in ancient times. The existence of many ancient sites, including rock-tombs and temples at al-Marāqī, Khamīsah, Abū Shurūf, al-Zaytūn and Abul-'Awwāf, proves that there existed at those sites, even in Roman times, other important, populated small towns in addition to the main centre, which was on the site of present-day Aghūrmī. According to some ancient Arab writers, there were one thousand springs in Siwa; but even if we admit this figure is much exaggerated, there is no doubt that the number of springs in Siwa in ancient times was much more than the 281 known today.(1)

Siwa's great present problem is not the scarcity of the water from its springs; rather, it is one of too much water and not enough drainage. There are many flowing springs whose water goes unused ; it drains into the salt lakes, whose water level rises with much harm to the neighbouring cultivated land because of the rise of subsoil water and the lack of an adequate system of drainage (Fig. 10).

As an example, the water of several springs — including 'Ayn Qurayshat, the largest spring in Siwa and one of the largest and most important springs in all the oases — is wasted, and flows into the salt lake of al-Zaytūn.(2) Thousands of cultiv-

(1) Map of Egypt: 1:500,000, Sheet No. 1 (May, 1937), and A. Azadian, «l'Oasis de Siouah et ses Sources,» **Bulletin de l'Institut d'Egypte**, T. IX (1926-27) pp. 105-44.

(2) The output of the spring of Qurayshat is upwards of 30,000 gallons a minute.

Fig. 7. New houses at the foot of the medieval Fortress (Shālī).

Fig. 8. The town of Siwa.

Fig. 9. A minaret of one of the mosques — the conical type.

able feddans (acres) are thus turned to **karshīf**; the presence of ancient sites near it, and in other places not far away, afford proof that the area which is now waste was cultivated in ancient times and supported a number of inhabitants, numerous and wealthy enough to raise such monuments. The same can be said of the district of al-Marāqī, which was populous and partly cultivated up to the 15th century, as we know from the description of al-Maqrīzī, the famous Arab historian.(1)

---

(1) A historian (1364 - 1442) born in Cairo and the author of many works, the principal one being **Al-Mawā'iz wa al-I'tibār fī dhikr al-Khiṭat wa al-Āthār** [Sermons and Learning on an Account of Settlements and Antiquities] (al-Milījī : Cairo), usually quoted as **Al-Khiṭaṭ.** Although reproached by his critics, his accurate and conscientious work is acknowledged without contradiction. (See Stephan and Nandy Ronart, **Concise Encyclopaedia of Arabic Civilization** (1959), p. 348. For his description of the district of Al-Marāqī, see below.

It is a great pleasure to visit some of the springs of Siwa in the midst of their gardens. They are generally surrounded by a circular stone wall, but the magnificent colours of the green moss and the air bubbles which emerge from the natural fissures in the rock, make us feel the beauty of the place; especially when we see in the deep green water the reflection of the sunlight and the palm trees nearby (Fig. 11).

One of the best examples is 'Ayn al-Gūbah, a short distance from the Temple of Umm 'Ubaydah in Aghūrmī. This large and beautiful spring is sometimes called 'Ayn al-Ḥammām (spring of the bath); it was the custom till the last century that in the early afternoon of the day of betrothal, brides came here to bathe in its waters; this takes place nowadays at another spring, 'Ayn Ṭamūsī, which is not so near to a public road.

'Ayn al-Gūbah is the ancient "Spring of the Sun," mentioned by Herodotus in his famous history written in the 5th century B.C., as one of the wonders in the land of the Ammonians: "They have another spring here, of which the water is tepid in the early morning and cools down toward the time when towns-people begin to go out; by noon it is very cold, and that is the moment when they water their gardens; then as the day draws towards evening, the chill gradually goes off it, until by sunset it is tepid again; after that it gets hotter and hotter as the night advances, and at midnight it boils furiously. Then, after mid-night, the process is reversed, and it steadily cools off until dawn. The spring is know as the 'Fountain of the Sun.' "(1)

Siwans still tell the story of the changing temperature to their visitors, but this cannot be taken seriously. The water temperature is steady; it is the temperature of the air which changes in this oasis; as for boiling water at midnight, this no doubt results from the bubbles of gas coming out of the fissures to make the surface of the spring look like boiling water.

The cultivated land in Siwa amounts to 1,300 feddans: 1,000 of which are gardens, while the remaining three hundred are cultivated with crops. The principal trees which grow in the gardens are the palms and the olives, which constitute the greatest source of income for the oasis; but besides these two there are many kinds of fruit trees. Almost all the varieties which grow in the Nile Valley or in the other oases can be grown here — with the exception of oranges, mangoes and gouava, which do not thrive because of the nature of the soil.

Vegetables of all kinds can also be grown, except for potatoes. Planting vegetables or crops, especially barley and wheat, needs much effort from the labourers because they have to hoe

(1) Herodotus, «The Histories,» Book IV, par. 182.

deeply, sometimes to the depth of one metre, in order to get fresher soil and remove the salt which accumulates on the surface and is disastrous for the young plants. Some of the rich owners of gardens grow flowers, especially roses and peppermint and love to offer them to their guests whenever they invite them to their gardens. It is a pleasure to attend such parties and sit on carpets and cushions while all kinds of seasonal fruits, biscuits, sweets and peanuts are piled on low tables in front of the guests. Green tea is prepared in their presence and served three times in small glasses. If the guest, or guests, are of importance to the shaykh who has invited them, he presents also the **gummār,** the white delicious heart from the top of the palm tree — generally an unneeded male tree which they can injure in this way without much loss.

The gardens are generally surrounded by fences; the lower part of the fence is made of mud, while the upper part is constructed of palm ribs; the height is about two metres. The visitor who expects to see in Siwa a well-kept garden or at least a half-clean one, will be greatly disappointed. Everything looks wild and untidy, but many people think that it is more beautiful this way because it looks more natural. Wherever we go, we find palm trees; there are about 240,000 of these in Siwa[1]

Fig. 10. The palm-groves of Siwa — view taken from Jabal al-Mawtā.

(1) The palm tree is one of the oldest plants in Egypt and is represented on monuments since Pre-dynastic times ; it has played a significant part in the art and religion of the ancients ; see Ingrid Wallert, **Die Palmen in Alten Aegypten** (Berlin, 1962).

100,300 are of the kind called **Ṣa'īdī,** supposed to be the best and greatly prized in the commercial markets throughout the towns and villages of the Nile Valley and among the Bedouin who live near the coast. Second to it is the **Friḥī** of which there are 6,854. The date called **Ghazālī** is renowned among the Siwans because they believe in its effectiveness for those who complain of lack of energy. Moreover, there are around 100,000 palm trees of the **'Izzāwī** variety, which is considered to be inferior to all the other kinds and is fed to donkeys; the **Washak** (the suckers), and the male palm trees, which are unproductive and are looked upon as useless, number about 23,000.

The palm tree is far and away the tree for which the Siwans care more than any other. It is a joy to hear a labourer singing in Siwan as he works on the tree. His melodius tunes are heard from a distance, and the moment he stops another labourer answers him from another garden (Fig. 12). For every kind of work there is a special song, and the Siwans can tell right away what the man is doing. The Siwans depend much on the palm; not only is its fruit their principal source of income and nourishment, but its different parts are also used in the construction of their houses. The trunk is used for rafters and sometimes in making doors, the ribs for the ceiling. The leaves are widely used in making mats and all kinds of plates and containers, especially the **margūnah** an essential item in the Siwan household (Fig. 13). The palm supplies them also with their favourite drink, the **labgī,** refreshing and delicious when it is fresh, intoxicating when it ferments. Some Siwans make from the **'Izzāwī** dates a kind of date wine, although this is forbidden by law. Thirty years ago a Greek used to come to the oasis in summer and extract alcohol from the wine.

The second tree in importance is the olive; there are some 25,000 trees in Siwa, some of them very old. The best olive tree gardens are now at Khamīsah; there is a hydraulic oil press in Siwa, besides several others which still follow the old traditional stonemill method, driven by hand. Many other kinds of fruit trees are grown, but they are for local use; they are not a source of income, nor are the fruit exported in large quantities.

The number of grapevines is a little more than a thousand; sweet lemons, figs, pomegranates, and citrus lemon can be grown with success. There are also peaches, plums, mulberries, pears, carobs and almonds, but the total number of each does not exceed a hundred trees and many of these produce an inferior crop. Attempts have been made to grow other kinds of fruit, such as mangoes, but without success.

The Siwans also grow in their gardens almost all of the vegetables known in the Nile Valley ; their favourites being

Fig. 11. The spring of Ṭamūsī.

milūkhīyah (Jew's mallow), okra, eggplant, pumpkin, pepper, **riglah** (purslane), tomatoes, cucumber, etc. Potatoes do not thrive in Siwa, and rice is not allowed now as a precaution against malaria. Barley, emmer wheat and maize are grown successfully.

Siwan Families

According to the Siwan Manuscript, the forty men who founded Shālī belonged to seven families; the number increased with time. Some of these families had close ties between themselves, and those who lived in the eastern section of the town, the Easterners, constituted one group, whilst the Westerners comprised another.

The inhabitants of Siwa love to tell their visitors that they are descended from Arab Bedouin and that some of the original tribes came from North Africa, or sometimes from Arabia. On one occasion, a Siwan boasted to me that his great-great-grandfather came from Makkah (Mecca). In fact, the original inhabitants of Siwa are one of the branches of the Berber group from the tribes of Zanātah, who mixed with Arab Bedouin from different tribes from the west. In the Middle Ages, Siwa was one of the important stations for caravans and a market for the negro slave trade, consequently, we find a mixture of negro blood among the inhabitants. The original families are the Zanāyin, al-'Adādisah and al-Ḥaddādīn, who constitute the group of Easterners generally called "al-Takhsīb", an expression which means pleasant, open-hearted and non-aggressive; the Westerners are the families of Awlād Mūsā, al-Sarāqinah, al-Shaḥāyim and al-Ba'āwinah, who were called al-Lafāyah which means almost the opposite of the nickname of the other group. Al-Ba'āwinah, after some time, left Shālī preferring to live at Aghūrmī. The Siwan Manuscript mentions that al-Ba'āwinah went there and lived with the remnants of the "Romans" who were living at Aghūrmī.

The Fights

There were feuds between the two groups and the Siwans had their own rules which they respected. Whenever there was a fight, all the able men of the two groups had to join in. On an appointed day they stood in two rows facing each other; each family had to take its place opposite a family of the other side. The middle part of the row was occupied by the Zanāyin of the Easterners and in front of them stood the two families of Sarāqinah and Shaḥāyim from the Westerners; on the right wing of the Easterners stood the 'Adādisah, and opposite them Awlād Mūsā. On the left flank stood the Ḥaddādīn who faced the people of Aghūrmī (al-Ba'āwinah). The women remained at some distance, in order to encourage their relatives and throw stones at those who showed cowardice and began to run away.

Before the use of firearms, they fought from sunrise to sunset, and, if neither side accepted defeat and ran away, they went home to spend the night in their neighbouring houses, then resumed their fight next morning. This continued until one of the two parties fled from the field. Following the use of firearms, they used to stand facing each other as usual; and at a signal they shot once only, then stopped to take care of the wounded and remove their dead. After a certain time had elapsed and they had re-loaded their flint muskets, they fired once again, and so on for as long as neither of the two admitted defeat and ran away. They fought their battles in that heroic way; in some of the battles the losses amounted to tens of lives on each side with many others wounded. However, after the hostilities —

which might continue for several days — they managed to live together once again. Many stories are still told about these "wars", as they call them, and I give here a few details of two battles to show the kind of chivalry which they admired and still remember with great respect.

A Siwan Hero : Among their favourite stories of these "wars" is the battle of 1712, called the "Battle of al-Ramlah". There was a rule that neither of the two parties, Easterners or Westerners, was allowed to change the width of any street in the town, without the approval of all the heads of the families of both sides (**al-agwād**) since they considered themselves partners in all the town. In that year, the Easterners wanted to widen a very small street which led to the gardens, because it was too narrow. At the time, the authority was in the hands of one of the Easterners; because of this, and out of sheer obstinacy, the Westerners refused to agree. This incident created ill-feeling on both sides and they began to destroy, stealthily and at night, one another's trees and crops. This did not please the **agwād,** who held a meeting at which the Westerners insisted on dictating their conditions ; the Easterners wanted peace and agreed to forget all about their losses and pay all that the Westerners estimated as indemnity. This attitude made the Westerners more arrogant ; they withdrew their acceptance on the grounds that their **zaggālah**[1] did not agree to this arrangement. They said the Easterners should pay double the indemnity — a very harsh demand — which the Easterners also accepted. The Westerners, believeing that their adversaries were afraid of them, became more aggressive, imagining that this was their chance to get the leadership of the oasis and subdue the others. They refused once more and insisted on pitching a battle.

Some of the Western shaykhs went to the head of al-Ba'āwinah at Aghūrmī, Aḥmad al-Ḥājj 'Umar, asking him to join them as usual, but he refused because he believed that his own people were unjust in their attitude. When he was accused of being afraid, he simply answered that he disapproved of their attitude and reminded them of the consequence of their aggressive and arrogant behaviour towards their peaceful neighbours. Several leading personalities among his own relatives at Aghūrmī sided with the others, believing that, according to tradition, they should take their usual place on the day of battle. He agreed, at last, to lead his people and join the battle, but on two

(1) The **zaggālah** are the unmarried labourers in the service of the landowners. This group of youths who took care of the gardens and fields during the day, were a kind of militia and night guards, and had their own privileges ; no agreement could be made without their approval. (For more details about this group of people, see below in the chapter on Customs and Traditions.)

Fig. 12. One of the zaggālah singing while collecting some dates.

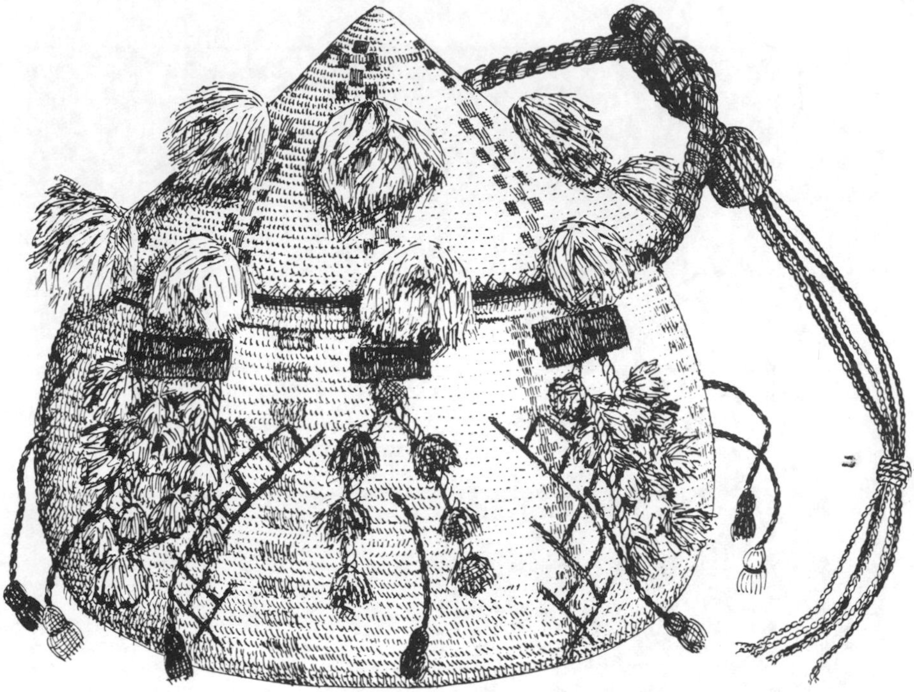

Fig. 13. A decorated margūnah used by the newly married.

conditions — the first being that none would ever attack their enemy in the night, as they had done in destroying their gardens, or try any tricks, but were to fight in the tradition of their fathers; the second condition was that they swear on the Koran that none of them would run away, but fight on. He said that with their new enmity and unjust attitude, one of the two parties must be eliminated and so they must go on fighting until all of them died, or their enemies were killed; the winning party would enjoy living alone and in peace. To this they agreed.

On the day of battle, Aḥmad al-Ḥājj 'Umar was at the head of his men and fought like a lion. But the Easterners were stronger and better fighters, and the Westerners began to run away to save their lives, including the people of Aghūrmī. All the Westerners ran away, leaving their dead and wounded, except one man who insisted on fighting to the death; he was Aḥmad, who continued to fight quite alone, and refused to stop. The warriors of the Easterners admired his great bravery and threw their weapons at his feet, rushed to kiss his hands and his head and called him the hero of the day. He felt ashamed of his own people, who did not keep their promise to fight to the death, and he refused to go back to his house at Aghūrmī. The Easterners offered to give him in marriage any daugther of the shaykhs he wanted, and urged him to come and live with them. He accepted the marriage but refused to live with them; he built for himself a new house in a garden which he owned between Aghūrmī and Shālī. He lived there for seventeen years, in almost complete seclusion, until his own people were able to persuade him to forget their cowardly attitude and forgive them. By then, he was advanced in years and agreed to return and spend the remaining years of his life in the house in which he was born and in which he spent his youth.

The reader might well wonder how Westerners and Easterners could live again as neighbours in their fortified town and in their gardens. The answer is that their defeat on the battlefield was not the last thing that day. The Westerners fled to their gardens, and the Easterners humiliated them further by attacking their houses, molesting their women and taking from their homes whatever they wanted. This continued for three days, at the end of which the victors allowed their adversaries to return to their homes on four conditions, which give us an impression of Siwan life at the time and also of the Siwan mentality. The first condition was that from that day on, whenever a caravan arrived at Siwa, bringing merchandise for sale, the Westerners must keep away until the Easterners had obtained all that they wanted to buy. The second condition was to forbid any Westerner to buy or sell anything directly; this had to be done through one of the Easterners. The third was no less humiliating because it stipulated that if an Easterner and a Westerner wanted to cross a bridge over a canal at the same time, the Westerner was obliged to give priority to the Easterner; if he did not abide by this rule, he was considered an aggressor and had to be punished. The fourth condition was more peculiar. The **ḥaṭīyah**(1) of Khamīsah was owned by Easterners and Westerners, whose gardens were very close. The condition stated that if one of the Western **zaggālah** was singing in a garden, while doing his work there, and stopped, then one of the **zaggālah** of the Easterners should begin to sing and then finish his song; the Westerner was not allowed to sing once more.

These conditions were respected and never broken for fifteen years; but in the year 1727 new disagreements and new arrangements arose. We must always bear in mind that the total number of all the Siwans in those days was not much more than 3,000 persons and many of them were related. They had always managed to live together in their oasis in the midst of the Libyan Desert; and in spite of all the disagreements and sometimes enmities, they were one in the face of any outside danger, such as when they were attacked by Bedouin.

---

(1) The **ḥaṭīyah** is some sort of a settlement or small hamlet with gardens irrigated by one or more springs.

Another Brave Man : The second story is of a different kind. In 1820 the soldiers of Muḥammad 'Alī conquered Siwa. They were accompanied by one of the shaykhs of the Westerners, 'Alī Bālī, who was appointed later as the Mayor of Siwa, as a reward. After a while, he began to abuse his authority and turned out to be a great despot; all the Siwans hated him, including his close relatives. At last, he was killed by one of his own cousins who was able, with his two brothers, to leave Siwa and flee into the desert. The murder of 'Alī Bālī took place in the year 1838; his murderer was called al-Mubārak. The son of 'Alī Bālī avenged the death of his father on his enemies, and after many intrigues managed to get authority into his hands; he became the favourite of the government and the head of all the shaykhs in 1853. Al-Mubārak suffered greatly in his banishment, since he was not welcomed anywhere in the desert. One day he arrived at Siwa, entered it and went in the late evening to the house of Yūsuf 'Alī Bālī and addressed him, saying : "If you do not recognize me, I am al-Mubārak, who killed your father. Here I come to you, giving you every right to kill me; my blood is your property. I surrender to you and you can kill me if you want, because I deserve it. This will not cost you anything because I have with me my shroud, in which you can wrap my dead body. Here is my pistol; I hand it to you to shoot me."

Yūsuf did not answer but ordered his men to lock him in the prison until the morning. When the **agwād** assembled as usual, Yūsuf told them the story, stating that it was against his honour to kill a person who surrendered himself; he ordered him brought from the prison. He then told the prisoner, in front of everybody, that he forgave him. Al-Mubārak answered that as long as he lived he would consider his own life as the property of Yūsuf Bālī, and from that day on he was his most faithful friend. Four years later, in 1857, the Easterners revolted against Yūsuf and assassinated him; the Westerners, to whom he belonged did not know what to do because they realized that their rivals were stronger. Furthermore, many of them hated Yūsuf and his tyranny and were pleased when he was killed. At the time, al-Mubārak was in Cairo; on hearing the news he rushed back to the oasis, and did all he could to persuade the great majority of the Westerners to avenge the murder of their shaykh.

On the day of the battle, he addressed the Easterners who stood in front of them on the neighbouring hill, Jabal Idrār, saying : "I owe my life to the man whom you have killed, as you all know, and it is my duty to avenge his murder. Anyone amongst you who will be hit by a bullet in his forehead should be sure that I am the person who shot him." He fought very bravely and at the end of the battle he was one of the twenty-eight persons who lost their lives that day. His name is not yet forgotten and is still mentioned as a noble example of a daring, brave and honest man.

The Language of Siwa

The Siwans have a language which they use among themselves. Nowadays, almost everybody understands Arabic as his second language, but thirty years ago it was quite usual to meet many elderly men who knew only a few words of Arabic, while most of the women and the very young children could not understand it. Until 1820 there was one family in Siwa who specialized in speaking Arabic and other languages; they could speak to the strangers in the caravans who were Arab Bedouin, or from the Nile Valley, or North Africa, or from the distant oases in the desert, who came to trade with the Siwans or buy their dates and olive oil; the head of this family was called "Shaykh al-Khabar".

The language of Siwa has always interested visitors, and many of them tried to study it and published in articles and books collections of words and sentences(1); but apart from these limited efforts, there are few books on the language and its grammar. The earliest of these is B. Basset, **Le Dialecte de Syouah** (Paris, 1890); this was followed by W. Seymour Walker, **The Siwan Language** (published in 1921), and the third is the work of E. Laoust, **Siwa : Son Parler** (Paris, 1932). In this last book we find a competent survey of the subject and the results of all the serious studies comparing the language with other Berber dialects, particularly those which are still spoken now in Suknah, Nifūsah, Ghadāmis, Sinid and other places in the Libyan Desert belonging to the Zanātīyah in North Africa.

The influence of Arabic is increasing, and more Arabic words and expressions are introduced; I hope that further studies will be made of this language before it is too late.

---

(1) We find these collections of words in the works of visitors to Siwa since the end of the 18th century. For example, in Hornemann, **Tagebuch seiner Reise von Cairo nach Murzuck...** (Weimer, 1802); in Frederic Cailliaud, Voyage à Meroé (1819 - 1822); in H.M. Von Minutoli, **Reise Zum Tempel des Jupiter Ammon,** (Berlin, 1820) ; in the manuscript of Bernardino Drovetti who visited Siwa in 1820 but whose work was published in 1935 by Giovanni Marro, «Un cimelio del viaggio di B. Drovetti all'oasi di Giove Ammone,» in **Bulletin de la Soc. Roy. de Geogr. d'Egypte** T. XIX (1935), pp. 8 - 16. We find more collections in the work of Brichetti-Robecci, **All'oasi di Giove Ammone Viaggio, 1889** (Milano, 1900); in C.V.B. Stanley, «The oasis of Siwa,» in **Journal of African Society,** (London, 1911) ; in J.E. Quibell, «A Visit to Siwa,» in **Annales du Service des Antiquités** (1917); and in the paper of Mustafa Maher, «L'Oasis de Siouah,» in **Bulletin de la Soc. Sult. de Géographie d'Egypte**, 9 (Cairo, 1919). He visited Siwa in the year 1893. A useful collection of words is published by Abdul-Laṭīf Wākid in his book, **Wāḥat Amun,** (Cairo, 1949).

New Projects

Visitors to Siwa cannot help thinking that it would be an easy matter to increase the cultivated land several times over, and profit from the wasted waters of its springs. These thoughts increase when they visit the remains of the ancient monuments and read something of its ancient history. But what most of these visitors forget is that the times have changed and the problem of Siwa is not simply the problem of lack of labour. It is, in the first place, the problem of drainage, an extremely difficult one in a depression whose floor is 18 metres below sea level. Moreover, the wasted waters have created many lakes in the oasis, whose water level is as high as the surrounding lands.

In the winter months of 1907, the Khedive 'Abbās Ḥilmī took great interest in Siwa and sought to reclaim some of its lands — especially the land which could be irrigated by 'Ayn Qurayshat, the largest spring in the oasis. The great success of his agricultural projects in Maryūṭ (Mareotis) made him think of Siwa, and he had, in his company, experts in land reclamation. The people of Siwa welcomed his plans and gave him, as a present to his son Prince 'Abdul-Mun'im, three springs among which was the spring of 'Ayn Qurayshat and all the land surrounding it; these amounted to not less than 2,000 acres. His engineers started on the project, but lack of labour and the great cost of making catchment areas for drainage made the work proceed very slowly; then came the First World War and nothing more has been done to this day.

From time to time, the government initiated some projects on a small scale, but always without much success, and they were discontinued. The most important was the project of al-Naqb, in the eastern part of the depression, which was begun with great success in the year 1951 by the General Inspectorate of Desert Irrigation and which succeeded in reclaiming 350 acres in the following years. However, it was discontinued later because of serious labour problems and the great expense involved. A second project was that of Khamīsah, which was also started by the same Department, but neglected subsequently.

In recent years, Siwa has been confronted by two difficulties. Formely, the inhabitants of the desert, Bedouin and oasis dwellers, were exempt from military service, but a new law cancelled this privilege and the Siwan youths were enlisted in the army, like everybody else in the country. The rich shaykhs were badly hit by this since it derived them of cheap local labour. Many of the ex-soldiers, who did not own land, preferred to get a job in one of the government offices if they could. Only a small proportion went back to their original work in the gardens.

Another problem for Siwa developed in 1962 when the discovery of the oil fields in Libya, and especially near neighbouring

Jaghbūb, enticed more than three hundred of the young men to go and work there. The high wages and less strenuous work made them leave their oasis. Fortunately, their jobs in Libya were not permanent, and most of them had to return after a while. In 1969 most of them were forced to come back, because new regulations made it difficult for those who entered Libya without legal papers to remain there.

The vacancy in the labour force was filled, to a certain extent, by workers from Upper Egypt; but their wages were too high and they were not used to the hard and strenuous work in the Siwan gardens. Moreover, some of those strangers were not of decent character and troubles began to arise. When I was in Siwa in September 1968, the daily wage of a labourer was sixty-five piasters plus his mid-day meal, with tea several times in the day — and labourers were scarce. In April, 1970, the wages were less; sixty piasters a day, from which the labourer got forty-seven and a half piasters in hand (the difference deducted for social security). There was no difficulty in getting any number to work, because there were many who had returned to Siwa from Libya.

The Change in Thirty Years

For about the last twenty years, Siwa has been the scene of exploration looking toward the possibility of finding oil in the depression. The preliminary studies showed that it was possible, but more practical steps were needed to establish whether petroleum could be found in commercial quantities, as in neighbouring Libya. Drilling began in the summer of 1969 and the great question cannot be answered for some time; so far, only water has been found. If oil exists in Siwa it will be, without doubt, a great boon to Siwa and Egypt as a whole, but it will have its consequences for Siwan life. The Siwans themselves are not very enthusiastic about the project.

In any case, whether or not oil is found, life in Siwa will change, as it has done over the last ten years. There is not the slighest doubt that the next generation will live a life different from that of their own parents; especially the girls, who are very keen to attend school and many of them look forward to finishing their education in Marsā Maṭrūḥ or Alexandria.

When I compare life in Siwa nowadays with what I saw in the year 1938, I can hardly believe the rapidity of the change which has taken place. The boys and girls who used to play in the streets of the quiet town, wearing their traditional clothes, have disappeared. The great majority are now dressed like the children of other places, such as Marsā Maṭrūḥ, or the Egyptian villages. Whenever a Siwan is reminded of a tradition or of one of the old customs, he merely smiles and says that this used to happen a long time ago, as if such traditions were a sign of backwardness. Only the elderly people still adhere to ancient customs and speak of them with restricted pride. But we should not forget that the Siwans, especially the women, are a very conservative people and I do not hesitate to claim that the Siwan women will be the guardian of the culture in the oasis. There is a great change already in the attitude of the men toward the new ways of life which differ from their own traditional patterns. There are new channels of culture which find their way through transistor radio-sets and increasing contact with the outside. There is also an inclination to imitate the officials and those who come to the oasis — as if this is the way to prove that they are advanced in their thinking. But all this is only on the surface, as far as most of the women are concerned.

And now, after this lengthy introduction to the Oasis of Amun, and the dilemma which hovers over it, we begin the chapter on its customs and traditions.

2

Siwan Customs and Traditions

The majority of the Siwans still preserve many of their old customs and traditions. The changing times, and the new currents of modernism, have influenced and to a certain extent modified some of their customs, but Siwan society has not yet broken down. A great number of the inhabitants, and especially the women, still find great pride in their old traditions and pity those who are drifting away from the traditional way of life.

The early travellers to Siwa (see below, chapter 4) were greatly interested in the life of the people and recorded in their writings what they heard from the inhabitants through interpreters who accompanied them; all of these travellers spoke neither Arabic nor the Siwan language, and none of them was in position to mix with the people freely during their short stays.

The Siwan Manuscript

Apart from these writings, we have an important source of information in the Siwan Manuscript, already mentioned in the previous chapter. It was begun some ninety years ago by the head of the family of Abū Musallim, the religious judge of Siwa at the time, who had studied, in his youth, at al-Azhar, in Cairo. He recorded in this book mention of Siwa and the other oases as recorded by some of the medieval Arab writers. He added to it oral traditions existing among the inhabitants concerning the origin of the different families, the wars which took place between the Easterners and Westerners, as well as a general account of some of their customs and traditions. His work was continued by his son after his death and afterwards by his grandson. The original, however, was presented to Prince 'Umar Ṭūsūn in the late twenties, after several copies had been made. The family still adds to it whatever they consider worth recording, such as the dates of arrival or departure of some of the prominent officials and very important incidents. I saw a copy, in 1938, and was allowed to keep it for two days and take from it all the notes I wanted. Other members of the same family and other families also started other books of the same type (Fig. 14).

The family says nowadays, that one of the Ma'mūrs of the oasis took away the copy which I saw in 1938 and sent it to Cairo and has never returned it, but in all probability they still have the copy and are unwilling to show it to every visitor who asks to see it. The important parts are those which give an account of local laws and regulations in Siwa and the detailed description of the ancient town and the old customs which were deeply rooted among the inhabitants. A number of the important points in it are included in the present work. However, in the following pages, I give only some of the customs and traditions which I consider necessary to an understanding of the social life of the oasis. The subject still needs more study.

The Zaggālah

This word is the plural of **zaggāl** which means, literally, "club-bearer". These are a special class of the inhabitants whose duty was, and still is, to work in the fields and gardens of the rich landowners during the day. A number of them were supposed to constitute a body of guards for the oasis during the night. A group of them were also chosen to be in attendance on the

Fig. 14. A shed at the side of ʿAyn Tagzirt.

heads of the families and the rich landowners. They used to be referred to as **khādim**, which means literally "the one who is in the service of another". Some of them were entrusted with the punishment of any person who transgressed against the law. They belonged to the same families as their masters, but were generally among the poor who owned no land and had to work for the rich.

When the Siwans were still living inside their walled town, none of these bachelors was allowed to spend the night in the town but had to sleep outside the gates, in caves cut in the rock or in the gardens. Their age varied between 20 and 40, for they were not allowed to marry before that age. With time, they turned into a large group of strong-bodied youth, (Fig. 15), who spent their leisure time in drinking an intoxicating drink, **labgī**, a special kind of fermented juice extracted from the heart of the date-palm, singing and dancing and indulging in all kinds of pleasures which suited their age and temperament. Under such circumstances it is not surprising that homosexuality was common among them.

The rich person who engages a **zaggāl** to work for him is responsible for all his meals the year round, clothes him with a shirt of cotton with short sleeves in the summer, and a shirt with long sleeves, a woolen hand-woven tunic, which they called a **gibbeh**, and a turban-cloth in winter. At the end of the year he must give him forty bushels of the best variety of dates (the **ṣa'īdī**) and twenty bushels of barley for his services. In return, the **zaggāl** cannot marry, but must give all his time to working for his master. The reason for their being forbidden to spend the night inside the town was to prevent them from having the opportunity to have relations with married or unmarried women.

The merry parties of the **zaggālah** were, and still are, the gayest in Siwa. Many of the sons of the rich joined them and soon became accustomed to their way of life. With time, the rich owners depended entirely on the **zaggālah**, not only for hard work in the fields and gardens, but also in their fights. In the middle of the 17th century, the **zaggālah** had become a powerful group and acquired the right to have their voice heard in any dispute concerning the gardens, or in the fights which often occured between the two factions of the town. In more than one place in the Siwan Manuscript we read that the council of the heads of the families had to change their decisions, or their agreements with others, because their own **zaggālah** did not consider them acceptable.

The following story shows that they were far from being under control. In the early years of the 18th century (circa 1705) a number of Bedouin women of doubtful character, under the leadership of one of their number, settled at Siwa and pitch-

Fig. 15. **Three zaggālah labourers in a garden party. One of them is playing a metal flute, the second is keeping tempo on a can, and the third one sings.**

ed their tents at the foot of the hill at a spot known nowadays as al-Manshīyah. This was during the season of selling the dates, when many caravans arrive in the oasis and business flourishes. They succeeded in giving many of the Bedouin "a home away from home", and managed also to attract some of the **zaggālah** who used to go there to enjoy their evenings. After the season, the shaykhs were forced to agree that the women continue to live where they were, because they thought that this would make their labourers happier and, in the meantime, help to ease the minds of the married Siwans. With the passing of time, the leader of this group of women had become very powerful and the majority of the **zaggālah** were under her influence. On more than one occasion, the proud, conservative shaykhs had to ask her to help them, when there were difficulties between some of the shaykhs and their **zaggālah.**

I attended, on many occasions, the parties of some of these groups, either in the day in the gardens, or in the evenings in the town square, or inside one of the houses. The parties held during the day were generally quiet and those who took part were happy, singing and playing their music. Their musical instruments are the flute, a drum and sometimes a pipe, or the beating on a tin with the hands or short sticks. Their songs are in their own Siwan language and are sung either by one person at a time or by the whole group.(1) Their gayest parties are those held in the evenings, when they get very drunk and begin to dance in a circle. Each one puts a girdle around his waist and another above his knees and moves round and round, jerking his body, leaning forward and putting his hands on the shoulder of the man in front of him. The musicians sit in the middle, or at one side, and the dancers are supposed to sing together, but in their excitement one hears shouts and shrieks as if they were wounded animals. It does not take long before the onlookers observe that some of the dancers come very close to those in front of them and the dance turns into erotic movements.

Morals

If the **zaggālah,** or some of them, behave in this way, can we say that all the Siwans share with them their attitude towards accepted principles of morals? I must say that most of the new generation of Siwan youth tell the strangers that they disapprove of it, but no one can say that it has completely disappeared. In almost every book or article written about Siwa, the author refers to the homosexuality of the inhabitants, but it must be made clear that this has become much less prevalent, and that the Siwans are now in this respect no better nor worse than any other community in the towns of Egypt, or elsewhere in other countries of the world.(2) The men of Siwa pay great attention to being seen performing their prayers and go very often to the mosque, but this does not mean that all of them abstain from drinking, or avoid committing other vices.

---

(1) For a detailed study of the music of Siwa and its songs, including several sung by the **zaggālah,** see Brigitte Schiffer, **Die Oase Siwa und ihre Musik** (Bottrop, 1936).

(2) Up to the year 1928, it was not rare that some kind of a written agreement, which was sometimes called a «marriage contract», was made between two males ; but since the visit of King Fu'ād to this oasis, it has become completely forbidden. Orders were issued to inflict the severest punishment on those who dared to commit such a crime. However, such agreements continued, but in great secrecy, and without the actual writing, till the end of World War II. Now the practice is not followed. The celebration of marrying a boy was accompanied by great pomp and banquets, to which many friends were invited. The money paid as **mahr** (i.e. dowry) for a boy, and the other expenses were much more than what was spent when marrying a girl. For this abnormal marriage, see G. Steindorff, **Durch die libysche Wuste Zur Amonsoase, (Bielfeld und Leipzig, 1904)** p. 111 - 2. Steindorff's visit took place in the year 1900.

The Siwan is by nature a conservative person, hates to be criticized or ridiculed by others and pays the greatest attention to avoid doing anything wrong in public. They are thrifty and always reluctant to encourage any intimate friendship with strangers, unless they know that it is in their own interest and that they can profit from it. In the meantime they are very keen to be on good terms with government officials and especially those in key positions in the oasis, and take great pride if these officials agree to visit them in their houses or gardens, where they do all within their power to impress their guests. In my long experience with the Siwans, I never had occasion for serious complaint. I have always taken them as they are; and I cannot understand why most of those who have written about them have been so unkind.

In one of the best books written on Siwa, the author — who spent a long time with them as District Commissioner from 1917 onwards — says of the Siwans : "They are not immoral, they simply have no morals." In another place in the same book he says : "They seem to consider that every vice and indulgence is lawful."(1) This is a very polite and fair criticism when compared with what was written by others, and especially in Arabic. I wish that people could remember the very wise saying: "Let him without sin amongst you cast the first stone."

As for the Siwan women, they used to live in complete seclusion and were not allowed to meet strangers, but there were no real barriers to prevent them mixing with their relatives and some of their neighbours. The **zaggālah** labourers working for the family had every opportunity to go into the houses at all times during the day, and in the evening whether their masters were at home or not. However, if we wish to compare the morals of the Siwan women with their sisters in the other oases, or in the Nile Valley, they are by no means the worst.(2)

Clothes and Ornaments

The clothes of the Siwan girls and their silver ornaments are generally the first thing to attract the attention of visitors.

---

(1) C. Darlymple Belgrave, **Siwa : The Oasis of Jupiter Amon** (London, 1923), pp. 149, 150.

(2) We cannot expect women to live the life of saints in a society where the husbands indulge in abnormal ways of pleasure and where the youthful labourers were supposed to have all their meals in the house and enter the houses whenever they wished. The following paragraph in the Siwan Manuscript is worth mentioning :

«The women who commit adultery were punished either by killing them, or by banishment to the Oasis of Baḥrīyah.» This used to take place in the past. None of the Siwans can remember nowadays that any one of the women who committed adultery was killed or banished. In the present century, all that is done is to divorce the woman if she is married, or to keep the whole matter a secret.

The young girls who play in the streets are dressed in garments of very bright colours, with wide, long, sleeves and they wear around their necks bead necklaces. Some of the girls nowadays dress their hair in many tresses in the traditional way (Fig. 16 and 17), but others simply let their hair fall on their backs, or make it up in two tresses only. It is a source of pride to every woman to have her hair done in many small, thin tresses, numbering as many as thirty or forty, and to do the hair of any of her daughters, who have reached the age of eleven or twelve, in the same way. Sometimes, a clever relative does the hairdressing, but more often it is one of the professional women who specialize in this work, who comes to the house and spends four or five hours in dressing only one person's hair. While the women make much fuss about their hair, the men cut it very short, or shave their heads completely. Only the **zaggālah** leave one tuft on the top of their heads. In the past, it was common to see the small children with several small tufts of hair on their shaven heads. Everyone of the leading families had a certain type of haircut for their children, and thus it was possible to identify them, even when they were playing in the streets. Nowadays, this practice is neglected and very few still follow it.

Whenever the women, or their grown up daughters, go out to attend a marriage, or to congratulate a relative or neighbour who has given birth to a child, or to make any important visit, they might well wear more than one garment. However, the outside robe must be black in colour, with rich silk embroidery of variegated colours around the neck and the front part of the dress, and they must wear a number of their traditional silver ornaments. The Siwan ornaments consist of broad silver bracelets (Fig. 18), finger-rings (Fig. 19), different kinds of necklaces — especially one called **al-ṣalḥāt,** which consists of six pieces of a special design, threaded with round silver and coral beads (Fig. 20). They also wear ear-rings, either light ones in their pierced ear-lobes, or heavy ones which hang from the top of the head at each side, over the ears (Fig. 21). There are many varieties of these silver ornaments; some of the very rich women may own not less than ten pounds weight of silver. However, the most essential and very typical silver ornaments of the Siwans are two — a circular silver bar which they call in the Siwan language **aghraw,** and which is used by all the well-to-do females. The unmarried girls hang from it a decorated disk, which they call **adrim** in the Siwan tongue (Fig. 22 and 23). The second important ornament is the **ti'lāqayn,** which hangs at each side of the head; it has silver chains ending with sleigh-bells, attached to crescent-like ornaments. The number of chains at each side varies between five and nine (Fig. 24).

When I first visited Siwa thirty-five years ago, two silversmiths were busy making silver jewelry for the women, besides what was imported through the Bedouin from Alexandria and

Fig. 16. A siwan girl of sixteen wearing some of her silver ornaments.

Libya, where silversmiths at Benghazi also used to make them. Nowadays, and indeed for fifteen years past, there are none; all the new articles are made in Alexandria, where one silversmith has specialized in making the same kind of ornaments for the Siwans. However, most of the rich Siwan girls are parting from the old tradition of wearing the heavy silver ornaments and prefer to use gold necklaces and gold finger and ear-rings, which they wear along with some of the traditional silver ornaments.

In their houses, the women wear garments of bright colours, always with wide, long sleeves. They give the greatest attention to the dressing of their hair, constantly smearing it with olive oil, and applying **kuḥl** for darkening their eyes. When they go out, they wear a black dress over the other coloured ones, and put on trousers of white cotton cloth tight at the ankles, the lower parts embroidered with coloured silk in beautiful, geometric designs. Whenever a Siwan woman leaves her house she wraps herself in a wide sheet of cloth (called a **milāyah**), striped in black and gray. It is not woven in Siwa, but is always imported from the village of Kirdāsah, near the pyramids of Giza where for hundreds of years some of the families have woven this kind of cloth for the Siwans. Kirdāsah was the starting point of all the caravans which used to travel between Cairo and Siwa up to the twenties of this century.

Whenever the women see a stranger, they pull the **milāyah** together over their faces, leaving only a small hole for one or both eyes, since they never use veils. It is not very common to meet an adult Siwan grown-up woman in the street, because they rarely leave their houses except to visit relatives, attend a funeral or a wedding, or to join in the festivities at the birth of a child. Shopping and any kind of work outside the house is the duty of the men.

Sometimes we see some of the women, especially the middle-aged or elderly, walking in the town or in the roads leading to the gardens. Up to ten years ago, many of them could be seen riding donkeys.(1) Nowadays almost every Siwan family owns a donkey-drawn cart, which they call a **karussah,** a word which apparently reached Siwa from neighbouring Libya when it was under Italian occupation. The **karussah** is always driven by a man or a boy, who sits at the front; behind him one or more

---

(1) The Siwan men ride donkeys with both legs to one side, and when they wish to mount they hold the reins in one hand then jump from the ground and seat themselves on the donkey's back. They say it is only the women and the very old and weak men who ride astride. All the donkeys one sees near the town of Siwa are males ; the females are grouped at the village of Abū Shurūf, to which the male donkeys can be taken. The conservative Siwan men of previous generations were very keen to keep their wives and daughters away from everything which reminded them of sex. This old custom is still followed.

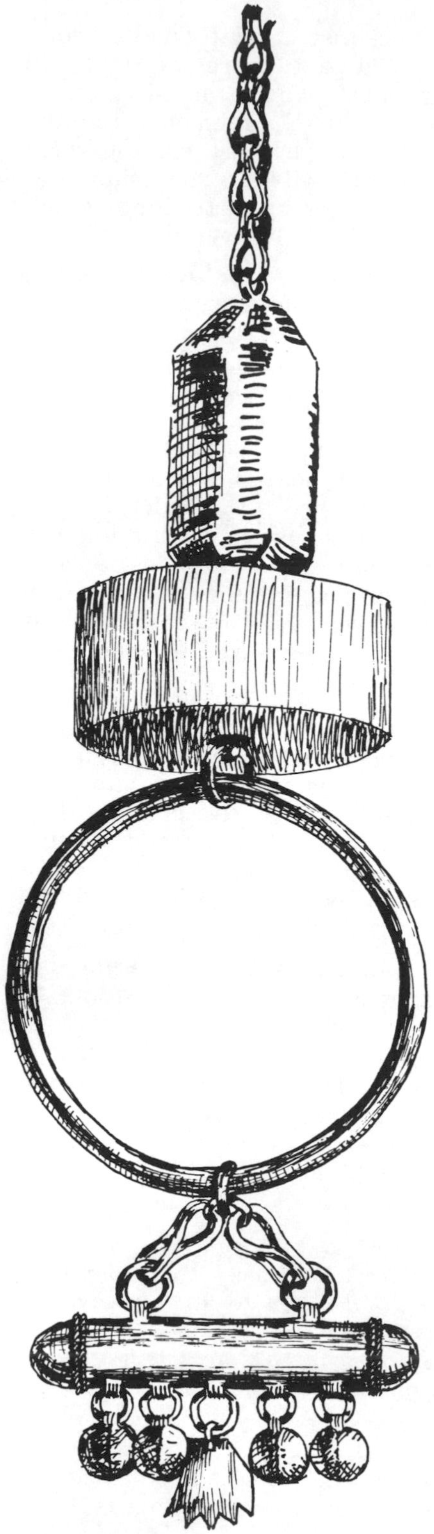

Fig. 17. The qaṣaṣ, an ornament for the hair tresses.

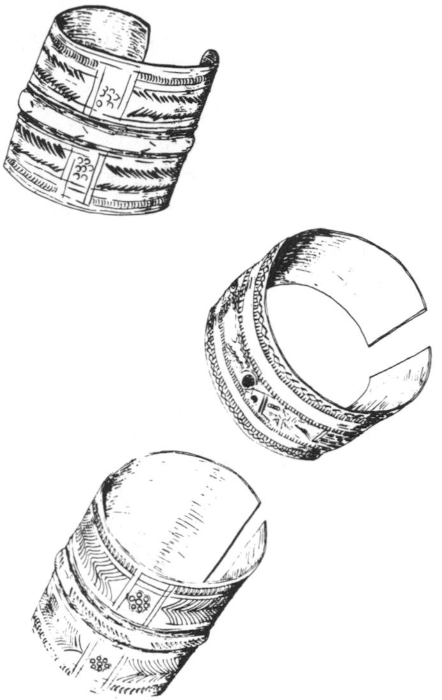

Fig. 18. Three different types of silver bracelets.

Fig. 19. Five different finger rings, the favourite types of the Siwans.

women and their children. Doubtless, it is more economical, more comfortable and useful, since it is used also for the other needs of transportation.

Apart from the black or dark garments, which the visitors often see, at home the Siwan women wear other coloured dresses. They treasure most the two dresses which are made for brides ; one is black silk and the other is of white cotton or silk. Both are very wide with long, wide sleeves and are richly decorated with silk embroidery and buttons of mother of pearl (Fig. 26).

In spite of the wave of modernism which is beginning to sweep over Siwa, there are certain things to which the Siwan women attach great importance. These are the celebration of the birth of a child, marriage ceremonies and the ceremonial when a dear relative dies. In spite of the modifications which are inevitable in these changing times, many of the old traditions are still respected.

The Birth of a Child

The birth of a child is celebrated with many festivities, particularly if the parents belong to rich families and the child is male. The most important occasion is, of course, the birth of a firstborn.

The midwife is still the principal person to take care of the pregnant women and delivers the infants, in spite of the presence of more than one government physician and the availability of a hospital. They appeal to the physician only very rarely and, when the midwife sees that her patient is at the point of death, she cunningly prefers to avoid all responsibility; thus she can later put all the blame on the physician if anything happens.

As a rule, the woman who gives birth must lie on a mat on the floor for seven or ten days.[1] The first six days pass quietly; only the very intimate relatives can call on her; the seventh day is the day of celebration. The female relatives, neighbours and friends, come to the house accompanied by their young children. All must share a meal prepared for the occasion, which must in-

---

(1) The numbers three and seven have a prominent place among the Arabs and have passed from the Arabs to all the African Muslims. Among the Berber, before their conversion to Islam, the two numbers five and ten had this place ; they are still very important and play a significant part in the life of the Berber, including the people of Siwa.

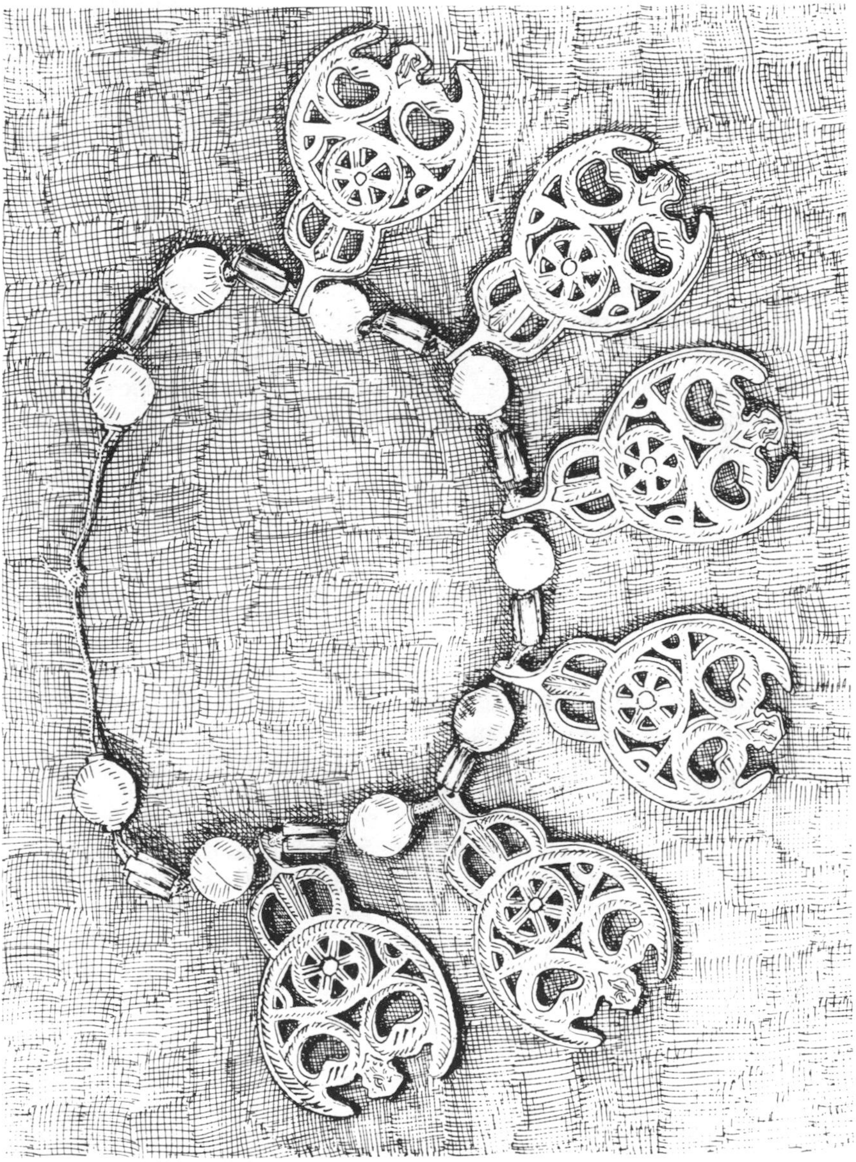

Fig. 20. The necklace called al-Ṣālḥāt used by Bedouin and Siwans.

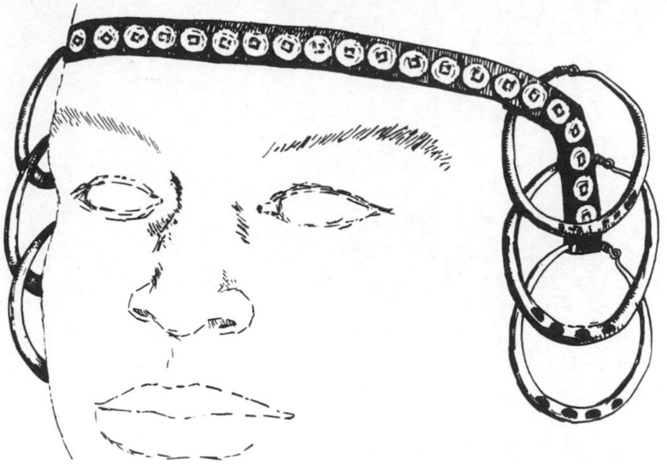

Fig. 21. The ornament called Lūgīyāt in Siwan; buttons on the forehead and silver rings hanging at the two sides of the head.

clude salted fish. This is a traditional dish connected with the miraculous birth of their local saint Sīdī Sulaymān (see below, p. 65). The ceremony of naming the child begins after the meal, if it is a boy, the father alone has the right to choose the name; if it is a girl, it is the mother who selects the name. After this, everybody may look at the baby; then the midwife marks the cheeks, nose and legs of the infant with a paste of red **ḥinnā**(1) then rush into the streets and the market place, calling out at the top of their voices the name of the baby and the name of the father.

After the departure of the children, a large earthenware bowl, especially made for this occasion, is brought into the room where the mother lies; it must be half filled with water. Each woman in the room throws into it her silver ornaments, and then the women make a circle around it, raising it from the floor while the midwife recites rythmically good wishes and prayers to God to make the child live and have a happy future. When she has finished, the women raise the bowl and lower it seven times and then drop it to the floor. It smashes to pieces, the women collect their ornaments and thus ends the ceremony; the smashing of the bowl is believed to drive away the evil eye and assure the child a happy life.

In the case of a firstborn boy, the father calls the barber after some time, to shave his head. He gives the barber the weight of the hair in silver, if the family is poor, and its weight in gold if he is rich. Mothers love to hang amulets around the neck of the child or attach them to his garments; the most pre-

---

(1) The **ḥinnā** (colloq. hinnah) plant is the «Lausonia inermis». It is a perennial shrub, which grows abundantly in Egypt; its leaves and flowers were used in cosmetics and also in the mummification in ancient Egypt. A paste of its leaves is used as a dye for hair, hands and feet.

Fig. 22. The aghraw, the silver circular ornament around the neck, and the adrim, the disk attached to it.

cious is that which is written by the shaykh of the mosque and is placed in a small leather bag. All such amulets are to protect the baby from evil and to keep him healthy.

All the boys are circumcised, not when they are very small babies, but when they reach the age of four or more. In the Siwan Manuscript, we read : "One of the old customs is the ceremony of circumcision. He who wants to circumcise his son informs his relatives, and if he is rich he informs the whole town. On the day preceding the circumcision, they shave most of the head of the boy and, in the evening of the same day, the relatives come to the house, and make a **qushaṭah** over his head.(1) They hang decorated paper above his head, and some of the relatives and friends of the family dye his hands with **ḥinnā.** The following morning they take the boy to the spring of Ṭamūsī,(2) where they wash him, and then bring him home to be circumcised.

(1) Meaning that each of the relatives must give some money to the barber in order to shave the small tuft or tufts which he leaves on purpose. This is generally done amidst the cheers of women and their singing.

(2) The spring of Ṭamūsī has a special significance in the traditional life of the Siwans. We shall hear more of it subsequently in the paragrapns on marriage in this chapter.

Fig. 23. A Siwan girl. Notice the silver ornament which hangs on both sides of her head.

"After three days, every person who was present at or invited to the **qushāṭah,** comes to the house with a small basket full of peas, pomegranates, cucumbers or watermelons. The relatives bring a pair of pigeons or a chicken, or give money." The Manuscript adds : "The father of the boy used to give a banquet, but nowadays he offers tea to all the guests."

Marriage

Marriage at Siwa can be considered as the most important of all the festivities; it is an occasion when tradition is still respected to a great extent.[1] I begin with what is recorded in the Siwan Manuscript and then add other details. "When an important marriage takes place, the whole town is invited. They eat **azqagh**, a Siwan food made of lentils and peas. The food is provided by the family of the bride, but the marriage feast is celebrated in the house of the bridegroom's family. On the marriage day, the women of the man's family go and fetch the bride; they struggle until they win and take her away from the women of the bride's family. The bridegroom goes into her room for about one and half hours and then leaves her. All who are present at the feast bring **gummār** with them. A woman accompanies the bride to the house of the bridegroom; the girl is brought wrapped up in a **jird**[2] and a sword hangs at her side until she reaches her husband. The custom of bringing **gummār** has ceased since the days of 'Abdul-Raḥmān Mu'arrif (one of the judges of Siwa in the 19th century). The presents had become in his time peas and cones of sugar; these are replaced in recent years by money. The old custom does not exist anymore."

These brief notes lack many important details and need commentary. A fixed **mahr** (dowry) — the sum of 120 piasters (six riyals, the equivalent of six dollars or one and third English gold sovereign) — is to be paid for any girl whether rich or poor, young or old, virgin, divorced or widow, because the Siwans consider them all as the daughters of the same equal forty ancestors. This **mahr** is taken by the father, or the relatives of the girl if they are very poor. As is usual, four are to be paid when married and two when divorced. The rich do not accept it. The difference lies in the gifts which the bridegroom presents to the bride; these include different kinds of clothes, expensive silver ornaments and, in recent years, also some of gold. To avoid all possible complications, many bridegrooms prefer to give the family of the girl a fixed sum of money and, if her family wants to make a show, they can add from their own money to what is actually paid.[3] In any case, the family of the

---

(1) For details of marriage customs see the works of Schiffer, **Die Oase Siwa...**, pp. 27 - 29; Steindorff, **Amonsoase...**, pp. 111 - 2 ; Mahmud Mohammad Abdallah, «Siwan customs», **Harvard African Studies, 1 :** 8-17; and the writer's **Siwa Oasis: Its History and Antiquities,** (Cairo, 1944), pp. 12 - 13.

(2) A large sheet of wool, or silk, in which Bedouin men wrap themselves; it is used by the well-to-do Siwan men.

(3) Thirty years ago, the presents offered by the bridegroom did not exceed 20 - 30 pounds, among the richest families; in very recent years 150 pounds is considered a modest and reasonable sum of money.

Fig. 24. Another girl wearing the tiʿlāqayn the adrim and aghraw ornaments.

Fig. 25. A decorated kuhl-pot. The bomboo tube is put inside cloth decorated with silk in different colours. Decorated multicoloured leather strips hang from it.

girl also spends large sums of money on her clothes and ornaments — more than they usually receive from the family of the bridegroom. Nowadays, the clothes alone cost more than a hundred pounds, if the bride and the bridegroom belong to well-to-do families.

When the bride is dressed in the evening of her marriage day, she must wear seven garments one over the other. The first, which is next to the skin, must be white in colour and of a thin transparent cloth; the second is red and transparent also; the third must be black; the fourth is yellow; the fifth is blue; the sixth is of red silk and the seventh is of green silk. Over these, she wears a special marriage dress, very richly embroidered with silk around the neck; over her head she puts a red silk shawl. The silver ornaments also cost a considerable sum of money.

The average age of marriage for girls is now sixteen years, and for men twenty-five. Until some thirty or forty years ago, the girls used to get married at the age of twelve to fourteen or less. A very strict custom forbade a man to have real intercourse with his wife for at least two years, since they believed that if the girl reached the age of puberty in the house of her husband, she would remain more obedient and faithful to him. Some Siwans (a small minority) still adhere partly to this custom, but they find that half a year or less is more than sufficient, since the brides are already mature.

However, it is very rare in Siwa to find a husband and wife who spend all their lives together; divorce is easy and occurs frequently. One seldom meets a man who is married to more than one wife living together in the same house; but it is not rare to hear some men boast that they have married several times, one after the other. Not infrequently, under these sad circumstances, many of the young girls who are not yet eighteen. have already been married and divorced once or twice.

When all the arrangements between the two families are made, generally by the women, and the family of the bride has had enough time to sew and embroider all the clothes and buy her ornaments, they fix a date for the marriage. This is generally after the season of selling the dates, or the season of selling the olives.

In the early afternoon of the day of betrothal, the bride puts on her best clothes and goes forth in the company of some of the women of her family and a few of the male relatives, to the spring of **Ṭamūsī**.(1) Previously, it was the custom that the bride would descend into the spring, wearing a single garment and wash herself in its waters, but nowadays she washes her face, feet and hands only. Here at the spring, the bride removes the decorated disk (the **adrim**) from its circular bar (the **aghraw**) and hands it to her mother or one of her aunts, to be used by her younger sister or any other young girl in the family.

The women constantly serenade the bride, from the moment they leave the house and during the so-called bath at the spring. On their way back, they continue their singing until they meet

(1) In previous times the brides were taken to «'Ayn al-Gūbah» the ancient «Spring of the Sun» which was also called «'Ayn al-Ḥammām» i.e. «Spring of the Bath» because of this ceremony. Since the middle of the last century, the Siwans prefer to take the brides to 'Ayn Ṭamūsī because it is far from the crowded roads and there the women can find more privacy.

Fig. 26. The flowing Siwan clothes.

the women of the bridegroom's family, who await them at an appointed place in the gardens on the outskirts of the town. Each of them offers her some money as a present, and the women of the two families continue their singing until they arrive at the house of the bride. There they spend their time in singing and dancing, waiting for the arrival of the bridegroom.

In the late evening, the bridegroom goes to the house of the bride accompanied by his relatives and friends. The bride waits in one of the rooms, guarded by some of her female relatives. A mock fight between the women of the two families ensues, ending in the "victory" of the bridegroom's party. They then take the bride to their house; joined by the other women where they resume their singing and dancing. The girl used to ride a led donkey, but nowadays they generally take her by car. When they reach the house, a woman carries her, helped generally by other women, until they seat her in her new chamber. It is very important that her feet should never touch the ground while she is being carried, since this is considered very unlucky.

Later on, the bridegroom goes to see his wife, taking with him a present of fruits and some biscuits, peanuts, peas and sweets; when he arrives, the other women are supposed to leave the room.[1]

The first thing he does, after entering the room is to take away the sword which hangs from the bride's right shoulder and put it under the bed. It was formerly the custom that he then removed her right shoe and struck her gently seven times on her right foot with his right hand; nowadays he presses very gently her right toe with his right toe. After this he opens the bag or basket, containing the fruits and sweets, and persuades her to eat some of them with him. After an hour, he descends to his friends. If he fails to do so, they knock on the door until he comes out. He spends the rest of the night with them, sharing their drinks and watching the singing and dancing until dawn. After this, he leaves the house with his best friend and spends two days in one of the gardens with him and his other friends.

On the third day, the family of the bride brings to her their presents and the rest of the furniture, including a carved red wooden chest which is made generally in Alexandria, and the

(1) It was the custom till some fifty years ago that the bridegroom took with him a stalk of a date palm and, before entering the room he removed his white garment, soaked it in oil, wrapped it around the stalk and lighted it. When it was half burnt, he placed it on two stones set apart until it burnt completely. If it broke, it was not a lucky omen. Nowadays, this is no longer done.

rest of her clothes, also the finely woven plates and pots which the girl has woven herself, including several conical baskets, the **margūnahs.** These, like the other plates, are made of the fine leaves of the stalks of the date palms and are richly decorated with silk, leather and buttons of mother of pearl.(1) They bring also the cooking pots and some food. On the same day, the bridegroom returns to his house and brings with him for his bride, the traditional present consisting of all kinds of fruit of the season on their branches and fixed around a **gummār**; these are arranged very nicely and decorated with flowers. The present is sometimes so heavy that more than one person is needed to carry it from the gardens to the house. The bride eats a little from it, and then they begin to cut pieces from the **gummār** and send them, together with some of the fruit, to every person who has provided a persent, or helped in the arrangements for the marriage.

On the seventh day, there is another small gathering at which the leading members of the two families have a meal in the bridegroom's house; after the seventh day the young couple begin their normal life together. These detailed ceremonies and festivities are performed only by the rich families when the girl marries for the first time.

Death

The Siwans bury their dead without any special ceremonies which distinguish them from other Muslims. They wash the body of the deceased according to the rules of Islam and wrap it in shrouds ; the number of the shrouds depends on the wealth of the family.

Among the things which attract the attention of every visitor to Siwa is the great number of graveyards, which he sees around the houses of the town and its suburbs. This is due to the fact that every large family has its own. Whenever a person dies, they dig for him a deep trench in the ground; the dead person, wrapped in shrouds, is placed in the trench which is then covered with logs from the trunk of palm trees and earth and small stones are piled over them. They mark the tomb with one or two larger stones and sometimes encircle it with a low mud enclosure. The women of the family and their relatives show all the signs of exaggerated mourning and shriek at the top of their voices. The signs of mourning reach their peak at the moment when the body of the dead person leaves the house, carried on a bier on the shoulders of the relatives. The women utter very loud cries, tear their clothes, beat their breasts, throw dust over their heads and, sometimes, smear their faces

(1) One **margūnah** is for the use of the husband, when he takes his food with him to the gardens during the first few months of married life.

with mud or some blue grit. At such times of excitement, the women forget the rule of avoiding being seen by any stranger and can be observed without any shawl covering the heads or faces. With their hair plaited in a number of small tresses and their exaggerated signs of grief, they present a living picture of ancient Egyptian women represented on the funeral scenes on the walls of the ancient tombs. They avoid, as much as they can, letting the body of a dead person remain in the house overnight; this is considered very unlucky and brings all kinds of misfortunes on the head of the family. If a person dies in the early afternoon, they prepare everything for the burial on the same day, even if they have to take the body to the grave and bury it by the light of lanterns or torches. Nothing is put in the tomb with the dead, but sometimes, a pot of incense, or a small vase of water is placed on the grave.

When a man loses his wife, it is considered very proper to marry another one, even during the same month, and nobody can criticise him; but when the contrary happens and a married man dies, the attitude toward his widow is quite different.

The Ghūlah

The word **ghūlah** means literally "the female **ghūl** (goblin, gobble), the devourer of humans".

When a man dies, his widow is called **ghūlah,** for the entire community believes that she has become possessed of a very strong evil eye which brings misfortune to any person upon whom she sets her eyes. The poor widow may be a child of sixteen or seventeen, but in any case, her misery begins at the moment her husband is carried to the grave. Some of her female relatives accompany her to the spring of **Ṭamūsī** where she removes her silver ornaments and ordinary clothing, washes herself and dons a white garment, a sign of mourning. Thereafter the unlucky woman is required to live in complete seclusion, for as long as four months and ten days in former times, forty days now. Her food, which must not contain meat, is brought to her by an elderly woman, the only person permitted to visit her personally during this period. She is allowed to speak, without opening the door, to her female relatives and those male relatives whom, by law, she is forbidden to marry, as for example, her father, brothers or uncles. Meanwhile, she is not allowed to change her white garment, wash herself, dress her hair, apply **kuḥl** to her eyes or use any kind of ornament.

When her period of seclusion has been fulfilled, the town crier, accompanied by a boy beating a drum, goes from street to street announcing that the **ghūlah** will reappear on the following day.

In mid-morning of that day, some of the children run through the streets announcing that she is coming forth; at noontime, a male relative climbs to the roof of the house and shouts at the top of his lungs that she is about to appear. Although her seclusion is over, the people still fear that some of the evil may yet remain. They believe, that even now, if she sets her eyes on a person, she brings him bad luck. Thus after all these warnings, she leaves the house, her face uncovered but her eyes bound. She is accompanied by a few relatives including children who keep repeating a phrase in Siwan, meaning: "Avoid your misfortune, the **ghūlah** comes to you." This warning is, in most cases, superfluous, because the men who live near her house, have long since disappeared into the gardens from early morning and the women and their children have shut themselves in their rooms.

If she lives in the town of Siwa, she goes to the spring of Ṭamūsī, or to the spring of Tiliḥrām, but if she lives in a distant place, she goes to the nearest spring or well, to wash herself with its waters. Thereafter she is considered free from the evil spirit which possessed her. On reaching her house she adorns herself with her ornaments, dresses her hair, puts on her finest apparel and receives her relatives and friends. At dawn next day she climbs to the roof and drops a piece of a palm-stalk on the first man or woman who passes in front of the house; if it finds its mark, the person can expect something unpleasant during this day. But whether the stalk hits or misses, the widow thus rids herself completely of all her misfortunes, and can resume her normal life. One year from the date of her husband's death she can marry again to any one she wants.[1]

This cruel custom is completely unknown anywhere else in Egypt, for it is in no way representative of the spirit and usage of the Muslim people, or the ancient Egyptians. However, it reminds us of other traditionally severe treatment of widows in some Asiatic and African communities. I wonder whence the Siwans inherited it, since no Berber or Arab community observes any custom of this kind nowadays.

Feasts

The most important feasts at Siwa are four; two are religious and are celebrated by all Muslims wherever they may be — these are the Lesser Feast, sometimes called the Lesser Bairam, celebrated at the end of the fasting month of **Ramaḍān**, and the Greater Feast known as Corban Bairam. The third is local and is celebrated in Siwa only ; this is the feast of Sīdī Sulaymān, a local Saint associated with the harvest. The fourth is the feast of **'Āshūrā.**

(1) This custom is mentioned in some detail by Maher, «**L'Oasis de Siwah**», p. 101 ; Steindorff, **Durch die Libysche...**, p. 112 ; Belgrave, **Siwa...**, p. 22, Schiffer, **Amonsoase...**, p. 29 - 30; Abdallah, «**Siwan Customs**,» pp. 11 - 13; and Wākid, **Wāḥat Amun**, pp. 130 - 2.

Siwa's celebration of the Lesser Bairam is not accompanied by any special traditions which make it different from the feast in the other oases, villages and towns of the Nile Valley, while the other three differ from festivals held on similar occasions elsewhere.

The Corban Bairam : Muslims celebrate the Corban Bairam on the tenth day of the Arabic month of **Dhul-Ḥijjah,** seventy days after the first day of the Lesser Bairam. On that day the Muslim pilgrims to Mecca celebrate it at the Mountain of **'Arafāt** where each pilgrim slaughters a ram in commemoration of Abraham's sacrifice of his son (according to Muslims, Ishmael not Isaac). At the same time the Muslims follow the same practice at home; the celebrant slaughters a sheep in his house, or at least cooks meat for his family. This tradition affords opportunity for the rich to express warmth and friendship towards their poor relatives and neighbours. Every family enjoys having a meal together, and while the methods of cooking or roasting or the number of plates might differ, everybody has his fill of the choicest pieces of meat on that morning.

But the Siwans have their special kind of celebration. From the first day of **Dhul-Ḥijjah,** the **zaggālah** stop most of their work in the gardens to go out and gather straw, dried weeds and stalks of date palm for use as fuel during the feast days. This continues for seven days, and on the eighth, they bring home large quantities of salt from a special district in one of the salt lakes. On the ninth day, every one seems busy, the women in housecleaning, putting the rugs, bedding and blankets on the roof of the houses. The **zaggālah** store fodder for the cattle.

Shortly after sunrise, following festival prayers in the mosque, the celebrants return home and slaughter the sheep. Instead of eating the choice pieces on the first day as everywhere else, they prepare this principal meal in quite a different way. They skin the sheep, and after removing all the hair from the hide, they cut it into long strips. These are cooked in olive oil together with the heart, liver and kidneys in an earthenware pot.

In 1941, when I happened to be visiting Siwa on the day of the Corban Bairam, one of its shaykhs insisted on inviting me to share this meal with him and his sons. I must admit that I was not accustomed to this kind of food, but I found it by no means very bad. The skin was not at all tough, and with thanks to my host for his kindness I ate as much as I could. My assistant, who was invited with me, could not continue to eat after the first mouthful when he understood what it was. He was sick all day.

On the second day of the feast the meal consists of the sheep's head, the legs and certain parts of the stomach, the meat being divided into portions weighing about one and a half pounds each. A large part of the meat is distributed to relatives and especially to newly married daughters. After eating as much as they can in the afternoon, the Siwans cut every left-over portion into very small pieces, mix these with plenty of salt, and thread all on strings. The strings are allowed to dry and then are stored for later use as needed. The remainder of the meat is cooked in fat and is stored in earthenware pots sealed with mud stoppers. Thus the meat can be preserved for months. This method of preservation is used also by the Bedouin of the desert whenever they are obliged to slay a camel. This stored meat is called **qiddīd**.

The Feast of Sīdī Sulaymān : The tomb of Sīdī Sulaymān which is situated at the side of the new mosque in the large town square, is the most venerated place in Siwa, because Sīdī Sulaymān is their patron saint, in whose sanctity and great miracles they firmly believe. The celebration of his **mawlid** (yearly festival) takes place after the corn harvest; apparently it replaces an ancient pagan feast of the harvest. But in recent years the festival has lost much of its gay spirit, since the government forbids the drinking of **labgī** or any other kind of wine, in public, during the week of the celebration. The intent of this prohibition is to avoid incidents and disputes between the **zaggālah** when they get drunk. Nevertheless, it is still the most important feast in Siwa; it is reminiscent of many aspects of the feasts of ancient times.

Before going into details I quote a literal translation of a description of the feast from the Siwan Manuscript : "Among the old customs, there was a day of the year when all the inhabitants used to meet at a place called al-'Āyid; everybody brought with him loaves of bread filled with **makhmakh** or **ghiyārin**." These are two Siwan words; the **makhmakh** is the purslane plant cooked together with beans or lentils ; the **ghiyārin** consists of cooked beans to which is added the Jew's mallow plant. "The food was put near one of the walls of the gardens which reach from a place now known as Jāmi' al-Durrah, to Khalīj Tanṣār. On this night, the men dance together and the women dance together till morning. They put all their food in one place and eat and drink the whole night, but this custom was discarded as a result of improper occurences which took place between them. This night was replaced by the evening of 'Āshūrā[1] during which the oil-pressers used to wrap tall, thick poles with old pieces of cloth soaked in olive oil. The people divided into groups; each group gathered around one of the poles which they ignited, and there they spent the whole night. The feast continued for

(1) The evening of the 9th day of the month of Muḥarram; see below.

seven nights of eating and drinking intoxicating beverages. It was discontinued on account of cost and was replaced by the yearly festival of the **mawlid** of Sīdī Sulaymān."

Thus the **mawlid** of Sīdī Sulaymān has replaced two older festivals of non-religious character. In fact, his festival still combines all the elements of the earlier feasts. But before describing the **mawlid**, it is essential to know more about Sīdī Sulaymān, and the Siwans' regard for his legendary personality — which, in its turn, reveals ancient non-Muslim influences.

The Siwans say that before his birth, Sīdī Sulaymān's mother felt an overwhelming desire to eat fish; she was unable to give birth and was almost at the point of death. There are no fish at Siwa(1), and the sea, over 300 kilometres away, cannot be reached in less than seven or eight days. Suddenly the miracle happened. A bird flew into the room through the open window and dropped a fish, which was immediately cleaned, cooked and eaten — and the child was born. This is the reason every pregnant woman in Siwa eats salted fish; she believes that thus she might have a similar boy. This also explains why the Siwans cook the salted fish in certain dishes on certain occasions.

The Siwans also tell another story. During Sīdī Sulaymān's lifetime, an army of savage negro tribes of Tibbu in the Western Sudan was on its way to plunder them. The saintly man called the people to the mosque to pray. His prayers were effective, and the whole army of the invaders was buried by a sandstorm. This is reminiscent of the story about the army of Cambyses which was sent against Siwa in the 6th century B.C. (see the chapter on history). In this later version, Sīdī Sulaymān took the place of the god Amun in rescuing Siwa by sending a violent sandstorm which buried the whole army before reaching the oasis.

The Siwans say that their great saint was very generous and preached hospitality to strangers. Some years after his death, a number of poor Bedouin pilgrims arrived at Siwa on their way to Mecca. Although they were in need, the people refused to welcome them and drove them away. The saint was very displeased, indignantly closed the door of his tomb and refused to let anyone inside. All their efforts to open the door were in vain, and the people wondered why their patron saint should be angry with them. Then they recalled their unfriendliness toward the poor pilgrims and at once sent out messengers to bring them back. Once the pilgrims were well fed and entertained, the door opened miraculously by itself.

---

(1) The small fish which can be seen in some of the small canals of the springs has been recently introduced in Siwa. It is of a special kind which feeds on the eggs of malaria-bearing mosquitoes.

The Siwans tell many tales about their saint; they consider his tomb a refuge and sanctuary for anyone who seeks his protection. They firmly believe in these legends; indeed, they become very indignant when anyone casts the slightest doubt.

Several days before this **mawlid,** every man or woman in Siwa is busied in preparations; sewing clothes, baking bread and biscuits, bringing fruit from the gardens, storing drinks, and putting all in readiness. On the preceding day they whitewash the tombs of Sīdī Sulaymān and other saints, and most of the men go out and make a general cleaning of the springs. On the day of the festival, the rich shaykhs slaughter sheep and distribute the meat to the poor; the women hang carpets, blankets and coloured mats from the roofs and windows of houses, and everyone dresses in his or her finest apparel. In the morning hours, the Siwans visit each other's homes for congratulation; in the afternoon the young men retire to the gardens to drink their favourite **labgī.** At dusk all return to the town square, which is illuminated with candles and lanterns and decorated with banners. Near the tomb of the saint, the pious and elderly men hold religious circles to perform their **dhikr.** In this they repeat the name of Allah and move their bodies to the beating of drums and the music of flutes and tambourines.

Some distance from the square, and nearer to the foot of the hill where the old town stands, most of the men and in particular the **zaggālah** celebrate in a different way. The festival continues for three days spent in eating, dancing, singing and drinking, despite the prohibition of alcohol. They enjoy themselves to excess, and when the festival is over, most of them need a few days' rest.

The Feast of 'Āshūrā : A few hundred years ago, this was Siwa's principal feast, but today it is second in importance, its place having been taken by the **mawlid** of Sīdī Sulaymān. Its origin is religious. It commemorates the martyrdom of al-al-Ḥusayn, son of 'Alī and Fāṭimah (the daughter of the Prophet Muḥammad) who was killed at Karbalā', in Iraq, on the tenth of the month of Muḥarram, thirty days after the Corban Bairam. A very important feast during the period of Fatimid rule in North Africa and Egypt since more than a thousand years ago; the day is celebrated now with great solemnity by all Shī'ite Muslims. Although its importance has long since greatly diminished in the towns of Egypt, it has retained the greater part of its old prestige in Siwa. In discussing the feast of Sīdī Sulaymān earlier, I quoted a paragraph from the Siwan Manuscript in which a reference to the feast of 'Āshūrā describes how the oil-pressers used to celebrate it by illuminating the town square. Nowadays it has given place to the **mawlid** of Sīdī Sulaymān and has become primarily a feast for the children.

Several days before the feast, the children begin to decorate the roofs of their houses with tall palm tree stalks, each fastened with a torch soaked in olive oil. At the sunset-call to prayers on the evening of the feast day, the children climb to the roofs and light the torches. When they finish, they stand together in groups and sing at the top of their voices a special old song, reserved only for this feast. For about ten minutes, the whole town is illuminated, and the pleasant voices of the children resound from every direction.

A large meal is prepared in every house, and all the members of the family enjoy the evening in their homes. On the following day, each child goes into the street dressed in his best clothes and carries a small framework of pieces of palm tree stalks from which hang fruits, nuts, sweets and different kinds of biscuits. Each child calls on his relatives of the same age, to exchange sweetmeats. The parents and the grown-ups, in general, take no active part in the feast; the men sit in front of the houses while the women ascend to the roofs to watch their own, neighbours' and relatives' children, as they go happily from house to house.

Other Customs and Superstitions

The Siwans have many other customs which space forbids description in detail here. I have discussed the typically important festivals of Siwa; the reader can find further information in the references listed in the footnotes. I refer now only in passing to the customs of pilgrims to Mecca, when camels were used for this journey. Use of cars in modern times has caused various ceremonies to be neglected.

Similarly, the ancient ceremonious slaying of a heifer when an epidemic disease had spread and distributing small pieces of the meat to all the inhabitants of the oasis, has also disappeared. The belief was that anybody who ate the meat would escape from the death which threatened him.(1)

The Siwans, men and women, are very superstitious; they believe firmly in the evil eye and do their best to arm themselves against it, as witness the charms, talismans and amulets carried by the children from birth. The grown-ups are no exception. There are professional men and women whose work is to make these charms and to recite certain incantations when someone is sick or threatened by evil. The Siwans believe also in magic, and the oasis is never without two or three magicians

---

(1) For details of these two customs, see Ahmed Fakhry, **Siwa Oasis...**, pp. 16 and 19.

whose help is always needed.[1] The danger of the evil eye is not limited to humans but extends also to animals and crops, and it is not uncommon to see the skulls of donkeys raised on long sticks and fixed to garden walls as protection from the evil eye. Many customs and ancient traditions of Siwa are beginning to change; some, indeed, are modified or have even disappeared. But superstitions still remain in spite of education and the presence of physicians. The Siwans believe — especially the women — not only in the evil eye, but also in the great power of unseen forces, such as the **jinn** which can injure them if they do not arm themselves. Apparently, many generations must pass before these superstitions disappear completely, if they ever do.

Now, enough of customs, traditions and superstitions. Let us proceed to the ancient history of Siwa.

(1) A number of these superstitions are discussed in the paper written by Abdallah, Siwan Customs, pp. 21 - 23, and that of Oric Bates, «Siwan Superstitions,» **Cairo Scientific Journal,** vol. 5. No. 55 (Cairo, 1911), and chapter iv, Belgrave, **Siwa...,** pp. 207 - 88.

3

From the Earliest Times to the Rise of Islam

The Name of Siwa

There are many speculations about the origin and meaning of the word "Siwa", but none of these is conclusive.(1) All that can be said is that the name is comparatively new, since it was not known before the Middle Ages. Al-Maqrīzī and other Arab writers called this oasis Santarieh. Al-Maqrīzī mentioned it under this name in the 15th century, adding that its inhabitants spoke a language called Al-Sīwīyah (the Siwan); in the 17th century the name Santarieh was forgotten completely among the inhabitants of the oasis and the Bedouin at the coast; it was known as Siwa only.(2) In the writings of the Roman and Greek authors, they referred to it as the Oasis of Jupiter-Ammon, after the oracle of Amun which was located there. In the famous text of the Seven Oases in the Temple of Idfū which dates from the 2nd century B.C.(3) this oasis is mentioned, but unfortunately the text is fragmentary; the preserved part says: "The oasis which is at the south-west of Sherep (i.e. Wādī al-Naṭrūn), "... Pnta... " This shows that the name began with the letters "ta ... ", probably one of two names, the religious one; the other, which can be called the popular name, is lost. The name "ta..." does not occur in any other geographical text in the temples of this period. Some writers think its ancient name is the "Field of Palm trees,"

---

(1) For a number of these speculations, and the places in the different parts of the world which are called Siwa, Siba or Siwi, see Schiffer, **Die Oase Siwa...**, pp. 85 - 86, footnotes 69 - 71.

(2) More details about Santarieh and the occurence of the word "Siwa" are found later in the section on the history of Siwa in the Middle Ages.

(3) K. Sethe, «Die Aegyptischen Bezeichnumgen fur die Oasen und Ihre Bewohner,» **Z.A.S.** 55 : 49 ff.

which occurs in several texts, but this expression is general for all the oases and not for Siwa alone;[1] it is, however, similar to the Arabic expression, Bilād al-Jarīd (the lands of the palm tree ribs), which was used in the Middle Ages for all the oases.[2]

If we turn to the monuments which still exist in the oasis, we find the name "Tha" or "Thay" mentioned three times ; on the wall of the Temple of Umm 'Ubaydah at Aghūrmī, and in the Tomb of Si-Amun, and the Tomb of Mesu-Isis in Jabal al-Mawtā, in connection with the gods Amenre and Osiris which were worshipped there. It is the name of this oasis or at least of its principal town.

We must also remember that the inhabitants of Siwa were originally from the Berber and the language which they use until now is one of the Berber dialects. Al-Ya'qūbī (deceased in 897) referred to a Berber tribe called "...Swa" and Ibn Khaldūn (1362 - 1406) mentioned "Ti-Swa" (the "ti" is the Berber article), one of the tribes of Banī al-Waswah a branch of Lawāṭah.[3]

Siwa in Palaeolithic and Neolithic Times

The prehistory of the oases of the Western Desert is not yet thoroughly studied, except for Kharga which has received some attention. All that we know about Siwa is based on the surface finds made by a very few prehistorians, among whom are H.W. Seton-Karr, who presented a number of the implements he found there to the Museum of Alexandria; and C.W. Cunnington, who gave a small collection to the same museum, but his best specimens are now in the Museum of Archeology and Ethnography in Cambridge (England). Oric Bates, during his work in the Western Desert before the First World War, collected more specimens. The study of these flints proved that some resemble finds in parts of Algeria and Morocco, in the Sahara, Cyrenaica, Nubia and some places in Egypt, and are definitely associated with industries of the late Upper and Final Palaeolithic Age.[4]

Among the specimens collected by Cunnington is a kind of knife made of tabular flint with marginal flaking usually on one

(1) **Ibid.**, p. 49 ff.

(2) Dr. Henry Fischer drew my attention to what is published in Gardiner, **Papyrus Wilbour II**, p. 31, N. 6 where both Newberry and Keimer point out that the rendering of ...i3m... as date-palm is wrong.

(3) Laoust, **Encyclopédie de l'Islam,** T. IV, p. 485.

(4) For more details see Suliman Ahmad Huzayyin, **The Place of Egypt in Prehistory**, pp. 243, 298 and 432, Pl. XIII, and Figs. 5 - 7. The arrowhead found by Bates is published in his book, **The Eastern Libyans**, p. 145, Fig. 56, and republished by Alexander Scharff, **Z.A.S.** 61 : 28.

edge and the tip only; this implement shows similarities to the **Fayyūm B-Culture which dates from late Neolithic but has certain radical differences. In Siwa, the broad willow leaf and the** narrow javelin assume a distinctly local character(1) (Fig. 27).

These finds prove that Siwa was inhabited in Palaeolithic and Neolithic times, and also that the culture of its inhabitants in those remote times was identified with the countries of west Egypt, and at the same time with the culture of the Nile Valley.

Siwa in Historic Times

At the end of the Predynastic times and during the Old Kingdom, there lived to the west of the Delta a people whom the Egyptians called "Teḥenu" in their texts. Later on, their land was invaded by people of another race called the "Temeḥu". They in-

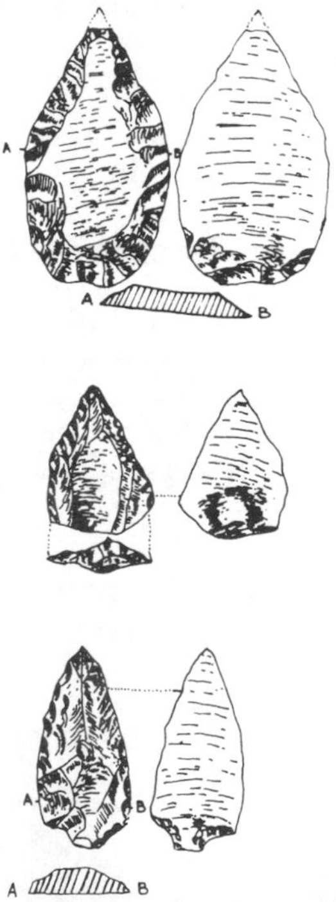

Fig. 27. Flint implements found at Siwa (now at the Museum of Archeology and Ethnography — Cambridge, England).

(1) Huzayyin, **Place of Egypt in Prehistory,** pp. 242 - 3 ; see also my book, **Siwa Oasis...,** p. 22.

habited the districts to the west of Egypt including, very probably, the coast and the oasis of Siwa as well as other ones; but what we know about them is limited and we cannot say with any certainty whether they were the ancestors of the Berber or of any branch, or whether their language had any connections with any Berber tongue or the present-day dialect of the Siwans. The question of who these two peoples were, and what their connection with the history of the Western Desert is, is important to the background of the history of Siwa, and I give it here in some detail.

The Teḥenu and the Temeḥu lived to the west of Egypt and, from the most ancient times, they sought to immigrate to the Nile Valley and settle in the Western Delta whenever there was a great drought in their region or when external or internal hostilities forced some of their tribes to search for a new home. The route of their immigrations was via the oases in some cases, and they reached Middle Egypt via Baḥrīyah or Farafra, but generally they went to Siwa or proceeded along the coast and the Maryūṭ district. The western part of the Delta, to the west of the Canopic branch of the Nile (which the ancient Egyptians called the Western River) was inhabited by people who were predominantly a mixture of Libyans and Egyptians, of the same origin as the brown Mediterranean race of the Nile Valley. This territory corresponds to the Third Nome of Lower Egypt (the Western), the Fifth Nome (the Saitic) and the Seventh Nome (the Barbed Harpoon Nome). The principal deity of the Third Nome (the Western Nome) was the falcon deity who was called "Horus from Libya with the striking arm"; the Goddess Neith, the chief deity of Sais (Fifth Nome) was characterized by the arrow, and was called "Neith from Libya".(1)

It seems that the Seventh Nome of the Delta did not extend further west than the lake of Maryūṭ. The region west of the lake, as well as the oasis in the desert, were not considered as part of any special Nome. Till the year 1971 it was generally accepted that the oases did not come under the control of the central government of Egypt before the Middle Kingdom, (20th century B.C.) and were Egyptianized only in the Eighteenth Dynasty (15th century B.C.). My recent excavations in Dakhla Oasis in the years 1971 and 1972 proved that the Governors of the Oasis had their capital since, at least, the Sixth Dynasty (2420 - 2280 B.C.) at the site of 'Ayn Aṣīl near Balāṭ, and continued to rule there during the First Intermediate Period (2280-2052 B.C.).

The tombs of five of those wealthy governors were excavated, and there were found very important inscriptions includ-

(1) Hermann Kees, **Ancient Egypt** (Chicago, 1961), p. 28.

ing inscribed stone doors, stelae, obelisks, offering-tables, etc... The style of the architecture of those tombs as well as the hieroglyphic texts and reliefs are more or less similar to what is known to us from the cemeteries of the provincial capitals in Upper Egypt at that period.

However, we have no evidence up till now that the region of the coast west of the Lake of Maryūṭ was considered as a part of any one of the Nomes of the Western Delta, although it was under the complete control of the government and many temples and fortresses were built there.

From the First Dynasty onwards, we find references to the inhabitants who lived to the west of the Nile Valley. They were called the Teḥenu (olive land)(1); and there were battles in which the Pharaohs captured great numbers of their men and their cattle. It is most unlikely that the Pharaohs of the Protodynastic period or the First Dynasty raided their land for the sake of conquest or booty; but it is probable that great numbers of those people came to the borders of the Delta with their cattle, intending to settle in the fertile lands of the Nile Valley.(2)

They came as immigrants, rather than as conquerors, but despite this fact their arrival in great numbers threatened the security of the land and the kings had to fight them and drive them back. Very likely these battles took place at the western edge of the Delta; but where the location of the land of the Teḥenu was, is still under discussion. Wilhelm Hölscher concludes that their home was in the neighbourhood of al-Fayyūm and Wādī al-Naṭrūn(3), but I believe that they lived further west in Maryūṭ and in the oases of Siwa and Baḥrīyah and in Barqah in Libya.(4)

They were of the same race as the Egyptians, brown in colour and, though the dress of the two peoples differed in some details, there were many similarities between them. Some of the names of the Teḥenu are Egyptian, such as Uni and Khuit-iotes,

---

(1) However, the interpretation of «Teḥenu» as olive-land is disputed by Keimer, BIFAO, 31 (1931), pp. 121 ff.

(2) The earliest reference to the land of Teḥenu is on one of the monuments from the reign of King Scorpion (Cat. Gen. 14238) in the Protodynastic period and depicts the booty brought from their land. Quibell, **Hierakonpolis I,** Pls. 15, 17 and p. 7. For other references from the early period of Egyptian history, see Wilhelm Hölscher, **Libyer und Aegypter** (1937), pp. 19 - 23.

(3) **Ibid.**, pp. 19 - 22.

(4) This point was discussed in some detail in **Baḥria Oasis,** vol. 1 (1942), pp. 5 - 10.

which occur on the famous scene from the Temple of Saḥure at Abūṣīr, which dates from the Fifth Dynasty.(1)

If we try to find out where there descendents live nowadays, we can think of some of the tribes who live nowadays in the west of the Sudan and in the southern desert of Libya.

It is very likely that the great immigration of the Teḥenu in the days of King Saḥure resulted not from drought but from internal difficulties caused by another people, the Temeḥu, who began to appear on the stage in North Africa and were pushing the Teḥenu from their territories. Very possibly some of their tribes tried to find a new home in the Delta. The unlucky Teḥenu were attacked from the west and beaten in the east until they ceased to exist as a nation. Their name, however, lingered for many centuries, almost until the end of the history of Ancient Egypt, but only as the ancient name of a geographical district or districts inhabited by other people.

The name, Land of the Temeḥu, appears for the first time in Egyptian texts in the reign of King Pepi I of the Sixth Dynasty; it is mentioned in the biography of Uni as one of the places from which he recruited soldiers for his army. The Temeḥu belonged to a race which differed from both the Teḥenu and the Egyptians; their skin was fair, they had blonde hair and gray (or blue ?) eyes and dressed differently, always having a lock of hair at the side of the head. Were those people native Africans or did they immigrate to North Africa from somewhere else ? It is almost impossible that such blonde hair and grey eyes could be native to African soil; it is very likely that they were the descendants of a European Nordic race who came in boats from the north or crossed the strait of Gibraltar, some of their tribes wandering later on along the coast and far into the south.(2) Such immigrations have occurred several times in historic periods. But however deeply we study the subject, seeking to determine from what part of Northern Europe they may have come, we cannot reach any definite conclusion; we find ourselves confronted with many problems. All that we read of their descent from Vandals or any other Nordic race is mere speculation.

Like the Teḥenu before them, the Temeḥu immigrated into the Nile Valley with their families, either to settle in the rich lands or probably for trade. In one of the tombs of Banī Ḥasan

---

(1) L. Borchardt, **Sahure** II, Pl. I. The third name is «Usa» which may be Libyan.

(2) Carlton Coon, **Races of Europe** (1939), pp. 464 - 65, believes that the Northern European origin of the Libyans is unlikely and suggests Central Asia which is rather unlikely as well.

(Tomb of Khnumhotep, No. 14, reign of Amenemhet I, circa 1970 B.C.) there is a scene depicting some of the Temehu with their women, children and herds. The men fix four or five ostrich feathers in their hair, wear long robes, the left arm is covered while the right is bare; they have short beards. The women wear a skirt with a fringe at its lower edge. The entire caravan is fair-skinned, coloured light yellow, with red-blonde, short hair and blue eyes.(1) The women carry their children on their backs, wrapped in part of their clothing; this custom existed in Egypt in prehistoric times, as well as among some of the Negro Sudanese tribes of antiquity. It is still in use nowadays in many parts of Africa, among some desert Bedouin in Egypt, and in Siwa oasis.

The ostrich feathers which we see fixed in the hair of the Temeḥu, and later among the Libyans, cannot be considered as a racial characteristic of these people. In fact, we see such feathers stuck in the hair of some Egyptians from the Predynastic period onwards. In historic times, they occur only in the determinatives of the ancient Egyptian words which denote soldier, military expedition or army, but were in use among the dwellers of Nubia, Libya and the desert Bedouin. Feathers are still worn in the hair in Central Africa and among some of the Hamitic tribes living in East Africa. Modern usage might throw some light on the subject. It is a mark of distinction. When a warrior of the tribe of the Danāgil (the Adels of Afars) succeeds in killing an enemy, he puts a white ostrich feather in his hair as a sign of victory. Some of these tribesmen wear many feathers. Perhaps in ancient times this was the custom among the Libyans, but with progress of time they used two feathers or only one.(2)

Sutekh-irdes, ruler of Siwa in the time of King Amasis and depicted with him on the walls of the sanctuary in the Temple of the Oracle, was a descendant of a Libyan family, and he has an ostrich feather fixed in his hair.

The Middle and New Kingdoms

Several Egyptian monuments prove beyond any doubt that Wādī al-Naṭrūn and the four oases of Baḥrīyah, Farafra, Kharga and Dakhla were known to the ancient Egyptians at least since the end of the Old Kingdom, and were visited by Egyptian patrols in the early Middle Kingdom. We can say, in general,

---

(1) Wreszinski, **Atlas II**, Pl. 50a, gives a detailed description of the clothes, weapons and amulets of these people; see also, P. Newberry, **Beni Hasan I**, Pls. 45, 47.

(2) See also the important details given by Jean Clére, «Fragments d'une Nouvelle Représentation Egyptienne du Monde,» **MDIK**, 16 (1958), pp. 40 - 43.

that these four oases were completely Egyptianized and brought under the direct control of Egyptian officials(1) even before the 6th Dynasty ; but does the same apply to Siwa, which lies much further to the west than any other oases, and at a distance of not less than eight days' march from the coast ? (Fig. 28).

To date, no monument of the Old Kingdom or the Middle Kingdom — or even the New Kingdom — has been found in Siwa. Moreover, the scenes on the walls of the tombs at Thebes, representing the chiefs of the two groups of the oases, the Northern and the Southern, cannot be considered as conclusive proof that the Northern group included Siwa as well as Baḥrīyah and Farafra. Until further evidence is discovered, this must remain an open question.(2)

It is very probable that Egyptian religion and Egyptian culture spread in Siwa in those days and that during the New Kingdom a temple for the God Amenre'stood there, but I must repeat that no monument of the New Kingdom has so far been found in this oasis, and that Siwa was not mentioned in the texts of the Libyan wars, or in any document dating from the 22nd Dynasty (Fig. 29).

The ancestors of the family which founded that Dynasty came originally from Libya, then lived for some generations in one of the oases, most probably in Baḥrīyah and paid great attention to its old home in the oasis; but to date, no monument from that Dynasty has been discovered in Siwa. We must wait until the 26th Dynasty; the oldest monument in this oasis dates from the reign of King Amasis.

Siwa in the 26th Dynasty

The 26th Dynasty of Egypt began in 663 B.C. and ended in the year 525 B.C., a period which witnessed very important movements and changes in the old world, not only in the Near Eastern countries, but among the Greeks and the Asiatic civilizations in Central Asia and China.

In the year 671, King Esarhaddon of Assyria invaded Egypt; some of the local princes of the chief towns accepted the new regime while others resisted, then fled to Ethiopia. After some years they returned and tried to repel the invaders. This state of unrest and rebellion affected, to a great extent, the position of Egypt as the center of commerce in the East,

---

(1) In April - May 1971, I discovered in the neighbourhood of Balāṭ in Dakhla Oasis the cemetery of the governors of the Oasis during the 6th Dynasty. (see above, pp. 73 - 74).

(2) In some of my previous writings on the Oasis (cf. for example, **Siwa Oasis...**, p. 25), I was convinced that Siwa was one of the oases of the Northern group and was completely Egyptianized in the 18th Dynasty.

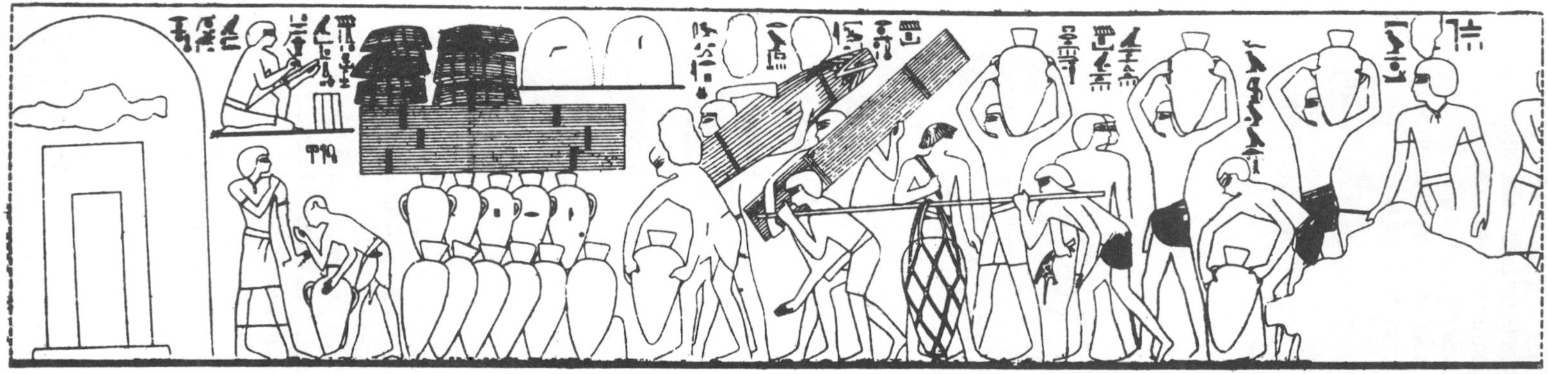

Fig. 28. The tribute of the oases (from the Tomb of Rekhmire. 18th Dynasty, Thebes).

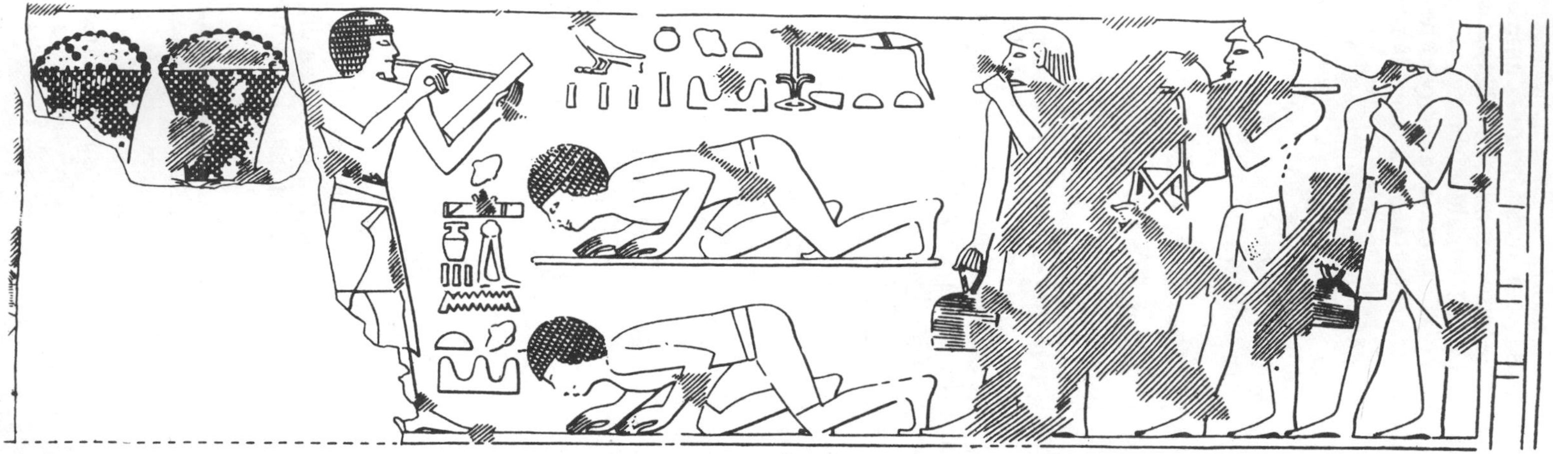

Fig. 29. The chiefs of the Southern and Northern Oases bring the tribute (from the tomb of Puyemre, 18th Dynasty, Thebes).

and trade with India was consequently directed to the Persian Gulf. Moreover, the trade of the Sudan and inner Africa was directed to the caravan routes via the oases, and thence to the coast of the Mediterranean where the merchandise was shipped in Greek or Phoenician vessels to Europe and elsewhere.(1) In other words, the Assyrian conquest of Egypt was in all probability responsible for the prosperity of the oases of the Western Desert of Egypt in those days, and also, to a great extent, for the establishment of some of the Greek colonies on the southern coast of the Mediterranean, the most important being Cyrene, founded in 631 B.C. After a short time, the Greek colonists of Cyrene became a threat not only to the inhabitants of Libya, but to Egypt itself. This was the reason why Apries and his successor Amasis started their new policy in all the oases.

The Temple of the Oracle, which still stands on the rock of Aghūrmī, was built in the 26th Dynasty, in the reign of Amasis. In all probability there were temples for the god Amun, and perhaps other local deities before that time.

The governors of the oases were descendants of Libyan tribes (the Mashwish) who held the power in their hands but recognized the Kings of Egypt as their lords. But the Egyptian rulers lived far away in their palaces in the capital, and each oasis was, in effect, a small kingdom, its ruler considered the local king.

Herodotus, who lived in the middle of the 5th century B.C., mentions that the King of the Oasis of Amun in those days was called "Etearchus". The inhabitants of Cyrene, who frequently travelled to Siwa for trade or to consult its Oracle, told the Father of History stories which they had heard from Etearchus concerning an adventure of five young people who undertook a dangerous journey. They sought to discover the lands south of the coast of Libya and its desert ; they reached a land inhabited by black people of small size and a large river which was thought at that time to be the Nile.(2)

The Oracle of Amun in the Libyan Desert

The Oracle of Amun in Siwa was already famous all over the Mediterranean countries by the beginning of the 26th Dynasty, but in seeking to trace its origin we can only guess that it must have originated some time during or before the 21st

---

(1) Khun B. de Provok, «Ancient trade routes from Carthage into the Sahara,» **Geographical Review**, 15 (1925), pp. 190 - 205, and W.B.K. Shaw, «Darb al-Arba'in,» **Sudan Notes and Records,** XII (1929), pp. 63 - 71.

(2) Herodotus, **Book II,** par. 31 - 32. The river which they discovered was apparently the Niger.

Dynasty when the power of the priests of Amun and the Oracles of that god played a prominent part in the religion and administration of the government in Egypt. It is probable that a temple to Amenre'was already built in Siwa in those days, to become, at a later date, the seat of an Oracle which was considered reliable. In the 26th Dynasty, this Oracle of Amun in the Libyan desert was widely known.

About the year 550 B.C., Croesus, King of Lydia, a contemporary of Amasis of Egypt, sought to test the knowledge of the oracles of the world in order to consult one of them concerning his future attitude towards Cyrus of Persia, then beginning to lay the foundations of the great Persian Empire. Croesus realized that a confrontation was inevitable; he wanted to inquire whether he should undertake a military campaign against Persia. Herodotus tells us : "With this purpose in view he (Croesus) at once prepared to try his luck with the oracles, and sent to Delphi, to Abae in Phocia, to Dodona, to the oracles of Amphiaraus and Trophonius, and to Branchidae in Milesia. These were the Greek ones which he consulted, but, not content with them he sent also to the Oracle of Ammon in Libya."(1)

He sent Lydian messengers to all seven, ordering each man to consult the oracle to which he was assigned, on the hundredth day after leaving Sardis, inquire what Croesus was doing at that moment, and record the answer. Herodotus tells us also that when all the messengers returned, "Croesus opened all the rolls and read what they contained. None impressed him in the least, except the one which contained the answer from Delphi. But no sooner had this been read to him than be accepted it with profound reverence, declaring that the Oracle at Delphi was the only genuine one in the world, because it had succeeded in discovering what he had been doing. And indeed it had; for after sending off the messengers, Croesus had thought of something which no one would be likely to guess, and with his own hands, keeping carefully to the pre-arranged date, he had cut up a tortoise and a lamb and boiled them together in a bronze cauldron with a bronze lid."(2)

---

(1) Herodotus, **Book I**, pp. 46 - 49.

(2) The prompt answer of the priestess of Delphi was given in hexameter verse :

I count the grains of sand on the beach and measure the sea;
I understand the speech of the dumb and hear the voiceless.
The smell has come to my sense of a hard-shelled tortoise
Boiling and bubbling with lamb's flesh in a bronze pot;
The cauldron underneath is of bronze, and of bronze the lid. (Herodotus, **Book I**, p. 49).

We are not told what answers the other oracles gave, or how far or near from the truth. In any event, this story shows very clearly that the oracle at Siwa was considered one of the seven most famous in the ancient world, and its answers were greatly respected and believed.

The Army of Cambyses

The Persians invaded Egypt in the year 525 B.C., and put an end to the 26th Dynasty. The army was led by King Cambyses, the son of Cyrus. While still in Egypt he decided to send three armies: one to Ethiopia, under his personal command; the second to Carthage (near the present-day city of Tunis), and the third to the Oasis of Amun. The first of these campaigns was a complete failure, and after many disasters a small part of the Persian army returned to Egypt. The second against Carthage could not be carried out because the Phoenicians who were helping Cambyses with their fleet refused to fight against their Carthagian cousins.

We can easily understand why Cambyses wanted to conquer Ethiopia and Carthage, but as for Siwa, we cannot find a satisfactory explanation except perhaps that Cambyses held a grudge against its oracles. It is possible that the Siwan oracle predicted the tragic end of Cambyses and his rule in Egypt after a short time, and he wanted to punish the priests and, in the meantime, show the Egyptians or Greeks who believed in the Oracle of Amun that the Siwan oracle and its priests were helpless. Again, Herodotus is our most ancient source of information. He reports that Cambyses, on arrival at Thebes en route to Ethiopia, "detached a body of 50,000 men with orders to attack the Ammonians, reduce them to slavery, and burn the oracle of Zeus."(1) He states further that the force sent against the Ammonians set out from Thebes with guides, and reached the town of Oasis, i.e. Kharga Oasis, which is, as Herodotus remarks, seven days' journey across the sand from Thebes and known to the Greeks as the "Island of the Blessed". After leaving Kharga, they disappeared; none of that large army ever reached Siwa, and none returned to Kharga or any other place in Egypt. Herodotus adds: "There is, however, a story told by the Ammonians themselves, and by others who heard it from them, that when the men left Oasis, and in their march across the desert had reached a point about midway between it and the Ammonian border, a southerly wind of extreme violence drove the sand over them in heaps as they were taking their mid-day meal, so that they disappeared forever."(2)

---

(1) Herodotus, **Book III**, p. 26.

(2) **Ibid.**, p. 28.

Amun avenged himself on those who wanted to destroy his temple and kill or carry his priests into slavery. The loss of the army and the tragic end of Cambyses himself must have increased the prestige of that oracle.(1)

While it is very possible that the number of the soldiers is greatly exaggerated, this does not change the historical fact that an army sent by Cambyses in the year 524 B.C. was buried under the sands of the Libyan Desert at some place mid-way between Kharga and Siwa.

The discovery of the site of this disaster has fired the imagination of many explorers of this desert for many years, especially after cars came into use in the present century, but no one has found any tracks which could lead to solving the mystery. Small aeroplanes have been employed, also without success. The explorers think of this lost army as a great hidden treasure worth millions of dollars; they spend hours calculating the price at which the arms could be sold to museums and collectors all over the world. They take it for granted that the dry sands have preserved all these weapons and equipment and personal property of the soldiers. Day dreams sometimes come true.

The sandstorms in the desert, and particularly in the areas of dunes can be disastrous to travellers. In the year 1805, a caravan of 2,000 persons with their camels, en route from Dārfūr in the Western Sudan to Asyūt, was buried under the sands of the same Libyan desert.(2)

In the Siwan Manuscript, we read twice of armies which were buried in sandstorms. The first was a Siwan force which went out to meet the Muslim invaders but was caught in a storm and completely buried in the sand; the second, an army of the black Tibbu tribe who intended to attack Siwa but lost their way in the desert. Both stories may be true; perhaps each is merely the ancient Cambyses in another context.

Cimon and the Oracle of Amun

The famous Athenian general, Cimon son of Miltiades, was besieging the Island of Cyprus with his fleet in 450 B.C., but the island resisted. Cimon had a great deal of confidence in the Oracle of Amun, and he was curious to know the result of that war. He sent some of his men to Siwa, and the oracle refused to give them any answer, but ordered them to leave the oasis as soon as possible, stating that Cimon who sent them was already with him. They left Siwa, boarded ship from Paraetonium (Marsā Maṭrūḥ) and set sail for Cyprus. When they reached Egypt they

---

(1) Plutarch (**Alexander, 26**), mentions the same story and says that Alexander was warned of going to Siwa lest he should meet with such danger and perish in the desert.

(2) Ritter, **Afrika, I**: 397; and Von Minutoli, **Reise...**, pp. 201 - 2.

learned from the resident Greeks that Cimon was dead. When they calculated the number of days, and checked the date of his death, they found that he died on the very same day that Amun had told them that "he was already with him". This story became famous throughout the ancient world, and Siwa's oracle became the most reliable. For how could the priests at Siwa know, on the same day, what had happened at such a distant place? Of course, modern communications were unknown in those early times.

Pindar

Pindar (518 — 438 B.C.) generally regarded as the greatest Greek lyric poet, was a great admirer of the Oracle of Amun. He sent, as a present to the god, perhaps after an oracle concerning himself, a hymn of praise which was carved on a three-sided stela. This was still standing in the temple, half-buried in its court when Pausanias visited Siwa 600 years later in A.D. 160.(1) When Pindar was very old, he sent messengers to the Oracle of Amun, asking the god to give him the greatest human luck, and in the same year, he died.(2)

The Athlete Eubotas

Many other stories about this oracle in the second half of the 5th century B.C. have reached us in the works of the classical authors; there is no need to mention them all. I prefer to refer to one which caused a great sensation at its time.

Eubotas, a well-known athlete from Cyrene, was told by Amun of Siwa that he was going to win the prize for running in the 93rd Olympiad (408 B.C.). He was certain of the truth of the oracle that he took with him to Olympia a statue of himself. He won, and consequently it was possible to see the statue of the champion on the day of his victory. This caused a great sensation among the Greeks and was not forgotten for many centuries. Diodorus, who lived in the 1st century B.C., and Pausanias, who wrote his work in the 2nd century A.D. repeated the story.

Lysander, who tried to bribe Amun

Lysander was a famous Spartan general, who won a great victory for his country in the year 405 B.C. when he captured the Athenian fleet and made Sparta the leading country in the

---

(1) Pausanias was a traveller and geographer, probably born in Lydia. His work «Description of Greece» is a valuable source on ancient Greek topography, monuments and legends. Pausanias saw also in the temple of Siwa other monuments presented to Amun, including an altar of Ptolemy I. (Pausanias, 9 : 16,1).

(2) Gustav Parthey, **Das Orakel** (Berlin, 1836), p. 161 ; see also August Boeckh, **Vita Pindaris**, p. 9.

Hellenistic world. A very ambitious man, he wanted to be crowned King of Sparta, but the laws forbade. He hoped to become king by election, but when he sought the support of the Oracle of Delphi, he failed. He tried the priests of the Oracle of Dodona, and with bribes received a favourable answer. Now he needed the support of the Oracle of Amun. A few years earlier, when he was besieging a city, the god Amun came to him in a dream, ordered him to attack and guaranteed his victory. Later, Lysander sent many presents to the temple in Siwa. Since Lysander was a friend of the King of Cyrene, the Spartan decided to go in person to visit him and ask his help with the priests of Amun; in the meantime, he sent them numerous presents, seeking to renew his old friendship and win the favour.

It seems, however, that the story of bribing the Oracle of Dodona was no secret and the priests of Amun at Siwa rebuffed his approaches. They not only declined to accept his presents, but took the further step of sending a delegation to Sparta, accusing Lysander of trying to bribe Amun. In the court trial which followed, Lysander was able to defend himself and prove his innocence. The priests left Sparta with broken hearts, but Lysander failed to realize his ambition.

During the 4th century B.C. the reputation of the Oracles of Delphi and Dodona declined, while the fame of Amun and his Oracle in Libya increased. In many towns of the Greek Islands and in Asia Minor, temples were built in Amun's honour and sacrifices and offerings were presented to him. In Athens, Sparta, Macedonia, North Africa, and in many cities of Asia Minor, the Oracle of Amun in Libya was mentioned with the greatest respect.(1)

Alexander the Great

The visit of Alexander to the Oracle of Amun took place at the early part of the year 331 B.C., after he laid the foundations of his own town of Alexandria. It is not only the most famous visit in its ancient history but is undoubtedly the principal incident which immortalized the name of this oasis in ancient and modern times.

After defeating Darius III, the King of Persia, at Issus in 333 B.C. and in order to protect himself from the strong Persian fleet in the Mediterranean, Alexander proceeded to conquer all the important seaports in Syria and Palestine. Thereafter he completed the conquest of Egypt, which fell to him without fighting when Mazaces, the Persian Satrap, surrendered to him the ci-

---

(1) For the subject of the worship of Amun and building of temples in his honour in the different kingdoms of Greece, see Parthey, **Das Orakel**, pp. 139 - 40; and also, Fakhry, **Siwa Oasis...**, p. 33, footnote 1.

tadel of Memphis, together with the garrison and the treasury ; and the Egyptians hailed him with joy as their deliverer from the Persian yoke.(1)

The Macedonian conqueror was recognized by the Egyptian priests at Memphis as king of Egypt and after the ceremonies in the Temple of Ptah he sacrificed to that god and to the other deities. Alexander was aware of the fact that nothing had enraged the Egyptians so much as the slaying of the Apis bull by Ochus and the disrespect shown to him by Cambyses. Alexander's respect for the gods of Egypt and the sacrifices he offered to them were not merely demonstration of tolerance to win the favour of the people; this attitude was, indeed, characteristic of the great leader of men.

From the 8th century B.C., and even much earlier, Egypt was well known to the Greeks, and many of the Greek writers of the 6th, 5th and 4th centuries wrote a great deal about Egypt and its religion. A great number of famous Greeks who laid the foundations of their civilization were proud to mention that they taught their pupils in Greece what they had learned from the Egyptian priests. We should also bear in mind that Philip, Alexander's father, took great pains to choose a number of good tutors for his son, because, as Plutarch observes, the king saw that the boy's education "was a matter of too great importance to be entrusted to the ordinary masters in music and the common circles of science." Thus he sent for Aristotle "the most celebrated and learned of all the philosophers". This was a fortunate choice, for Aristotle inspired in Alexander a passionate love for Greek culture and a deep religious feeling. For about three years the great philosopher taught Alexander, together with a number of noblemen's sons who later became his intimate friends. He read with him the Iliad, the book of books for Alexander until the end of his life; he introduced him to Euripides, Philoxenus, Telestes and many others. Alexander had a special reverence for Pindar, the great lyric poet.(2)

The Oracle of Amun was very famous, reports of people who had consulted it were mentioned in many works, and its answers were highly respected. Plutarch tells us that after marrying Olympias, Philip dreamed that he closed the queen's womb with a seal, the impression of which he thought was a lion. Most of the interpreters believed the dream suggested some reason to doubt the honour of Olympias; others declared the dream meant that she was pregnant and that the child would prove to be a boy of bold, lion-like courage.

---

(1) Uhlrich Wilcken, **Alexander the Great,** (Berlin, 1930), p. 113.

(2) Wilcken, «Alexanders Zug in die Oase Siwa,» **Z.A.S.**, 30 (1928), and idem, **Alexander the Great** (1930), p. 57.

On another occasion, the king looked through a chink in the door of Olympias' bedchamber to see his wife sleeping with a serpent at her side. After this vision, Philip sent a messenger to consult the Oracle of Delphi; in the answer, Apollo commanded him to sacrifice to Jupiper-Ammon and to play hommage principally to that god.

Alexander inherited his father's daring courage, but from his mother her love of mysticism and the exercise of extravagant and superstitious observances. He had a complete belief in oracles. More than a year before coming to Egypt he visited Gordium in Asia Minor. There the local oracle held that the person who unfastened the famous knot in the yoke of the ancient chariot of King Gordius in the citadel, would become lord of Asia. When Alexander learned of this his interest in the unknown and the mysterious seized him; he proceeded to inspect the chariot; after trying in vain to find the end of the strap, he drew his sword and cut the knot. In that night, thunder and lightning followed; this he took as a divine indication that his method of untying the knot was approved by the gods. From that day forward, he was possessed by the dream of world sovereignty and firmly believed that he was going to win every battle. In his first letter to Darius, he called himself "King of Asia".(1)

Alexander in Egypt

Many writers in ancient and recent times have suggested various reasons for Alexander's trip to Siwa which took him from his headquarters in Egypt for several weeks at a time when the military situation necessitated his being on the spot. Darius was reorganizing his forces and his fleet was still unconquered; Alexander was eager to meet him as soon as possible; preparations were essential for the coming battle. It is difficult to believe that he made the journey at so critical a time, to be crowned at Siwa or to be addressed as the son of god, since these ceremonies had already occurred in the Temple of Ptah at Memphis, and could be repeated at any time he wished, in the same temple or any other temple in Egypt.

Callisthenes,(2) Alexander's court historian, who accompanied him on the journey and left us a detailed, eye-witness des-

(1) **Ibid.**, pp. 96 and 107.

(2) Callisthenes is a Greek historian born about 360 B.C. He was a relative and student of Aristotle from whom he received instruction at the same time as Alexander the Great. He accompanied Alexander on his earlier campaigns and was with him in Asia, after Egypt, and died in prison in 328 B.C. Although his historical writings dealing with the exploits of Alexander are preserved in fragments, he is responsible for the romantic narrative of Alexander's life, which grew up in the following centuries. After its translation into Latin in the 3rd century A.D. this became the main authority for the medieval adaptation of the myth of Alexander.

cription, states that he made the journey not only on account of the oracle but also because he had the ambition to rival Perseus and Hercules who had likewise formerly consulted the god. In analyzing this statement, Wilcken finds it quite credible when one considers how vividly Alexander conceived his relations to the heroic ancestors of his race.(1)

Arrianus, a Greek author who lived in the 2nd century A.D., produced what is considered to be a complete history of Alexander from his accession to his death; it was drawn from the best available sources, particularly Ptolemy and Aristobolus. Arrianus explains the trip to Siwa much more simply. He wrote that while Alexander was at the coast after laying the foundations of his new city, a "longing" to see the Oracle of Jupiter-Ammon seized him and he decided to proceed on his journey. Considering the character of Alexander and his sudden decisions, I feel inclined to favour Arrianus' explanation.

For five hundred years or more before Alexander, Egypt had relationships with the Greek states and had been open to Greek traders. As early as the eighth century B.C. a Greek trading-station had been established at Naukratis in the Western Delta, and in the seventh century Greek mercenary soldiers were in the service of Egyptian monarchs. When Cyrus overran Lydia and Ionia, Egyptian troops fought on the side of the Lydians and Greeks, and in the first Persian invasion of Egypt, Greek mercenaries fought side by side with the Egyptians.

Many Greek philosophers came to Egypt to study in the schools attached to the temples, and such men as Solon of Athens, Kleobolus of Lindos, Phales of Miletus, Pythagoras of Samos and Endoxos and Plato were among those who resided for long periods in Egypt and later spread the fame of the Egyptian wisdom. Through these contacts, the Greeks came to believe that Egypt was the very home of philosophy, mysticism, music, sculpture and the arts in general. Meanwhile, numerous temples of Amun sprang up in the Greek cities, and even at Athens a temple dedicated to Amun was ceremoniously opened in the year 333 B.C., less than two years before the date of Alexander's visit to the Temple of the Oracle at Siwa. Alexander was well aware of all of these facts, as well as the stories circulated about his direct relation to Amun and the rumours of his divine birth.

His march along the coast west of the site of Alexandria was not an anticipated journey, but was known a long time beforehand. At Paraetonium (Marsā Maṭrūḥ) he was met by ambassadors from Cyrene, who brought him various gifts including three hundred horses, several chariots and a golden

(1) Wilcken, **Alexander the Great,** pp. 122 - 3.

crown, and offered him their friendship and allegiance. His companions tried to dissuade him from visiting the Temple of Amun, but all their warnings were in vain. According to Plutarch, "...it was a long and laborious journey and besides the fatigue, there were two great dangers attending it. One was that their water might fail in a journey of many days' travel in a desert which afforded no supply; and the other, that they might be surprised by a violent south wind amidst the wastes of sand, as had happened long before to the army of Cambyses. The wind then had raised the sand and rolled in such waves that it devoured full fifty thousand men. These difficulties were considered and represented to Alexander, but it was not easy to divert him from any of his purposes."

Ptolemaic and Roman Times

The visit of Alexander to this oasis and his great devotion to Amun must have added to its fame; and it is quite logical to suppose that some monuments to his name were built there during his lifetime, or later by the Ptolemies who were anxious to demonstrate their devotion to his memory. But to our astonishment, no such monument, large or small, has so far been found in Siwa, save a few coins now in the museum of Alexandria.(1) But the hope prevails; it is entirely possible that the excavations begun in the Temple of the Oracle in April 1970, will reveal one day new material which might add to our knowledge.

However, some of the inscribed tombs at Jabal al-Mawtā (see below) can be dated in the early Ptolemaic times, which proves that this oasis was prosperous at that period.

At the end of the last century, a few small antiquities were found which date probably from the time of the Ptolemies; these were acquired by Steindorff when he visited Siwa in 1900. The same can be said of the few small objects found in the pillaged tombs near 'Ayn Qurayshat in the year 1907, which were presented by Khedive 'Abbās II to the Cairo Museum.

Several records of visitors to the Oracle are preserved in the writings of the time; the most important is that of the messengers of Hannibal at the end of the 3rd century B.C. After his victory over Sagnuta, the great warrior sent messengers to inquire of the Oracle of Siwa when the war would end. The answer was cryptic and could be explained in two ways, but Amun assured Hannibal that he would die in Libyan territory. When he died in Libyssa it was considered as a fulfillment of the oracle, and that it was Libyssa and not Libya that was meant.

Toward the end of the Ptolemaic period, Rome and Roman culture ruled supreme, and new methods of fortune-telling spread

(1) Steindorff, **Amonsoase...**, pp. 132 - 3.

among the people. The oracles, in general, lost much of their old prestige and very few people cared to go and consult them; Siwa was no exception. When Cato the junior (died 46 B.C.) was marching in Libya along the coast near the abode of Amun, his friends tried to persuade him to visit it, but he refused; he did not care; so much had the great reputation of the oracle declined.(1)

Strabo, who visited Egypt in 23 B.C. mentioned the oasis of Siwa in his Geography observing that "The Oracle had almost altogether disappeared which had previously enjoyed such high reputation."

This does not mean that the Oracle of Siwa ceased altogether or that the priests closed the doors of its temple; we are certain that it continued until many centuries later. Plutarch mentions that a rich man called Kleombrotus from Lakedaemonia visited the Oasis of Amun but found nothing of importance except an oil lamp which burned the whole year round. He reported that the priests of the temple told him the lamp required less oil from year to year, which proved that the years were becoming shorter.

When Hadrian visited Egypt in A.D. 130 many towns in Egypt hastened to honour him by erecting statues of the Emperor in their temples. The priests of Amun expressed their loyalty by placing an inscribed stela in the temple. A fragment found there is now in the Museum of Alexandria.(2)

The last important, well-known personage to leave an account of his visit to the oasis, was Pausanias, the famous Greek traveller and author who arrived in Siwa in A.D. 160. The oracle was still active and the priests were officiating in the temple. Pausanias entered the temple and according to his report, many stelae stood in the temple court, among these the one inscribed with the hymn of Pindar, the famous Greek poet. Pausanias also mentions seeing a stela in the name of Ptolemy I.(3) One of the two inscribed fragments found in 1970 in this temple dates from the 2nd - 3rd century A.D. We can say that despite the decline of the oracle, and of Egypt itself in the second half of the Roman rule, Siwa continued to worship its ancient god, and its priests continued to offer to Amun until the 6th century and even later.

---

(1) For all the references to the visitors to Siwa at the end of the Ptolemaic period and during Roman times, see Parthey, **Das Orakel,** and in particular pages 142-43 and 169-71.

(2) E. Breccia, «With King Fuad to the Oasis of Ammon,» **The Swallows** (April - May, 1929), p. 30.

(3) Pausanias, 9 : 16,1.

Did Christianity Spread in Siwa ?

No Christian monuments have thus far been discovered in Siwa, and I know of no reference which can throw light on this question; but I believe that Christianity did reach Siwa. According to Laoust[1] it penetrated into Siwa in the 4th century, although no monument, has been found which makes us accept this date as decisive. The only monument in Siwa which can be mentioned as possibly Christian is the brick ruin in the neighbourhood of Bilād al-Rūm.[2] Some parts of this construction still remain; its facade is the only standing part; until it is excavated, we cannot say whether it was the enclosure of a Roman fortress or a Christian church. The Siwan Manuscript mentions it in the following words : "Bilād al-Ṛūm is a church at the foot of the hill from which some remains still exist and which was built with burnt brick; it is the abode of prostitutes. Khamīsah, Mishandid and Dahībah as far as the white mountain belong to their dwellings."

The neighbourhood of Khamīsah is a very rich part of Siwa, and it is not improbable that Christian families lived there; the uncouth description of those who live near the "church" results from fanaticism. However, none of the Siwan families of the present day ever refer to themselves as descendants of Christians. In one instance, the Siwan Manuscript mentions that at Aghūrmī lived people who were descendants of the "Romans" which, in my opinion, meant "Christians". This expression in those days was applied to people who did not speak the language of the Arabs and were not converted to their new religion.

When Justinian ascended the throne (527 - 565) he issued instructions to close the remaining pagan temples and schools everywhere in Egypt. His agents were enthusiastic in carrying out his orders to the extent of converting the inhabitants of Ujaylah in Libya, to Christianity. Before these agents came, the people of this very small oasis worshipped Amun and Alexander.[3] It is impossible to imagine that in those days Justinian's men would have failed to close the Temple of the Oracle and the other pagan temples in Siwa, if their enthusiasm in carrying out the orders of their imperial master did not spare a far-off small place like Ujaylah. Whether some of Siwa's inhabitants were

---

(1) **Encyclopaedia of Islam,** I, IV, p. 485.

(2) In this neighbourhood, we find rock tombs, quarries, the brick ruin called the «church» and the ruins of the stone temple which was called the «Doric Temple» by the travellers of the 19th century. The cross which was seen on one of its blocks is a quarry mark and cannot be considered as the symbol of a Christian monument.

(3) Jean Maspero, **Organisation Militaire Bizantine** (Paris, 1912), pp. 12, 13 ; See also Parthey, **Das Orakel,** p. 155.

already Christians, or whether the agents of Justinian succeeded in converting a part of the population to Christianity, the new religion does not seem to have achieved a great success in Siwa as it did at the coast or in the other oases such as Baḥrīyah or Kharga.

Since the 4th century, the power and authority of the Romans had greatly decreased and anarchy and disorder were everywhere in the desert. The power of the Blemmyes was increasing in Nubia, and the power of the Masacaes was growing in the oases, and both were fierce pagan tribes who lived on pillaging the oases and the villages at the edge of the desert in the Nile Valley itself. The real power over the oases of the Western Desert was in the hands of the Masacaes from the end of the 4th century. They kept threatening the caravans, and raided the towns and villages of Upper Egypt (The Thebaid) from time to time.

We read in the life of Saint Samuel of Qalamūn[1] that about the year 633, when he was at Jabal al-Qalamūn (at Wādī al-Muwayliḥ, between the south of al-Fayyūm and Wādī al-Rayyān) the Berbers (the Masacaes) came from the west. After treating him very badly they took him away with them but when they found him useless they left him half-dead on the road to die. He managed to return safely to his church after a four days' walk. Shortly afterward, other Berbers came and pillaged all the villages, and on their way back they took Anba Samuel with them as a slave; he was to spend three years with them.

The home of these Berbers is seventeen days' march from Wādī al-Muwayliḥ in a westerly direction, which puts it in Siwa oasis. We read in Saint Samuel's biography that these pagans worshipped the sun. He was released from slavery as the result of many miracles in curing the sick, among whom was the wife of his master. The man asked the saint to pray for his wife to give birth to a child and promised him his liberty if this should transpire. When the boy was born the Berber fulfilled his promise and gave Anba Samuel a camel and five servants to show him the way home.

We know from the ancient authors that the Libyans worshipped Amun as the setting sun,[2] and thus we can say that

(1) Amelineau, «Samuel de Qalamoun,» **Revue de l'Histoire des Religions,** T. XXX (1894), pp. 1-47, and my paper, «The Monastery of Kalamoun,» **Annales du Service,** T. XLVI, pp. 63-83.

(2) For the different references to these authors, see Parthey, **Das Orakel,** p. 140

very probably the worship of Amun continued in Siwa until the introduction of Islam, and that it might have existed there side by side with Christianity.

The Muslim troops invaded Egypt in 640 and the army of 'Amr captured Alexandria in 641. Some of his troops later proceeded westwards to invade North Africa and the oases of the desert.

4

From the Rise of Islam to the Present Day

The Introduction of Islam

No fixed date can be given for the introduction of Islam into Siwa, but we cannot be far wrong if we say that the new religion found its way into Siwa in all probability before the end of the first century of Islam. Some Muslim writers have assumed that the Siwans had already been converted to the new religion when the Army of 'Amr marched into North Africa in 641, but this cannot be taken as an historical fact.

Some of these books relate the origin of the town, by whom it was built, and descriptions of its gates, walls and squares — all mere imagination of the writers. Study reveals that the authors had never seen the place, and their reports were simply invented, as for example the statements of Ibn Wāṣif Shāh and Ibn Duqmāq. However, other writers were more truthful, such as al-Mas'ūdī (10th century), al-Idrīsī (12th century), Ibn al-Wardī (14th century) and al-Maqrīzī (15th century).

Ibn al-Wardī mentioned in his work, **Kharīdat al-'Ajā'ib** that when Mūsā ibn Nuṣayr was appointed as a governor of North Africa (al-Gharb) in the days of the Omayyads, he marched to al-Wāḥ al-Aqṣā (Siwa, literally the distant oasis) guided by the stars. After seven days' march in a south-west direction, he found a town protected by a great fortress with iron gates. He was determined to capture it but failed. He ordered some of his men to climb the walls, but every one who reached the top and looked into the interior of the town uttered a loud cry and threw himself inside. No one knew what happened to him or what he had seen. Observing his failure, Mūsā ibn Nuṣayr decided to give up and went away without capturing it.

The march of Mūsā ibn Nuṣayr, the famous Arab general, was in the year A.D. 708. This proves at least that until that date Siwa was neither conquered nor converted to Islam.

In another part of his work, Ibn al-Wardī relates the story of a man who claimed to have discovered a strange city in the desert. He came to 'Umar ibn 'Abdul-'Azīz, then the governor of Egypt, to report that while he was searching for a stray camel near Santarīyah (Siwa), he came upon a town, mostly in ruins. He went on to say that inside, he found a large tree bearing all kinds of fruit, many of which he ate. Upon further investigation, the governor learned from a Copt (Egyptian Christian) that this must be one of the two towns of Hermes of Hermeses (Hermes was the god of knowledge), and that it contained great treasures. 'Umar selected a group of his most trusted men, provided a month's supply of food and sent them out with the Copt to search for the place. They roamed the desert for some time but found nothing to corroborate the story.

However, Islam found its way into Siwa, and the inhabitants were converted, as in the other oases in the Libyan desert. The Arab geographer al-Idrīsī (A.D. 1099 - 1154) travelled much in North Africa and visited the oases. He referred to the Small Oasis (Baḥrīyah) as uninhabited, stating that caravans stopped only for water, and that he saw nothing there except the palm trees and the ruins. As for Santarīyah, he mentioned only that it was inhabited by Muslims who had an **Imām** (religious leader).

Al-Maqrīzī (A.D. 1364 - 1442) left us a description of this oasis; the first part based on the writings of the Arab authors who preceded him, the last part his own. Because of its importance for the history of this oasis in the Middle Ages, I give here a literal translation of these paragraphs: "The town of Santarīyah is a part of the oases and was built by Manqayūsh, the builder of the town of Akhmīm, who was one of the ancient kings of the Copts. Ibn Wāṣif Shāh[1] said he had the capacity of his father and his experience was highly acknowledged by the Egyptians. He was the first to build an arena and ordered his attendants to do their exercises in it. He was the first builder of a hospital to cure sick persons and invalids. He provided it with medicines, appointed physicians, provided salaries sufficient for their living, and appointed curators to look after it. He created a festival for himself which was called the King's Festival. His subjects used to come to him at a certain time of the year, where they spent seven days eating and drinking while he observed them from a balcony raised on pillars. The pillars had gold rings

---

(1) Ibn Wāṣif Shāh was the author of a book on the wonders of the ancient history of Egypt, which he filled with legendary details. The book has perished but a great part of it has survived through the quotations of later writers like al-Maqrīzī. None of the kings of ancient Egypt was called Manqayūsh, but Ibn Wāṣīf Shāh wrote that he was buried in the pyramid opposite Atfīḥ. The statements of this writer cannot be taken seriously, and have no historical value.

and were covered by magnificent cloth woven with threads of gold; the interior of the dome over the pillars was inlaid with alabaster, glass and gold.

"In the days of this king, Santarīyah in the desert of the oases was built. He constructed it on a square plan and its houses were built of white stone; there was a gate in every one of its four walls which led to another wall built parallel to it. In every street, on the right and the left hand sides, he constructed gates which led to the interior of the town. In the middle of the town there was a square surrounded by seven terraces; it was covered by a dome of painted wood supported on great marble columns. Over the dome there was a tower of marble surmounted by a statue made of hard black stone which turned round, always facing the sun. Everywhere in the dome there were statues which whistled and shouted in different tongues.

"The king used to sit on the uppermost terrace of the town square surrounded by his sons, relatives and the sons of kings. On the second sat the chief priests and the ministers, and on the third sat the chief officers of the army. On the fourth sat the philosophers, astronomers, physicians and scholars. On the fifth sat the landowners, and on the sixth sat the artisans, and on the seventh terrace sat the public. It was said to every group : 'Look at those who are beneath you and not to those who are above you, whom you cannot reach' ; this is a kind of education. His wife stabbed him with a dagger and he died after ruling for sixty years."

Al-Maqrīzī continues : "Santarīyah is now a small place inhabited by six hundred persons of Berber origin known as 'Siwa' and their language is called 'Sīwīyah' which resembles the language of Zanātah. It has gardens of palm trees, olives, figs, other fruits and vineyards. It has now about twenty springs which flow with good water. It is eleven days' march from Alexandria and fourteen days from Giza. The inhabitants suffer much from the 'jinn' who take away whomsoever they find alone. The inhabitants hear their murmuring."(1)

There is no need to comment on the description of that fairy town or to waste any time on comparisons with the actual remains in Siwa. Manqayūsh and his town had existed only in the imagination of Ibn Wāṣif Shāh. In any event, from the few remarks of al-Maqrīzī we gather that although this oasis had greatly declined, and its inhabitants in the 15th century were reduced to only 600 people, some springs were still flowing and gardens produced dates, olives and other crops.

According to the Siwan Manuscript, Siwa had suffered severely at the hands of the raiders of Arab and Berber Bedouin,

(1) Al-Maqrīzī, Al-Khiṭaṭ..., pp. 379 - 80.

and the inhabitants were reduced to a mere forty men (circa year A.H. 600), whereas the whole population was approximately 200 people at the beginning of the 13th century. Consequently we can say that Siwa saw its worst days of decline in the period between the 9th and 12th centuries, and that it began to revive only in the 13th when the forty remaining men decided to build a fortress at Shālī, the present site of the Town of Siwa, to protect themselves from the raids.(1)

The inhabitants of Shālī, who were living now in some security, began to prosper and their numbers increased. They were divided into several families and the oasis was ruled by the heads of these families, more or less independent in their oasis until the end of the 18th century. In spite of the competition between the two main groups of the population, the Easterners and the Westerners, the Siwans had some kind of "law" which they enacted for themselves and invested authority in the hands of their shaykhs whom they called **al-agwād.**

In spite of their seclusion in their oasis, the Siwans used to trade their crops of dates, olives and olive oil with the Arab Bedouin of the coast, Fezzan, Alexandria, al-Fayyūm and Cairo and some of them used to go thence to market their produce. However, from the 13th century till the 19th, some of the pilgrims of North Africa used to prefer the ancient caravan route via the oases in their journeys to Mecca. This was used from very ancient times because it was shorter, and in those days much safer than that of the coast. They travelled in large, powerful caravans in the company of merchants, traders and other travellers, all under the protection of the caravan guards.

These caravans used Siwa as one of their important way stations, and from Siwa they reached Baḥrīyah. After Baḥrīyah some of the travellers continued their desert trip to the Nile Valley, either by way of Cairo if they wanted to visit there, thence directly to al-Bahnasā to take a boat for Qūṣ or Qifṭ, then cross the Eastern Desert to al-Quṣayr on the Red Sea. Others, who had no intention to visit Cairo, travelled from Baḥrīyah to Farafra and then to Dakhla, and came at last to Kharga which was always a very important caravan station on the famous caravan route of Darb al-Arba'īn. From Kharga they travelled either to Asyūṭ or went to Farshūṭ on the Nile, thence to Qūṣ or Qifṭ.

---

(1) In the Siwan Manuscript, reference is made to the Muslim conquest and the rulers' decision to resist; they thought of poisoning the water of the springs by throwing in mummies. No date is mentioned but we learn also from the same manuscript that some tribes, mostly from Jabal Yafrīn in Tunis, settled there and lived at first in tents near al-Zaytūn and then moved to Aghūrmī where some of the original population still resided. Later on, the forty men decided to build the fortress.

Siwa and the other oases were visited by many thousands of people in those centuries, but unfortunately we have no records of their trips and none of the great majority cared to give us any description of what he had experienced. One of the exceptions is the Arab, Leo Africanus, who travelled throughout North Africa in the first quarter of the 16th century (he died in 1526) and visited Siwa on one of his trips. He described its inhabitants as almost black, very rich and thrifty.(1) They were trading also with the inhabitants of the other oases and especially with Jaghbūb and further west with Fezzan; although they did not recognize the authority of any government in Egypt or Libya, they were no doubt aware of what was going on politically in Libya and the Nile Valley.

Siwa in the 17th and 18th Centuries

The same conditions prevailed during the 17th and 18th centuries; this oasis was more or less independent, paying no tribute to Cairo nor anywhere else, but as Muslims they recognised the authority of the Sultan of Turkey as the Caliph, and this was the only tie. The caravans continued to visit Siwa and trade with its people; the German traveller, Wansleb, who visited Egypt in the second half of the 17th century, mentioned that he saw at Alexandria the date caravans coming from "Sibah" and described the dates as the best of their kind.(2) The only available information we have about Siwa in those days is recorded in the Siwan Manuscript; here we find local records of the families and their feuds, the names of some of the heads of the families who distinguished themselves and seized power and authority, and the local law which they made for themselves.(3)

The manuscript details the constant feuds between the Easterners and the Westerners, with emphasis on the deeds and personalities of the Easterners, to whom belonged the family of Musallim, composers of this work over several generations. Detailed local records begin with the year 1697 when Ibrāhīm Bāghī, the head of the family of al-Zanāyin, had become the leader of all the **agwād** and ruled Siwa more or less as a local prince. During the time of his authority (1697 - 1711) Siwa flourished and its inhabitants felt secure in their oasis and the

---

(1) Pierre Langlés, «Mémoire sur les Oases,» **Voyage de F. Hornemann** (Paris, 1808), Append. II. p. 354.

(2) Parthey, **Das Orakel,** p. 173.

(3) This part of the Siwan Manuscript which is kept with the family of Shaykh Musallim was shown also to one of the officials in Siwa who quoted parts of it in his book — Wākid, **Wāhit Amun,** pp. 31 - 48. Wākid supplies the details which he copied from the Manuscript and the material which he collected from Shaykh 'Umar Musallim, his informant on some of the details in the year 1938 and the subsequent years.

trade caravans increased. After his death in the year 1711, no other chief could fill the vacancy and the old rivalry between the two factions of the oasis caused wars between them. Unsettled conditions in Siwa prevailed for more than a century, but the caravans continued to arrive, and the oasis remained an important way station on the caravan route. It was governed by a body consisting of the heads of the families, **Majlis al-Agwād.**

European Travellers

But while Egypt was suffering under the tyrannical rule of the Mamluks, Europe began to develop interest in the East, and many European travellers of the intelligent, adventurous type began to travel in its different countries at that period. Toward the end of the 18th century, Siwa was visited by two European travellers who left us an account of their visits.

Browne in the year 1792 : W.G. Browne, an English traveller, was the first European to penetrate the desert to Siwa and give us an account of his journey.(1) He left Alexandria in the company of a guide, an interpreter and some Bedouin on February 24th, 1972 and arrived at Qāret Umm al-Ṣughayyar on the 7th of March; he described it as a "miserable place, the buildings being chiefly of clay; and the people remarkably poor and dirty." At last he arrived at Siwa. Browne's description of the place and its inhabitants throws much light on the Siwans and their character and, because of their importance, I give here in detail some of his remarks in his own words.

"When we arrived at the town of Siwa", he says, "we dismounted, and seated ourselves, as is usual for strangers in this country, on a **mesjed,** or a place used for prayer, adjoining the tomb of a **marabut,** or holy person. In a short time the chiefs came to congratulate us on our arrival, with the grave but simple ceremony that is in general use among the Arabs. They then conducted us to an apartment which, though not very commodious, was the best they were provided with. After a short interval, a large dish of rice and some boiled meat were brought, the Shechs attending while the company was served, which consisted of my interpreter, our conductor, two other Bedouin, our companions and myself."

His attendants thought it safer for him to say that he was a Muslim Mamluk, but he could neither speak Arabic nor was he able to attend the evening prayers with the others in the mosque, and consequently the Siwans suspected him, and his interpreter was obliged to explain the next morning. "The

---

(1) W.G. Browne, **Travels in Africa, Egypt and Syria, from the year 1792 to 1798** (London, 1799) ; the part about his visit to Siwa is chapter ii. pp. 14-29.

Shechs seemed surprised at a Christian having penetrated thus far, with some expense and difficulty, and apparently without having any urgent business to transact. But all, except one of them, were disposed to reconciliation; inclined thereto, no doubt, by a present of some useful articles that had been brought for them. This one was the head of the people, violently exasperated at the insolence of an unbeliever, impersonating and wearing the dress of a Mohammedan."

At first the Siwans insisted on his instant return, but at last the more moderate among them prevailed and he was permitted to remain for two or three days to rest. But "whenever I quitted my apartment, it was only to be assailed with stones, and a torrent of abusive language." At last the chiefs were able to calm the inhabitants, and he was allowed on the fourth day to go out and see what he wanted. On that day he visited the ruins of the Temple of Umm 'Ubaydah (see below). On the following day he was permitted to see tombs cut into the rock, whose number he estimated to be about thirty; he referred to the skulls, bones and other parts of bodies which were scattered about the place but failed to mention observing any inscriptions on the walls; this was Jabal al-Mawtā.

These are the antiquities which he visited near the town of Siwa. When he inquired from the shaykhs for a "place of the name of Santarieh," they professed ignorance. When he asked whether they knew of any ruins of any kind farther westward or southwest, one of them replied that there was a lake called "Araschie" where there were ruins. But, he added, these were inaccessible because the site was surrounded by water and there were no boats. This informant entered into "an enchanted history of this place" which caused Browne to insist on visiting it. At last he left Siwa on the 12th of March, after making secret arrangements to reach the site in spite of all the difficulties. Browne mentions that he marched for two days, until his party arrived at the place proscribed to him. He reported : "I found it an island, in the middle of a small lake of salt water which contained misshapen rocks in abundance, but nothing that I could positively decide to be ruins; nor indeed was it very likely that any such should be found there, the spot being entirely destitute of trees and fresh water. Yet I had the curiousity to approach nearer to these imaginary ruins; and accordingly forced my horse into the lake. He, from fatigue and weakness, or original inability to swim, soon found himself entangled, and could not keep his head above water. I fell with him, and was unable immediately to detach myself; at length, when I found myself again on dry ground, the circumstances I was under prevented me from making further observation on this island and lake." This lake is known nowadays as the lake of Khamīsah, and it was the scene of an incident to another traveller to Siwa in 1819.

On his way from Siwa to Araschie, at about six miles distant, Browne passed "a small building of the Doric order, apparently designed for a temple. There either has been no inscription on it, or it is now obliterated." This is the so-called "Doric Temple" in the district of Bilād al-Rūm. When Browne's book was published, the English geographer John Rennel identified Siwa with the Oasis of Jupiter Amun which was mentioned by Herodotus and had enjoyed great fame in ancient times.(1)

Browne's account provides other valuable information. He observes for example, that "the people of Siwa have communications equally with Egypt and Fezzan, and the wandering Arabs pass the desert in all directions, in their visits to that small territory, where they are furnished with many articles of food at a cheaper rate than they can be in the towns of Egypt. They pass thither from Elwah (Baḥrīyah Oasis) from Feium (Fayyūm) and the district of Thebes, from Fezzan, from Tripoli, from Kahira (Cairo), and from Alexandria." He describes the oasis in these words: " A large proportion of this space is filled with date trees, but there are also pomegranates, figs, olives, apricots and plantains; and the gardens are remarkably flourishing. They cultivable a considerable quantity of rice which, however, is of a reddish hue, and different from that of the Delta. The remainder of the cultivable land furnishes wheat enough for the consumption of the inhabitants."

Browne also made very useful notes about the dress of the male inhabitants, the character of the people (which, of course, was not very favourable), and the food on which they lived. His opinion of the women was not very high: "While I was there, a newly born infant was found murdered, having been thrown from the top of a house. I understood that these accidents were not infrequent. It would seem an indirect proof of libertinism in the women, which, however, no other circumstance led me to suppose. Inquiry was instituted, but no means offering to identify the perpetrator to the crime, the matter was dropped."

Among his other observations, Browne noted that the Siwans used no coffee or tobacco, and their other needs were supplied from Cairo or Alexandria whence their dates were transported. He observed also that the government was in the hands of four or five shaykhs who, although they enjoyed external respect, in reality lacked adequate authority for the preservation of public order: "On the slighest grounds arms are taken up; and the hostile families fire on each other in the streets, and from the houses." No such fights took place during Browne's

---

(1) J. Rennel, **Geographical System of Herodotus** (London, 1800), pp. 574, 601 ff.

short visit but evidently this is what he heard from his guide or interpreter.

In general, the account is extremely useful and we must be grateful to him, for his notes supply the first detailed picture of Siwa to reach the world for almost 1700 years. They provide at the same time an impression of the daily life of the Siwans in the later years of the 18th century.

Frederick Hornemann : Six years later, in the year 1798, Hornemann, a German traveller arrived from Europe. Unlike Browne, he was not an independent explorer; rather, he was assigned by the London African Society to journey through North Africa and bring back a report, including a description of the places he visited and any available information about trade. In preparation for the trip, he learnt to speak Arabic and acquired adequate knowledge of Islam and Muslim practices. When he arrived in Egypt, the army of Napoleon was in the country, but the German explorer experienced no difficulty in obtaining from the French authorities all the required documents to travel wherever he wished.

With a caravan of pilgrims returning from Mecca to North Africa, he left the Nile Valley from the village of Kirdāsah near the Pyramids of Giza. The caravan departed on the 5th of September and reached Siwa on the 21st, after spending a few days at Qāret Umm al-Ṣughayyar. Together with the caravan, Hornemann spent eight days at Siwa during which he visited the ruins outside the town and made many useful notes on the life and customs of the Siwans. His description of the monuments is more detailed than that of Browne, but the two agree on all the main points.(1) He was eager to see the ruins and study them carefully, and it was this unusual eagerness which brought him trouble later on. He could speak Arabic and performed prayers with the others, but some of the Siwans suspected him because of his lack of punctuality in attending prayers and his great interest in the monuments of the ancient pagans; no true Muslim, the Siwans declared, would do such a thing.

His caravan left the oasis in the early morning, proceeding westwards, but after some hours they were overtaken by the Siwans ; as Hornemann describes it, "the braying of three hundred donkeys announced the arrival of the Siwan army." The Siwans wanted to kill him, together with his attendant who was also of European origin, accusing them that as Christians they made fun of the Muslim religion. It was only the intelligence of

---

(1) Hornemann, **Tagebuch...** . It was translated into French with commentary by Langlés and published under the title, **Voyage de F. Hornemann** (1808).

Hornemann which saved him; at once he took out the documents supplied by Bonaparte, written in French, handed them to the shaykhs and asked them to read them and see that he was a Muslim. His attendant who had become deeply interested in Islam after living twelve years in Turkey, knew by heart several verses and paragraphs from the Qur'ān (Koran); now he began to repeat them in a loud voice. Some of the Siwans began to think their suspicions might be unfounded, and at this moment Hornemann made another very successful move. He took out from his baggage a copy of the Koran and began to read aloud in Arabic; this was final proof that they were Muslims. The "Siwan Army" apologized and returned home. Hornemann continued his journey, and from the coast in North Africa he forwarded his reports by ship to London. But he lost his life later in another adventure and never saw Europe again.

The important points in his observations made at Siwa include his description of the town as a fortress lying on a hill, houses built one on top of another and crowded with inhabitants; the pilgrims compared the place with a beehive. He noticed also that the language was not Arabic but resembled the tongue of the Ṭawāriq, which is spoken throughout North Africa. He made a large collection of Siwan words, which he lost afterwards, only twenty-eight words being preserved. He described the Oasis of Siwa as a small independent community comprising the town and several small villages. Siwa paid no tribute to the Sulṭān of Turkey ; its wealth depended largely on the date trade, and whenever a caravan arrived the shaykhs negotiated in the name of the whole community.

Butin's Visit in 1819 : In the year preceding the arrival of Moḥammad 'Alī's troops, the oasis was visited by two Frenchmen. The first was an adventurer, an officer named Butin who heard from some of the Siwans in Alexandria the legendary story of the great treasure buried in the island in the middle of Araschie, the salt lake; the same stories Browne had heard twenty-seven years before. Butin brought with him a small portable boat, but once he had arrived at Siwa and the inhabitants discovered his intentions, they became infuriated. They seized his boat and pillaged everything he had with him; after many difficulties, he was lucky to escape with his life. He was killed later in Syria. Butin left no account of his journey to Siwa; Cailliaud (**Voyage..., I, 81**), Von Minutoli (**Reise..., p. 83**) and Jomard (**Voyage à Syouah,** pp. 3, 23) mentioned his visit and referred to his misfortunes.

Cailliaud, 1819 : The second Frenchman was the energetic, talented mineralogist and explorer, Frederic Cailliaud. He arrived in Siwa a few months after Butin's visit; he reached it from al-Fayyūm in fifteen days and spent twelve days there from the 10th of December till the 22nd. As mentioned earlier, Egypt at that time was under the rule of Muhammad 'Alī; but while Siwa nominally acknowledged the suzerainty of the Sulṭān of Turkey, it paid no tribute or taxes to the Sulṭān or the Egyptian ruler. The Siwans were certainly well aware of Muḥammad 'Alī's authority, but when Cailliaud arrived, accompanied by his friend, the painter Letorzec, they were perplexed, for he presented to the shaykhs an official letter from the Pasha addressed to the people of Siwa, instructing them to facilitate his mission and render all assistance. After discussions which lasted for days, they allowed Cailliaud to visit the gardens and some of the ancient sites, and to use his instruments to determine the longitude, latitude and height of the place, but always under supervision.

He did not deny his nationality or his Christian faith, but kept on reminding his host that he was working for the Pasha. They permitted him to visit the gardens, and the ancient sites of Jabal al-Mawtā, Jabal al-Dakrūr, Khamīsah and Bilād al-Rūm, but denied him the right to visit the ruins of Umm 'Ubaydah or to enter the town. Cailliaud insisted on seeing both, and at last, and only on the day preceding his departure from the oasis, they allowed him to visit these places.

Cailliaud's description of the monuments of this oasis is much better and more accurate by far than the reports of Browne and Hornemann; his observations on the life of the Siwans are very important.(1) The inhabitants lived inside their fortified town which they permitted no stranger to enter; the members of the visiting caravans were required to spend the night outside. When it was necessary for the shaykhs to meet a stranger, he was brought by the **zaggālah** to a chamber near the gate. The shaykhs represented the several families, but the real power was vested in only two, the heads of the two rival groups of the oasis, the Easterners and the Westerners. Though the enmity between the two groups was constant and bitter, they were always able to live in neighbouring houses and in the face of danger from outside, they managed to forget their enmity, close ranks and meet the enemy together.

---

(1) Frederic Cailliaud was by profession a mineralogist and a traveller who came first to Egypt in 1815 and was employed by Muḥammad 'Alī to locate some of the mines used by the ancients. He explored the oases in the years 1819-20, and later on ascended the Nile to Meroe. He wrote several books; the best is his **Voyage a Meroé** (1923-7) in four volumes of text and three volumes of plates; his notes about Siwa appear in Volume I. In addition to this work he wrote another book, **Voyage à l'Oasis du Syouah**, published in 1823.

Cailliaud mentions that the Siwans opposed his visit to the interior of their town because they firmly believed in an old prophecy that the long sojourn of a Christian in their town would bring misfortune; thus they wanted to get rid of him as quickly as possible without offending the Pasha in Cairo. Cailliaud himself wondered if the prophecy might not be true; only a few months after his departure from Siwa, the troops of Muḥammad 'Alī arrived. Great damage resulted when the town was hit by artillery and many Siwans were killed ; the oasis lost its independence. What was worse, they had to pay taxes.

The Years Preceding the Conquest of Siwa

For twenty years after Hornemann's visit, no traveller attempted to journey to Siwa despite publication of his book and Browne's narrative; perhaps their description of the Siwan attitude toward non-Muslim visitors was responsible.

After the withdrawal of the French in the year 1801, Egypt entered a new period of relative discipline and prosperity under Muḥammad 'Alī. This brilliant ruler opened the country to foreigners, welcomed all Europeans and extended every possible protection. Busy with national reforms and wars against the Mamluks and outside Egypt, Muḥammad 'Alī made no attempt for the conquest of Siwa until 1820.

The Conquest of Siwa in 1820

Muḥammad 'Alī had planned to seize control of the oases of the Western Desert before undertaking the final step of sending his army to the Sudan. He entrusted the subjugation of all the oases to one of his ablest men, Ḥasan Bey al-Shamāshirgī, the governor of Biḥīrah Province at that time. Prior to his march to Siwa in 1820 he had already accomplished the conquest of the other oases; Siwa, the westernmost, was left until the end. Some books mention that the conquest of Siwa was undertaken because Drovetti, the French Consul-General in Egypt at that time, spoke to Muḥammad 'Alī about its importance and his wish to visit it. Drovetti was deeply interested in antiquities, in fact, he was making a collection; he had in his service many persons including Cailliaud. It may well be that in his conversations with the Pasha, he referred to the importance of this oasis. But we cannot accept the interest of Drovetti alone as the reason for this campaign. The Siwans have another story. They say that from the days of Ibrāhīm Bāghī in the 18th century the Easterners oppressed the Westerners, and at last the leader of the Westerners went to Cairo, did his best to persuade the Pasha to put an end to the anarchy then prevailing and assured him of the loyalty of all the Westerners. In fact, however, Muḥammad 'Alī had already decided for the conquest of Siwa as part of the control of the oases and the cavaran routes of the Western Desert.

When al-Shamāshirgī received orders to proceed, the troops comprised 400 Bachi-bouzoucks (irregular troops), 200 Bedouin of the tribe of Awlād 'Alī and a hundred Bedouin of the tribe of al-Jimay'āt.(1) The small army was accompanied by Drovetti, Linant de Bellefonds, Muḥammad 'Alī's famous engineer, the painter Ferdiani and the physician Ricci, a group of learned people interested to visit the oasis and its world-famous antiquities. 'Alī Bālī also accompanied the expedition. After fourteen days' march from Tirrānah (at the edge of Biḥīrah Province) they arrived at Siwa; the inhabitants withdrew into their fortified town and refused to surrender. They resisted for three hours; finally they realized that if they continued longer the cannon would reduce the whole town to ruins; thirty-three Siwans had already been killed as against three Bedouin with al-Shamāshirgī.

The Siwans surrendered, and during the negotiations which followed they agreed to pay tribute as subjects of the Pasha but they refused to permit any of the invaders to enter the town. Only when al-Shamāshirgī insisted on complete surrender and threatened to turn the town into ashes if they persisted did they finally accept.

Drovetti and his companions entered the town and were allowed to go wherever they wished. They visited the monuments of Umm 'Ubaydah, the tombs of Jabal al-Mawtā, Aghūrmī, the ancient well and some of the stone walls near it. At a distance of three hours' march from Siwa in a north-west direction, Drovetti inspected the remains of a temple called al-'Amūdayn which he said seemed to be of non-Egyptian architecture.(2) He gave the dimensions of this monument as 90 feet in length and 25 feet in breadth with no hieroglyphs on its walls. This differs from the Doric Temple visited by previous travellers, which he also visited on his way to lake Araschie.(3)

The Siwans agreed to pay 12,000 riyals(dollars) as the war fine and a yearly tribute of two thousand camel loads of dates. 'Alī Bālī was appointed as the 'Umdah of Siwa and a force of forty soldiers was left with him. For a short time the Siwans changed their attitude toward visitors, and the German Consul, Von Minutoli, was not molested when he visited Siwa in November of the same year. But this new attitude did not prevail long.

---

(1) Maher, «L'Oasis de Siouah,» p. 55.

(2) The results of their work were published later on by the French archeologist Jomard who identified Aghūrmi with the Acropolis visited by Alexander the Great and as mentioned by Diodorus and Curtius.

(3) Minutoli, **Reise....**

Eventually they refused to welcome more visitors and declined to pay the tribute. Thus Ḥasan Bey al-Shamāshirgī returned in the year 1829 with a force of 600 men. The Siwans elected to fight, but the town was occupied after a brief battle. Eighteen of their shaykhs were executed, and twenty were banished. Ḥasan Bey did not leave Siwa this time before appointing a governor; the first Ma'mūr was one of his officers named Faraj Kāshif. He built the first government house on a rock to the south of the town, and remained there with the garrison while 'Alī Bālī continued as a mayor of the oasis, assisted as usual by the other heads of families as shaykhs.

Between 1820 and the End of the 19th Century

The modern history of Siwa reveals a constant feeling of unrest among the inhabitants; more than once they refused to pay the tribute levied upon them, and consequently punitive expeditions were sent out, as in the years 1839, 1844, 1852 and 1893. The post of the Ma'mūr of Siwa was very unpopular; every officer so assigned considered it as a sort of exile, and did all in his power to shorten his stay; one cannot expect much from such officials. Meanwhile, family rivalries continued and, during those eighty years, fierce battles frequently occurred between the Easterners and Westerners. As for their attitude toward foreign visitors, this remained as before, and even worse in some instances.

Von Minutoli, 1820 : After Siwa's conquest in 1820, the German Consul in Cairo decided to make a trip to the coast and to Siwa, together with a number of friends. He was accompanied by Ehrenberg, Hemprich, Scholz, the painter Liman, the topographer Gruoc and the draughtsman Boldrini. The party left Alexandria on the 5th of October, 1820 and marched along the coast. On the 26th, Von Minutoli, accompanied by Gruoc, arrived at Siwa while Ehrenberg, and the others proceeded to Cyrenaica and Derna, later to rejoin Von Minutoli and Gruoc at Siwa. Von Minutoli arrived at Siwa on the 7th of November and remained until the 12th; no one dared to prevent him from going wherever he wanted. He was able to take the dimensions of the Temple of Umm 'Ubaydah and make many drawings of its walls; his drawings are the only documents we have to identify the builder, because the temple was blown up and many of its stones removed in the year 1897 (Fig. 30).

Von Minutoli visited Bilād al-Rūm and Khamīsah; to the west of the town of Siwa, he found a building called Dayba(1)

(1) This place was not mentioned by the other travellers, and its name is unknown to the Siwans in the this century; I have not come across any ruins in the north of Siwa which could be identified with it.

which, he reports, dates from the Arab Period, and the site of Qaṣr al-Ghashshām at the west of the town. He entered the tombs of Jabal al-Mawtā and refers to hieroglyphs and paintings in red, yellow and blue colours on the walls of some of the tombs; he mentions also an effaced Greek text in one of these.

Ehrenberg and his companions wasted much time at the frontier, waiting in vain for permission to visit Derna, and at last gave up the hope of visiting Tripolis and proceeded to Siwa. They arrived there on the 18th of November, six days after Von Minutoli's departure, and the Siwans were very unfriendly. The party waited five days for permission to enter the town and visit the monuments; they had to leave the oasis disappointed.[1]

Bayle St. John : For twenty-seven years thereafter we hear of no European who went to Siwa. The first of whom we have any record is an Englishman, Bayle St. John, who journeyed there in September 1847 with three of his friends. They were not permitted to enter the town but were allowed to visit the gardens and the ancient sites. At the time of his visit, Bayle St. John reports that there was neither a Ma'mūr nor 'Umdah in Siwa. 'Alī Bālī was stabbed to death by members of his own family in 1838, and his son Yūsuf requested appointment by the Egyptian Government in place of his father, but without success for many years. However, when Bayle St. John visited Siwa, it was Yūsuf Bālī who welcomed him to the oasis and extended to him and his companions every assistance.[2]

James Hamilton, 1852 : Yūsuf Bālī hoped that once the authorities in Cairo learned of these good deeds, he might be successful in gaining the appointment, but his hopes were not fulfilled. Another opportunity occurred a few years later, and this time Yūsuf followed another tactic. When James Hamilton arrived at Siwa and pitched his tents near the Police Station, the Siwans made it clear that they resented all foreign visitors.

It was Yūsuf Bālī who inflamed the rage of the **zaggālah** and urged them to attack Hamilton's camp at night. In the meantime, he warned Hamilton secretly and persuaded him to come to his house for protection. The Siwans fired on his tents, attacked the camp and pillaged everything they found, but Hamilton was safe in Yūsuf's house. Yūsuf also assisted his foreign guest in sending two messages to Cairo outlining what had occurred, and the Khedive 'Abbās I immediately sent a force to Siwa.

---

(1) Victor Ehrenberg published a book called **Reisen in Aegypten,** where he mentions all the difficulties he met on his journey, illness of the members of the mission, his disputes with the Bedouin, falls of camels, breaking the baggage, bad weather and worst of all the unfriendly reception of the Siwans.

(2) Bayle St. John, **Adventures in the Libyan Desert** (London, 1849), p. 149.

Fig. 30. The fortress of Aghūrmī and the ruins of the Temple of Umm ʿUbaydah in 1820 (After Von Minutoli, Atlas, Pl. VII, 1).

For six weeks Hamilton remained secure in Yūsuf's house until the arrival of the government force on the 14th of March. He was then set free, entered the fortified town of Siwa and the smaller fortified town of Aghūrmī; he was the first traveller to mention the existence of the stone temple there, the famous Temple of the Oracle. He observed the hieroglyphs in its sanctuary, the **cella,** and noted the corridor at the right-hand side. In referring to the temple ruins of Umm 'Ubaydah, he mentions that one of the Ma'mūrs carried out an excavation in the ruins and found a lion and three bronze statues.

After a week's stay, the armed force left Siwa, taking Hamilton with them. The shaykhs supposed responsible for the incident, mostly Easterners, were ordered to present themselves in Cairo in two months' time, and this they promised to do. When the time limit expired, a new force was sent to Siwa, consisting of 200 regular soldiers and 200 Bedouin from the tribe of Awlād 'Alī under command of their own shaykh, who had already visited Siwa several times and knew its shaykhs. Meanwhile, on his arrival in Cairo Hamilton met the Khedive and described the prevailing disorder and anarchy; he added that the only person who could restore order and government prestige was Yūsuf Bālī, whose late father had served as the first governor of the oasis. Consequently Yūsuf Bālī came back with the armed force, the letter of appointment as 'Umdah of Siwa in his hand. When the party arrived at 'Ayn Mijāḥiẓ (the first spring in the depression called by some Siwans 'Ayn Rāṭī) they camped there while Ḥusayn Dughghār, the Bedouin chieftain, went to the town and by his eloquence, lies and sly manners convinced the people to change their minds. They had already retired to their fortress and prepared for battle, but he assured them that the officer in charge had only good intentions; it was only necessary that a delegation accompany him to the camp, assure their loyalty to the government and all would be well. Forty of the shaykhs and notables returned with him, but as soon as they set foot in the camp they were put in chains and the force moved toward the town. On learning that the lives of their shaykhs were at the mercy of the force and that all would be hanged if any soldier was injured, the people surrendered. The commander presented a list of twenty-two more hostages and returned to Cairo with all sixty-two. They appeared before a court; two were executed, Shaykh 'Umar Musallim, Siwa's judge and Muḥammad Mu'arrif, one of his relatives ; the other sixty were sentenced to hard labour. Yūsuf Bālī was now in full authority as the 'Umdah of the oasis, while Dughghār, his accomplice, was appointed to the post of Ma'mūr and with a garrison of soldiers at his disposal. Understandably, all the Easterners now looked upon the new 'Umdah as their enemy and the source of all their misfortunes, but Yūsuf did not spare a moment to avenge himself, crush his opponents and to enrich himself in every way. When voices were raised in protest, he simply arrested more people and sent them to Cairo where they were imprisoned.[1]

But less than two years later, in 1854, 'Abbās I died and Sa'īd followed him on the throne; on this occasion all prisoners, including all the Siwan shaykhs, were set free and sent home. We can imagine now the position of Yūsuf when all the Easterners and some of the Westerners stood against him seeking revenge. The resultant battle between the two groups lasted for three days; it ended with victory for the Easterners. They besieged Yūsuf's house, but he managed to escape to the small nearby hamlet of al-Manshīyah and take refuge in a friend's home. Once there, he sent a message to his old friend the Ma'mūr, but the latter was in need of protection himself. At last the Easterners found him and put an end to his life.

After less than a year another battle took place between the two sides, in which al-Mubārak, a cousin of Yūsuf, showed exceptional courage (see above) but the Easterners won again. At last, in the year 1857, a new Ma'mūr came to Siwa, accompanied by a number of soldiers to restore order. It was thought at that time that the appointment of two 'Umdahs, one for the Easterners and one for the Westerners, might ease the situation. This was tried, but without success, and the authorities finally cancelled the order.

G. Rohlfs, 1869 : Rohlfs, the famous geographer employed by the Khedive Ismā'īl to study the deserts of Egypt, visited Siwa twice, first in 1869 and later in 1874. His popular book[2] on his travels in all the oases is an important work for all times. The part concerning Siwa is filled with important details of the ancient sites, and contains information about Siwan life and a description of the interior of the town. From his work we see clearly that the influence of the Sanūsī order, whose headquarters were at Jaghbūb, was increasing steadily in Siwa, and their representatives in the oasis had great power and influence among the people, especially the families of the Westerners.

Other Visitors to Siwa : Siwa was an unpopular post for the Ma'mūrs, and records reveal almost nothing about any special activity of any one of them. The rivalry and enmity between the two groups of the population continued and the authority of the shaykhs was decreasing; more than once the Siwans refused to pay the taxes due.

In the year 1886 Robecchi visited Siwa, where he completed the paintings and drawings published later in his atlas. In the early nineties, a certain Mr. Blundell and a journalist called

---

(1) Hamilton, **Wanderings in North Africa** (London, 1856). In this book Hamilton narrated the details of his visit; as for the sequences of that visit, see Belgrave, **Siwa...**, pp. 105 - 9.

(2) G. Rohlfs, **Drei Monate in der libyschen Wüste** (Berlin, 1876).

Ward spent one night in Siwa. The inhabitants were not very friendly, but they were not harmed.

In the year 1893 the authorities in Cairo decided to make a thorough investigation to determine the cause of constant troubles in Siwa and why the inhabitants had refused to pay taxes for the previous three years. Muṣṭafā Māhir Bey, the Governor of Biḥīrah Province, was sent to Siwa with a force of fifty soldiers. The majority of the Siwans preferred to show their loyalty but a section of the Westerners under the leadership of one of their shaykhs, Ḥassūnah Manṣūr, refused to pay any taxes. The shaykh retired to his house, a fortress-like structure built on a rock to the south of the city. Māhir Bey laid siege to the place, but the shaykh's relatives and friends succeeded in supplying Ḥassūnah and his men with their needs. In consequence, the siege became extended and Māhir Bey finally appealed to al-Sanūsī at Jaghbūb for help. When al-Sanūsī's deputy ordered Ḥassūnah to surrender, the shaykh complied at once, together with his followers; all were pardoned and agreed to pay taxes regularly to the government, but on the condition that the Egyptian Government would not claim the taxes unpaid for the past three years. The agreement was signed by Māhir Bey, Ḥassūnah Manṣūr and the deputy of al-Sanūsī as witness; this illustrates the influence of al-Sanūsī brotherhood in Siwa in those days. This incident convinced Ḥassūnah Manṣūr that he was the leading personality in the oasis, and the Westerners considered themselves superior to their adversaries. The disputes between the two groups were revived and inflamed; Ḥassūnah and many others lost their lives in another battle between them.

In 1895 there was unrest again in Siwa and some of the visitors were turned away; in October 1896, Jennings-Bramley was sent to the oasis on a mission concerning taxes but was forced to leave on the same day.(1) Shortly afterwards, Blunt visited Siwa but he was very badly received. The Siwans fired at his tent, stole his guns and luggage, and he narrowly escaped with his life.

---

(1) W. Jennings-Bramley, «A Journey to Siwa in September and October 1896,» **Geographical Journal,** 10 (London, 1897), pp. 597 - 608. He is the same Mr. Bramley who spent over forty years in the service of the Egyptian Government in the army and in the Frontier Administration, and the one who founded the settlement of Burj al-'Arab in Maryūṭ. Mr. Bramley built himself a stone house on a ridge near Burj al-'Arab ; it resembled a medieval European castle. There he lived after his retirement until 1956 when he had to leave the country. His knowledge of the genealogy of the different tribes of the Western Desert of Egypt, their customs and their laws was second to none in Egypt or anywhere else. He was always generous with his knowledge and it is greatly regretted that he did not write any books on this subject nor even his memoirs.

A new punitive expedition sent to the oasis provides the reason that the Siwans did not treat A. Silva White(1) badly when he arrived. In March 1898 White started from Cairo, passing by Wādī al-Naṭrūn, al-Qaṭṭārah Depression and Qāret Umm al-Ṣughayyar, intending to visit Siwa, thence to move on to Jaghbūb. He was allowed to enter the town; in fact, he mentions that he visited it five times during his stay which lasted from the 2nd of April until the 8th, and thus had to give up his plan to visit Jaghbūb, and returned to Cairo. His book adds little to our knowledge of Siwa, but he stresses the bad effect of the rivalry between the two groups of inhabitants and the increasing influence of the Sanūsī representative there. The house of Ḥassūnah Manṣūr was confiscated in 1896, and Maḥmūd 'Azmī, the Ma'mūr at the time, turned it into an office for the Police Station. In 1897, he committed the crime of placing dynamite under the sanctuary of Umm 'Ubaydah, blowing up one of its walls and the ceiling in order to obtain stone for his office steps and a house for himself. The photograph of White taken in 1898 shows the temple after its destruction.(2)

At the turn of the century, Siwa was becoming less revolutionary and its inhabitants wiser. The Sanūsī order encouraged marriages between the Easterners and the Westerners; and the two groups agreed that whenever a misunderstanding developed they would send to Jaghbūb; one of the Brethren would come and settle the quarrel without use of weapons. In the meantime the authority of the Ma'mūr had increased and the oasis was essentially as secure as any place of its size in Upper Egypt at the time. In fact, G. Steindorff found Siwa peaceful when he visited it; in December 1900, he was permitted to go wherever he wished; no one interfered with his work as he copied inscriptions in the tombs of Jabal al-Mawtā or Umm 'Ubaydah or even on the walls of the Temple of the Oracle which had been inhabited until that time.

From the Beginning of the 20th Century until the End of the First World War

Thereafter Siwa remained quiet, and the wars between the Westerners and Easterners became stories of the past. A limited number of shaykhs, the heads of their families, were responsi-

(1) Arthur Silva White, **From Sphinx to Oracle** (London, 1899).

(2) **Ibid.**, p. 224, White inquired about the destruction of this temple. The inhabitants told him that this was caused by an earthquake in the second decade of the century; they were referring to the earthquake of 1811. In the same book he wrote that when he compared his photograph with those of previous travellers. the destruction «has beeen wholesale, even within the last ten years».

ble for the good conduct of their relatives and directly responsible to the Ma'mūr who held supreme local authority. Differences between the families existed but the inter-marriages between them had good results. The influence of the Sanūsī brotherhood helped a great deal in turning a formerly riotous people toward peace and the observation of religious rules. Moreover, al-Madanīyah, another religious order was established in Siwa, with headquarters in Istanbul, Turkey. Its founder was Shaykh Ẓāfir al-Madanī; its purpose was to spread the good principles of Islam among the people of every community in the Ottoman Empire. Its hidden aim, however, was to strengthen the position of the Caliph, by enabling his agents to expand their ability to obtain information concerning any sign of disloyalty to his person or to the Empire anywhere.(1)

The new movement was readily accepted by the Easterners as a counterpart to the Sanūsīyah movement among the Westerners. Surprisingly enough, the existence of the two movements among the two groups of quarrelsome inhabitants caused no trouble; the contrary was true. Siwa had become more peaceful, its inhabitants began to be more reasonable and more inclined to the observation of the doctrines of Islam; the two parties competed in demonstrating their obedience in following the good principles.

Khedive ʿAbbās II Visits Siwa

Since Alexander the Great, no ruler of Egypt visited this oasis until February 1904 when the Khedive 'Abbās II journeyed there. After his great success in reclaiming land for agriculture in Maryūṭ, he decided to begin similar projects in Siwa. After his experts had completed all the necessary investigations, he expressed his wish to see the place, and the essential arrangements were made for his state visit. His caravan consisted of two hundred and twenty eight camels, a great number of them mounted by Sudanese soldiers of the camel-corps, twenty-two

(1) Just before the First World War, a delegation of a number of Siwan notables from the Madanīyah brotherhood travelled to Istanbul, after performing the pilgrimage at Mecca in order to pay their respects to Shaykh Ẓāfir. They were well received there and some of them married Turkish girls who accompanied their husbands on their return to Siwa. It did not take them long to discover that the code of life at Siwa did not suit them at all and somehow they contacted the Turkish Consulate in Cairo, who sent a representative to investigate the situation. They were divorced from their husbands, and the consul took most of them back with him to Cairo, and thence they returned to Istanbul. Anyone who knows Siwa and the Siwans can understand the nightmare in which those wives lived during their short stay in the oasis.

horses for his person and his companions, and twenty-eight horsemen as his bodyguard.(1) During the seven days' march between Marsā Maṭrūḥ and Siwa, the Khedive rode one of his horses or was driven in a sand-car especially built for this trip. On arrival, the camp was pitched at 'Ayn Rāṭī (Mijāḥiẓ) and there he received a delegation of all the heads of the families. He entered Siwa the next morning, riding a horse and surrounded by all his company. All the Siwans crowded to welcome him and cheered him with great enthusiasm. The shaykhs were presented with cashmere shawls, many others received clothing and money; banquets were provided for the poor. He visited several places ; as a gift, the Siwans presented him three springs together with all the land which could be irrigated by their waters: 'Ayn Qurayshat, the largest in the oasis, 'Ayn al-Shifā, and the Ḥaṭīyah of Tawīnī. The Khedive gave instructions for the property to be registered officially in the name of his son, Prince 'Abdul-Mun'im. He directed the government to restore the springs and help the inhabitants in every possible way. Three years later, in 1907, he paid a second visit to Siwa to witness the progress of the work at Qurayshat, and during this stay he ordered the foundation of the great mosque which is now called the mosque of King Fu'ād. In fact, the mosque was built by the government and neither 'Abbās nor Fu'ād contributed in building it. Its walls were a little over one metre high when the war broke out in 1914, and the work was stopped. In 1928, on the occasion of his visit to Siwa, King Fu'ād gave instructions to complete the construction.

During the work of reclamation and excavation for the drains at Qurayshat, the labourers digging in its ancient cemetery discovered some small objects, mostly of glass inlay; the Khedive presented eight of these to the Cairo Museum.(2) In the course of this visit, one of the inhabitants presented the Khedive with a lion's head(3) of Roman date, which had been built into one of the walls of the town of Siwa; the Khedive gave it to J.C.E. Falls, who accompanied him.

On his second visit the Khedive was anxious to push the work forward at Qurayshat. Noting that labourers brought from the Nile Valley would not stay long in the oasis and usually

---

(1) The details of the visit are published by one of his companions, J.C. Ewald Falls, **Siwa : Die Oase des Sonnegottes in der libyschen Wüste** (Cairo, 1908), p. 15 ff. Some interesting details were published in G. E. Simpson, **The Heart of Libya, The Siwa Oasis: Its People, Customs and Sport**, pp. 23 - 25.

(2) These eight small objects are registered in the Cairo Museum Journal d'Entrée under numbers 37934 - 37941.

(3) The photograph of this head is published in his book **Siwa...**, p. 35.

ran away after a short time, he encouraged the Siwans to work for him by raising their wages from one piaster to three piasters per day. But in spite of all efforts, the work went very slowly for lack of sufficient labour ; the outbreak of the war, and the forced absence of the Khedive from Egypt put an end to the project. To this day, the waters of 'Ayn Qurayshat are wasted; they flow to the salt-lake of al-Zaytūn.

Siwa during the First World War

In 1841, al-Sayyid Muḥammad al-Sanūsī, the founder of the Sanūsī order, visited Siwa on his way from al-Ḥijāz to his native land. After spending some months in Cairo he continued his journey westward to the oasis; taken ill there, he spent several months recuperating and instructing the people in the faith.(1) His **zāwiyah**(2) at Siwa was one of the earliest and most important centres in the Western Desert of Egypt.

In 1856, the Grand Sanūsī established at the Oasis of Jaghbūb an Islamic University second in Africa only to al-Azhar (the famous mosque in Cairo and the most celebrated seat of religious teaching for a thousand years) which became in a very short time the seat of learning for all the followers of his order. Until that time, Jaghbūb was almost an uninhabited oasis, in which the water was brackish, highly sulphurous, and insufficient to irrigate more than a small area of gardens; it became dependent for supplies largely upon Siwa which was not very far distant. The relations between Siwa and Jaghbūb increased with time and the influence of the Sanūsīyah order was dominant among the Siwans.

Since 1911, Sayyid Aḥmad al-Sharīf(3) the head of the Sanūsīyah at that time, had been allied with the Turks, who ruled Tripolis when the Italians landed on the coast of Libya in 1912. He sided with the Turks, but when the Italians succeeded in oc-

---

(1) E. E. Evans-Pritchard, **The Sanusi of Cyrenaica** (Oxford, 1949) pp 13, 14.

(2) A centre of the order, consisting of a mosque, a school, a guest house for travellers and a house for the representative of the order and his family.

(3) The Grand Sanūsī died at Jaghbūb on September 7, 1859 and was buried at Jaghbūb ; he was followed by his son Sayyid al-Mahdī, under whose leadership the order reached its greatest expansion. Al-Mahdī died in 1902 and was succeeded by his nephew Sayyid Aḥmad al-Sharīf who had to leave the country after the war and lived in exile till his death in 1933. After 1917, the struggle against the Italians was led by Sayyid Idrīs al-Sanūsī, the son of al-Mahdī. Sayyid Idrīs had become King of Libya in 1950. After the declaration of the Libyan Republic in 1969, he left Libya and now lives in Egypt.

cupying the coast, he became more or less independent in the interior. When war broke out in 1914, al-Sanūsī was on good terms with Egypt and had no problems with the British. But it was quite natural that his sympathies should lie with the Turks who were at war with the British, who in turn were occupying Egypt, and also against his enemies, the Italians, who were the allies of the British.

It was arranged that al-Sanūsī forces should threaten Egypt's western frontier in order to keep a large number of the British forces occupied there; the Turks and their German allies supplied guns and munitions.

The forces of al-Sanūsī proceeded to the Egyptian frontier at Sallūm and attacked it in November 1915. Consequently, the British and Egyptian garrisons were withdrawn from Sallūm and Sīdī Barrānī on the coast, and the Egyptian authorities began defensively to fortify Marsā Maṭrūḥ; in December 1915, the Sanūsī forces were beaten and lost a great number of their untrained Bedouin soldiers.(1) After another defeat at al-'Agāgīr near Sīdī Barrānī, Sayyid Aḥmad decided to leave the coast and proceed with his men to encamp at Siwa. The small troop of Egyptian camel corps soldiers stationed there received instructions to leave the oasis before the Sanūsī forces arrived. But the Siwans suspected their intentions and decided to attack the small force and sieze their equipment and personal property. When they attacked the barracks, the soldiers had already departed ; the Siwans in great numbers hurried after them ; they found them at 'Ayn Rāṭī, captured a few while the others escaped.

When Sayyid Aḥmad and his men arrived at Siwa, they were welcomed by the Siwans who offered their loyalty. They thought that this was their chance to regain their old independence and be rid of the discipline and taxes imposed on them for almost a century, but they were mistaken. Sayyid Aḥmad settled at Qaṣr Ḥassūnah, and his second in command, Muḥammad Ṣāliḥ Ḥarb(2) was appointed commandant of Siwa. The Siwans were required to put their men and resources at the disposal of al-Sanūsī; many of these joined the troops and proved

(1) Many interesting details of the battles which took place at the coast, and at Siwa in this period can be found in Belgrave, **Siwa...**, pp. 122 - 32 ; and in M. T. Butt and A. R. Cury, **Mersa Matruh** (Cairo, 1925), pp. 47 - 49.

(2) Muḥammad Ṣāliḥ Ḥarb was an Egyptian coast-guard officer stationed on the north coast in 1915. Accompanied by Bedouin and Egyptian soldiers, he went to Sayyid and fought at his side. He was an honest and pious man, with great talents as a soldier. Twenty-four years later he became Minister of Wạr in Egypt; after his retirement from the service he headed the Young Men's Muslim Association until his death in the sixties.

themselves good warriors and excellent policemen. Their love of discipline and sense of duty demonstrated their superiority to the Bedouin; they were appreciated by their superiors; Muḥammed Ṣāliḥ Ḥarb, in a private conversation with me in 1944 about those days at Siwa, spoke very highly of their abilities. Some of the notables of Siwa were given the titles of Bey, others were presented with Turkish medals and a number were appointed officers. But after a short time, the thrifty Siwans began to resent paying money or offering part of their products to the Sanūsī; in the resultant altercations, some of them received harsh treatment. On the 15th of April 1916, the head of the order, followed by several thousands of Bedouin and Siwans, left Siwa on his way to Dakhla Oasis, passing by Baḥrīyah and Farafra. During his absence the money complaints among the Siwans increased, and they were still more badly treated. In some cases, their wealth was confiscated, and the followers of the Madanīyah order, the rivals of the Sanūsīyah, succeeded in organizing a small rebellion.

Meanwhile, the situation at Dakhla Oasis was not favourable to Sayyid and he decided to retreat to Siwa. The news of the rebellion reached him when he was on his way; but on his arrival at Siwa, all the rebels laid down their arms and showed their loyalty to his person. But they complained bitterly about the behaviour of his men. The situation at the coast was becoming serious; Sallūm was captured, and the British troops were making preparations to march against Siwa. Many of the soldiers of al-Sanūsī deserted him and in January 1917, he began to arrange for withdrawal to Jaghbūb; but on hearing that the British forces were advancing in tanks and armed cars on the 2nd of February 1917, he hurried with 500 of his men on camels to Jaghbūb. Muḥammad Ṣāliḥ Ḥarb, with the remaining 800 men, decided to stop the British advance at the uninhabited oasis of Girbah. He succeeded in holding them off for two days until Sayyid was safe in Jaghbūb; then with all his men he retreated in the night to join him. The British forces entered Siwa on February the 5th, and were welcomed by the cheering Siwans who declared their loyalty as they always did with every new victorious conqueror. A new camel corps was re-stationed at Siwa during that year and the oasis became a district in the newly founded Frontier Administration. The use of motor cars in the desert made the journey to Siwa an easy matter, and after the end of the war the oasis received more attention from the government, and many officials were stationed there to look after its people.

The Visit of King Fu'ād (Fouad) in 1928

On the 14th of October 1928, King Fu'ād started his journey to Siwa by car, using the same old route used by Alexander the Great and Khedive 'Abbās II before him. He spent the night in a wooden house specially built at al-Buwayb, 125 kilometres from Marsā Maṭrūḥ, and arrived at the oasis before noon on the 15th. Arrangements for the royal visit had been made some months in advance. When the cortege arrived at the borders of the oasis, the royal cars were joined by all the force of the camel corps mounted on their dromedaries; the male inhabitants lined both sides of the road, beneath triumphal arches decorated with palm ribs and flowers all the way from the town limits to Qaṣr Ḥassūnah where a wooden rest-house was constructed for the celebration. The women grouped on the housetops and street corners, all attired in their finest apparel. They joined the men in greeting the king of the land amidst the thunder of cannon, while a military band played the national anthem.

During a small ceremony in the early afternoon, the two sons of 'Uthmān Ḥabbūn were released to the great joy of all the families of the Westerners.(1) The shaykhs, as the heads of their families, received tunics of honour, and His Majesty presented each with a gold watch and a sword; great quantities of clothing and purses of money were distributed to the poor. Evening brought a fireworks display and a film show, seen in the oasis for the first time, and the Siwans enjoyed themselves in performing their dances, singing and playing their traditional music. Next morning, the King inspected the troops, gave audience to the shaykhs and the leading members of their families and laid the foundation stones of the hospital and other government buildings. In the afternoon he visited the ruins of the Temple of Umm 'Ubaydah and listened to the explanations of Dr. Breccia, then the director of the Museum of Alexandria. He visited two gardens, one belonging to the Westerners and the other to the Easterners; in the evening ardent followers of the religious orders of the Sanūsīyah and the Madanīyah held their **dhikr** circles.(2)

King Fu'ād left Siwa at dawn on the 16th amid the firing of cannon and the cheers of the inhabitants who lined both sides of the road as far as the edge of the town, and all the members

---

(1) They were sentenced to twenty-five years' imprisonment for taking sides in a riot started by their father in 1910, in which the Ma'mūr of Siwa was killed. 'Uthmān Ḥabbūn was hanged, and his two sons and other relatives, all from the families of the Westerners, were sentenced to imprisonment.

(2) These are religious gatherings where the people sit in a circle or stand in rows and recite together certain prayers, or repeat the name of God, sometimes to the beat of some musical instrument, at the same time swaying and shaking their heads, often until they become insensible.

of the camel corps escorted the royal car. The king arrived at Sallūm before midday of the 17th, where the Maḥrūsah, one of the royal yachts, was waiting in the harbour. After several receptions and ceremonies during the day, the Maḥrūsah departed at 5 a.m. the next day en route to Alexandria.

The visit of Fu'ād to the Oasis of Amun had immediately good results. He gave orders to complete the mosque begun by the Khedive 'Abbās, to build stone walls around the flowing springs, and to do all possible to instruct the inhabitants in the best agricultural techniques and assist in selling their crops of dates and olives. Several specialists from the Ministry of Agriculture, who arrived shortly afterwards, built a modern oil press and a factory employing modern, hygenic methods of packaging dates. Education was not neglected; a school was started; nor was morality overlooked. When the king learned that some of the Siwans still practiced certain customs forbidden by religion and the accepted moral code, and that superstitions were spreading among them, he ordered a resident scholar of religion brought to Siwa, evetually to be appointed as the **Imām** of the mosque.

Fu'ād's visit, the government's new interest in the oasis and the increasing use of motor cars helped to Egyptianize Siwa in subsequent years more than ever. However, the conservative Siwans retained their own language and to a great extent many of their customs and traditions. They never showed any enmity toward visitors; but while their shaykhs from the early thirties did their best to show hospitality to officials as well as visitors to the oasis, the ordinary people kept to themselves and rarely encouraged strangers to enter their houses, or to mix in any way with the women of their families.

However, I cannot end these chapters on the history of Siwa without two other references: the first is the history of Siwa during the years of the Second World War; the second, a fourth royal visit in 1945.

Siwa Oasis during the Second World War

When the Second World War broke out in September 1939, Siwa was enjoying a period of peace and everything was going smoothly. I remember with the greatest satisfaction my visits to this oasis in 1938 and 1939, even in the early months of 1940 and how much I enjoyed my work there. But the situation began to change when it became known that the Italians and Germans were preparing to attack Egypt from the west. Adequate forces of the allied troops were stationed on the coast and especially at Marsā Maṭrūḥ; and it was also decided to station some of the troops in Siwa against the possibility that the Axis forces might occupy the oasis as well. With the arrival of these troops, the military authorities did not encourage any civilian visits to Siwa.

The troops stationed there in the later months of 1940 were mostly Egyptian, with some Australian, New Zealand and British units which garrisoned the oasis and took all necessary steps for its defence. The Italians frequently bombed Siwa from the air, and the inhabitants were forced to leave their houses. They found the rock tombs of Jabal al-Mawtā the best shelters to keep them and their families out of danger. Those who moved in at an early date occupied tombs which were already open; others digging caves in the sides of the hill discovered new tombs. During this excitement, numerous mummies and small ancient objects were found.

In December 1940, Colonel Bather, one of the British officers in the Frontier Administration, was stationed at Siwa as political officer. He brought to Cairo fragments of gilded Roman coffins which he presented to the Palace, but King Fārūq (Farouk) forwarded them to the Cairo Museum. On examining these objects, and on learning from Bather that new painted tombs had been found, I requested permission to go to Siwa to inspect them. I was required to sign papers stating that I was making the journey at my own risk; if I were killed no one could be held responsible. I found almost all the families living at Jabal al-Mawtā; the rock tombs were packed with men, women, children, chickens, pets and other animals, all living together.

Bather's report was true; among the newly discovered dozens of rock tombs, three were inscribed, including the tomb of Si-Amun. I was horrified to find that many of the soldiers used to come to visit that tomb; on payment of a few piasters to the family living in it, they were allowed to cut away any part of a painted scene to take home as a souvenir ! This went on for almost two months and caused the destruction or disfiguration of the best preserved scenes; eventually I had to leave the oasis before finishing my work. There was objection to the prolonged stay of an archeologist who, according to the mentality of the responsible military authorities in Siwa and Cairo, was busied with a work of no value, which could as well be postponed until the end of the war. My stay there was from the 5th of January 1941 until the 20th. The Siwans profited economically from the presence of the military troops, and many of them were making fortunes.

In the meantime, hostilities at the coast increased and with the approach of the summer months of 1942, it was expected that the attack on Egypt might begin at any time; but for some reason, the troops stationed at Siwa for its defence for two years, received orders to leave the oasis. The last soldier departed on the 30th of June, leaving the oasis to its destiny, without sufficient supplies to feed the population, now to be cut off in the midst of the desert for more than a month. By messenger mounted on a camel, the Ma'mūr sent an urgent message to Bahrīyah Oasis on the 19th of July requesting supplies and five policemen, since famine began to threaten the inhabitants.

Next day, on the morning of the 20th, two small Italian aircrafts landed at the airport near the rest house, three officers stepped out and began to walk in the direction of the police station. No one showed any kind of resistance, in fact according to the reports published later, the Ma'mūr even sent the government car to fetch them to his office.(1) The officers informed the Ma'mūr that the Italian forces were on their way to Siwa from Jaghbūb; at 1 p.m. two large trucks arrived loaded with forty soldiers and four officers. At once, in the presence of the Ma'mūr and all the shaykhs, they raised the Italian flag beside the Egyptian ensign at the top of the police station. The commandant of the force announced, through an interpreter who was with him, that the Italians had come to Siwa as fighting men, with no intention of interfering with the administration. Three days later other troops began to arrive, and now the total number was slightly more than 2000 Italians. The Germans who accompanied them consisted of one unit of armoured cars, with not more than ten officers. The Italian troops occupied the former allied barracks and some of the houses of the inhabitants.

The Siwans made good business with the Italians, and there were no serious complaints about the behaviour of the soldiers from the day of their arrival until their departure. On the 21st of September, Field Marshal Rommel visited Siwa and was received officially, not only by the troops but also by the Ma'mūr and all the shaykhs who invited him to tea in one of the gardens. At the end of the visit, which lasted for only a few hours, Rommel presented the shaykhs with two boxes of tea weighing three and a half kilogrammes, and 10,000 Italian liras.

When the disastrous news of the Battle of 'Alamayn reached the Axis forces, the Italians decided to retreat to Jaghbūb without a fight. Before departure they offered to sell their surplus supplies to the inhabitants and at the same time announced that they were ready to exchange any Italian liras which the inhabitants might possess for Egyptian or English pounds. The total sum amounted to fourteen thousand pounds. On the 8th of November, the last Italian force left the oasis; the period of the occupation was three months and eighteen days.

King Fārūq Visits Siwa

After the defeat of Rommel's forces at 'Alamayn, the coast and the Western Desert in general were no longer threatened,

---

(1) The story of the Italian occupation of Siwa is told in detail by 'Abdul-Laṭīf Wākid in his book, **Wāḥit Amun** (Cairo, 1949), pp. 65 - 71. Wākid's statements are based on official reports and private information supplied by the Ma'mūr himself.

and the people in Siwa and the other oases resumed their normal life. In 1945, King Fārūq accompanied by a few friends, made a trip to the oases in a caravan of twenty-four powerful, well-equipped desert cars. They started from Cairo on the 4th of January, and returned by the 14th. The king went first to Baḥrīyah, spent the night there, then proceeded to Siwa to remain for one day. Even now, the people repeat what they heard from their fathers about the details of the visits of Fu'ād and 'Abbās, and how the inhabitants of the oasis were impressed by the dignity and the beautiful uniforms of his courtiers and his bodyguard, and the valuable presents given to the heads of the families and the clothes and money distributed to the poor.

When the shaykhs learned that King Fārūq and his companions had arrived and were staying in the government rest house, they lost no time in going to pay him homage and extend a warm welcome. Everyone rushed home to dress in his best apparel; the older shaykhs donned the beautiful robes of honour and the swords given to them by King Fu'ād seventeen years before.

When they stood in front of the king; they could hardly believe their eyes. The picture they had in mind differed completely from the stout young man who stood in front of them in shorts and a simple open shirt. He listened to the phrases of greeting from their spokesman, Shaykh Mahdī Abū Gīrī the shaykh of Aghūrmī, the oldest one amongst them; thanked them and asked if there was anything they wished the government to do for them. The spokesman replied that the best service that could be rendered to Siwa, and from which everyone in the oasis would profit, was to macadamize the road between Marsā Matrūh and Siwa. The king ordered a servant who stood near him to take note of this. He then addressed them, inquiring if it were true that the Siwans still practiced a certain vice. The shaykhs bent their heads, none uttered a word; and they left the rest house without receiving any presents.

Later, whenever the visit was mentioned, the prudent and cautious Siwan shaykhs had little to say; their harshest comment was only that the King was unlike his father. One of the young shaykhs, whom I had known for several years and who was always frank with me, told me in 1946 that Fārūq "neither looked like a king nor behaved like one". The conservative Siwans could not understand that times were changing, and that the visit of King Fārūq to Siwa was not a formal one. I have always wondered if their disappointment was because they did not see or hear what they had imagined, or because they did not receive the presents they expected.

5

The Antiquities of Siwa

The majority of visitors to Siwa are attracted by its great reputation in ancient times, and look forward to visit what might be left of its monuments. It is true that the severe hand of time, the ignorance and fanaticism of the inhabitants, and the disastrous effect of the salt in the soil are responsible for the ruinous condition and sometimes the destruction of many of these monuments; but no doubt what still remains of them repays the visit. Wherever he goes, the visitor finds reminders of a great past, and he will enjoy his stay in spite of his sadness at the condition in which these monuments are completely neglected, unprotected and constantly exposed to destruction.

The reader cannot expect to find in the present book a detailed description of every scene on every wall of the tombs or temples; this can be found in the publications which deal with the archeology of Siwa as the main subject, but I hope to provide an adequate description of the principal monuments most likely to be visited.(1)

This chapter is a general survey of all the ancient sites in and around the oasis, including the uninhabited oases between Siwa and Baḥrīyah. The Temple of the Oracle, the Temple of Umm 'Ubaydah, and the tombs of Jabal al-Mawtā will be discussed in the following chapters.

---

(1) Those who want to study in detail all the archeological remains at Siwa, including the inscriptions on the walls of the temples and tombs, can read my book **Siwa Oasis : Its History and Antiquities**, where the scenes and inscriptions in this oasis are published.

The Ancient Sites of Siwa : A General Survey

The centre of the ancient town of Siwa was at Aghūrmi, clustered about the rock which stands there; the Temple of the Oracle stood upon it, while the town itself was scattered all around. There were, no doubt, other chapels for the god Amun and probably other gods, but none of them thus far have been discovered; only the remains of the second largest temple in the oasis still stand in the midst of the palm groves, not far from the rock. This is the Temple of Umm 'Ubaydah. These two monuments, as well as the necropolis of Jabal al-Mawtā will be discussed later in greater detail, as already mentioned.

These three sites are undoubtedly the most important antiquities in Siwa and can be visited easily as they are near the rest houses; but there are still many sites and ruins of temples scattered about the oasis, and it might interest the students of history and lovers of archeology to know where they are, and to have some information about them.

The Spring of the Sun : Before leaving the town of Siwa, I must refer to other sites which are close to the town; one of them is 'Ayn al-Gūbah, close by the Temple of Umm 'Ubaydah; this is the famous "Spring of the Sun" mentioned by Herodotus and other ancient visitors, and the most beautiful spring in the oasis.

Jabal al-Dakrūr : Jabal al-Dakrūr lies about five kilometres southwest of the centre of the town; it is the healthiest place in Siwa and has good water. Until thirty years ago, many of the Siwans were accustomed to spend several days there in the full moon of the Muslim month of Rajab. They used to build booths or pitch tents for this purpose on the sandy sides of the hill and at its foot. They considered their stay there as a holiday during which everyone, men and women, ate the largest possible quantity of garlic. They believed that this would keep them healthy all the year round. This custom is no longer observed, but the sand of the same neighbourhood is still used to cure people who suffer from rheumatic pains. There are certain persons there who specialize in burying the bodies of the sufferers in sand from the neck down for a few hours. The heads are protected from the strong heat of the sun, while the hot sand absorbs the sweat of the body.

At Jabal al-Dakrūr there are rock-cut tombs; the two most easily accessible are quite large. One has been cut into the middle of the hill, has six pillars and opens west; its walls are void of any ancient paintings but visitors of recent times have inscribed their names on them. Near the summit of the hill, another rock tomb opens north. It had four papyri-columns whose shafts have since been quarried away; parts of their capitals remain; in the Siwans' opinion or imagination they resemble large turbans. The shape afforded opportunity to invent many stories about the treasures which are still hidden there. Opposite this tomb, to the left of the pass, there is a Greek inscription in three lines.

These tombs are larger than those of Jabal al-Mawtā and differ from them in plan. There is great possibility that other tombs still exist. They date in all probability from the Ptolemaic period or earlier. Near the top of the hill there is a good layer of limestone, used in ancient times as a quarry. This is one of the places in which the stones were quarried for the construction of some of the temples built in this oasis; other quarries are at Bilād al-Rūm.

Visitors can see many openings in the hillsides near the town; most are small undecorated tombs which date from the late Roman period, since this was the site of the cemeteries of the town; the ancient capital was where Aghūrmī now stands. However, many of the openings in the hillsides were cut by poor people for dwellings, in ancient as well as in recent times. Hewing out caves for living quarters occured in ancient times in many parts of the world and still continues almost everywhere. These rock-cut chambers offer good and useful shelter in cold seasons, and are cool in the summer.

Other ancient tombs were cut in the side of the ridge known as Qaṣr Ḥassūnah, on which the rest house for King Fu'ād was built in 1928. When the Grand Sanūnī came to Siwa in 1838, he preferred to live in one of these; he used a neighbouring tomb as a place of worship. With his own hands he cut a **miḥrāb** (niche for prayer) in its rock and spent there most of the hours of the day and a great part of the night praying or teaching. No Siwan can be tempted to spend the night in it because they believe that if a person sleeps in this place and in future commits any sin, even a small lie, great misfortune will befall him. The pure place of worship of their holy man cannot be polluted by a sinner.

Sites West of the Town of Siwa

On our way to Ḥaṭīyat Khamīsah we pass by two sites of ancient tombs cut in rock; in the one called Ghayṭ Abū Manṣūr twenty-eight tombs are cut near the top of the ridge. None of these has any decorations; ancient tomb-robbers entered and many fragments of bones, shrouds and potsh rds are scattered around. The second group appears at Ḥaṭīyat Zāwah less than two kilometres south of the spring of Khamīsah. One of these tombs is larger than the others and contains two square pillars and a niche. Fragments of pottery show that both cemeteries date from the early Roman period.

Khamīsah : Ḥaṭīyat Khamīsah is considered one of the most fertile parts of Siwa, with the best olive gardens; it is famous also for other crops. None of its rich landowners live there; they have their houses in the town; the houses seen at Khamīsah belong to some of the labourers. Near the spring stands a small stone temple, in a ruined condition; its walls are not decorated. At the edge of the gardens there is a ridge called "Khamīsah". Although no tombs have been cut in its side, the inhabitants believe that the treasure of Queen Khamīsah is buried there. At the top a shaft has been cut but in all probability this is the work of treasure hunters. Another ridge at a distance of less than a kilometre west, contains about one hundred and fifty small tombs cut in the southside. They call it Mishandid now, but in the last century it was known as Khamīsah; it was mentioned under this name in the books of the 19th century travellers.

To the south of Khamīsah, and about five kilometres from Jabal Amilāl, there is a site called al-Ma'ṣarah; not far from it stand the remains of a stone gateway and a part of a surrounding wall. It was there that Rohlfs found, in 1869, a small marble statue of a ram, which he presented to the Berlin Museum; it is of Roman date.(1) This site is mentioned in the Siwan Manuscript as Bāb al-Madīnah, the entrance in a great girdle-wall surrounding the kingdom of a queen called Bilīsah; the Manuscript adds that the old name Bāb al-Madīnah is replaced by the name of al-Ma'ṣarah.

Bilād al-Rūm : Another important district lies to the west of Khamīsah, where we find rock-tombs and remains of a brick building at the foot of the hill. The Siwans believe that it is the site of a church.(2) Not very far away, are ruins of a stone temple, and a short distance behind the temple are the quarries from which the stones were taken (see the plan, Fig. 31).

This temple was standing in the last century, at least until 1869 when Rohlfs visited it; Cailliaud described it in some detail, stating that this was the most beautiful monument he saw in this oasis.(3) It has fallen down and is now a heap of ruins. This is the famous Doric Temple of the early travellers : facing south, it consisted of three halls preceded by a colonnade, thirty-four metres long; the temple itself was twenty-five metres long. The entrances to the halls were decorated but there were no wall inscriptions; it dates in all probability from the 1st century of our era and not from the late Roman period.

---

(1) G. Rohlfs, **Von Tripolis nach Alexandrien, 2** : 85 and 106.

(2) These ruins are known now as Qaṣr al-Rūm; Rohlfs gave its name as «El-Amoudein».

(3) Cailliaud, **Voyage à Meroé**, pp. 72 - 74, and Minutoli, **Reise...**, p. 173.

The entrances to some of the sepulchres are decorated with the cavetto cornice; and in the quarries are several unfinished blocks, among which is the capital of a column. The study of these quarries shows that large quantities of stone, much more than was needed for the Doric Temple, were extracted here. The stone is of very good quality and these two facts raise the question of the possibility that the stones used in building some of the temples of Amun in the capital of the oasis were quarried here as in the quarries of Jabal al-Dakrūr.

The District of al-Marāqī : The district of al-Marāqī occupies the western part of the depression; it was known for its fertility in the Middle Ages and is still famous for its good pasturage. Most of its present inhabitants are from the Bedouin tribe of al-Shihaybāṭ who live here with their flocks; very few Siwans live among them.

The place must have been thickly populated in Roman times because a great number of the ridges, after we leave the district of Khamīsah, are honey-combed with tombs cut in their sides, — a fact which proves that there were many inhabitants who lived there for a long time. The most important of these sites are Qāret al-Wazīdī, al-Zāwiyah, Jallātī, Abū Māḍī, Gharghart, Ḥaṭīyat 'Abdul-Jabbār and lastly Quwayret Shīzah. Among these the only site which preserves any ancient monument is Ḥaṭīyat Gharghart, where we find the remains of a stone building. Treasure hunters left not a single stone in place; the plan is beyond recognition. The distance between the town of Siwa and the last site in this district is about thirty-four kilometres.

In the Siwan Manuscript, we read that there were thirty flowing springs at Khamīsah; but those still in use are very few and their waters are mostly wasted and flow into the salt lakes of Khamīsah and al-Marāqī; the majority of the ancient springs are now sanded-up.

It seems that this district continued to flourish after Roman times. Al-Maqrīzī, who compiled his famous works in the 15th century, referred to it in one of his books, **Al-Khiṭaṭ,** stating that the "town" of Marāqīyah (the land of al-Marāqī) stands at the edge of the frontier of Egypt, after which begins the land of Intablus[(1)] at a distance of two **barīds** (i.e. 24 miles) from the town of Santarīyah. He describes it as a large country with many palm trees, cultivated lands and flowing springs, its fruits were of very good quality. He says further that emmer wheat was grown with great success, and its inhabitants grew rice and had many gardens. In the 10th century (the Muslim month of

---

(1) «Pentapolis» is meant; this name was sometimes given to the Land of Barqah (Barca) in Libya.

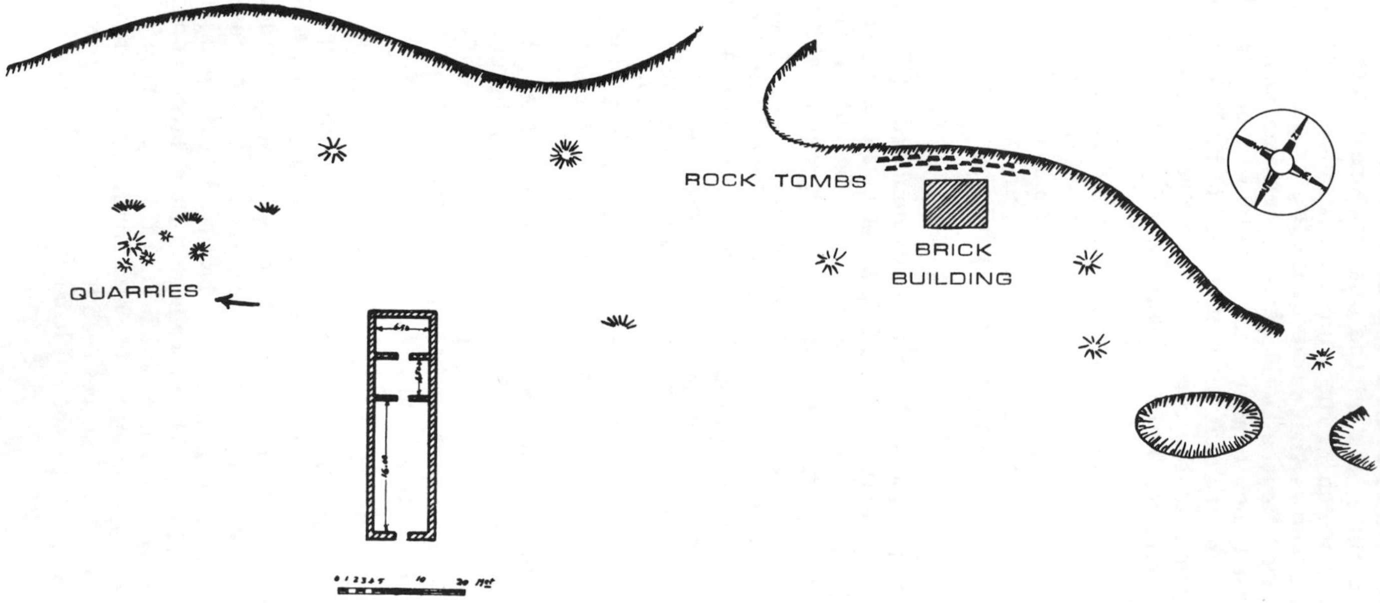

Fig. 31. The site of Bilād al-Rūm showing the place of the Doric Temple, the brick building, the rock tombs and the quarries.

Shawwāl, year A.H. 304, i.e. the year A.D. 922), according to al-Maqrīzī, the people of Marāqīyah deserted their district and immigrated to Alexandria in fear of attacks of the ruler of Barqah who occupied their territory; thereafter, he adds, it greatly deteriorated although up until his day it was still populated.

In 1950 the Inspectorate General of Desert Irrigation started cleaning out some of the ancient sanded-up springs in this district, among these the important spring of Mirkidah. The intention was to begin a pilot project for reclaiming land and drying-up a part of the salt lakes, at Khamīsah and al-Marāqī. Unfortunately, the project was discontinued.(1)

Sites East of the Town of Siwa

The cultivated lands in the eastern part of the depression were apparently larger than those of the western side, and the small towns were more populous. There are four very important sites : Qurayshat, Abū Shurūf, Abul-'Awwāf and al-Zaytūn.

The District of Qurayshat : 'Ayn Qurayshat, has already been mentioned several times in previous chapters; although its flowing waters are now wasted, the situation was different in ancient times, especially during the Ptolemaic and Roman periods.

Qaṣr al-Ghashshām: Not far from the spring we find two ancient sites about one hundred metres apart. One is the ruin of a stone temple which dates in all probability from the latter part of the Ptolemaic period. In 1900 when Steindorff visited this oasis, its walls were still standing. He published its photograph(2), mentioning that the entrances were decorated with the representation of the sun-disk, a serpent at each side; he noted also that its architecture combined Greek and Egyptian elements. When I visited this site thirty-eight years later, I found no more than a few stone blocks, and in 1970 almost

---

(1) For the problems of irrigation and the projects of drying-up parts of the salt lakes of Siwa and the depression of al-Qaṭṭārah, see the book of 'Alī Shāf'ī, **Siwa Oasis and its Relation to the Qaṭṭārah Depression** (Cairo, 1954), in Arabic. The author is the Egyptian pioneer in desert irrigation and served as Inspector General of Desert Irrigation for several years. In this book we find discussions of all the problems and possibilities in Siwa Oasis and details of his two pilot projects at Khamīsah and al-Naqb.

(2) Steindorff, **Amonsoase...**, Fig. 78 p. 104, his description of the ruins of this temple is on page 125.

nothing remained; all that we see now is a heap of debris and the signs of illicit digging are everywhere, especially in the ancient houses which surrounded the temple.

At the other neighbouring site stood the remains of a brick building, probably a fortress or a large mansion. The ancient cemetery is not far distant. This site is mentioned in the Siwan Manuscript, where we read one of the legendary stories about it. Qurayshat, according to the Manuscript, was the abode of a king called al-Ghashshām whose realm extended from this place to Ḥaṭīyat Arsanīn.(1) The land of Arsanīn (location unknown) had a yellow soil containing many stones, which when broken revealed a material resembling gold inside. The Manuscript also mentions a hill in the middle of which stood a statue of a man which could be reached from neither the top nor the bottom of the hill. In this hill, there was a small spring, whose waters fell on the ground over the gold, but no one could see the statue or locate the spring unless he drank from the water of another special spring at Ḥaṭīyat Arsanīn; if he failed to drink from it, he saw nothing at all. The king's place of recreation was at al-'Awwāf; his gardens were al-Zaytūn, Abū Shurūf, al-Naqb, al-Ma'āṣir and Tamīrah.

I now leave the statue in the middle of the hill, the spring and the gold inside the stones to those who care to search for them, and will now describe the ruins which still exist at some of the places mentioned as the gardens of that legendary king.

Abū Shurūf : After visiting the ruins at Qurayshat, the next site is the small hamlet of Abū Shurūf where a stone temple still stands, hidden in the midst of the poor brick houses of the inhabitants. Facing north, it has several chambers in good preservation; to the right of the entrance, (Plan, Fig. 32) there is a small corridor, in which we find a recess in the wall; the corridor leads to a staircase which reaches to the roof. Facing the narrow entrance there is a niche 1.20 cms above the floor measuring 70 by 50 cms; here was placed a statue of the god worshipped in the temple. All the walls are coated with a layer of plaster, but no inscriptions of paintings are preserved; we cannot even say if they ever existed. Most of the stone blocks of the arched ceiling are **in situ.** The entrances to the four rooms are 1.6 metres high and decorated in the Egyptian cavetto style. Like all the monuments to the west of Siwa, this one can be dated in the period between the 1st century B.C. and the first half of the 3rd century A.D.

---

(1) Qurayshat is known to the Siwans as a good place to find antiquities ; since the last century it has been a favourite ground for illicit diggers ; to this day they dig in the ruins of the temple, the houses of the ancient village and the cemetery.

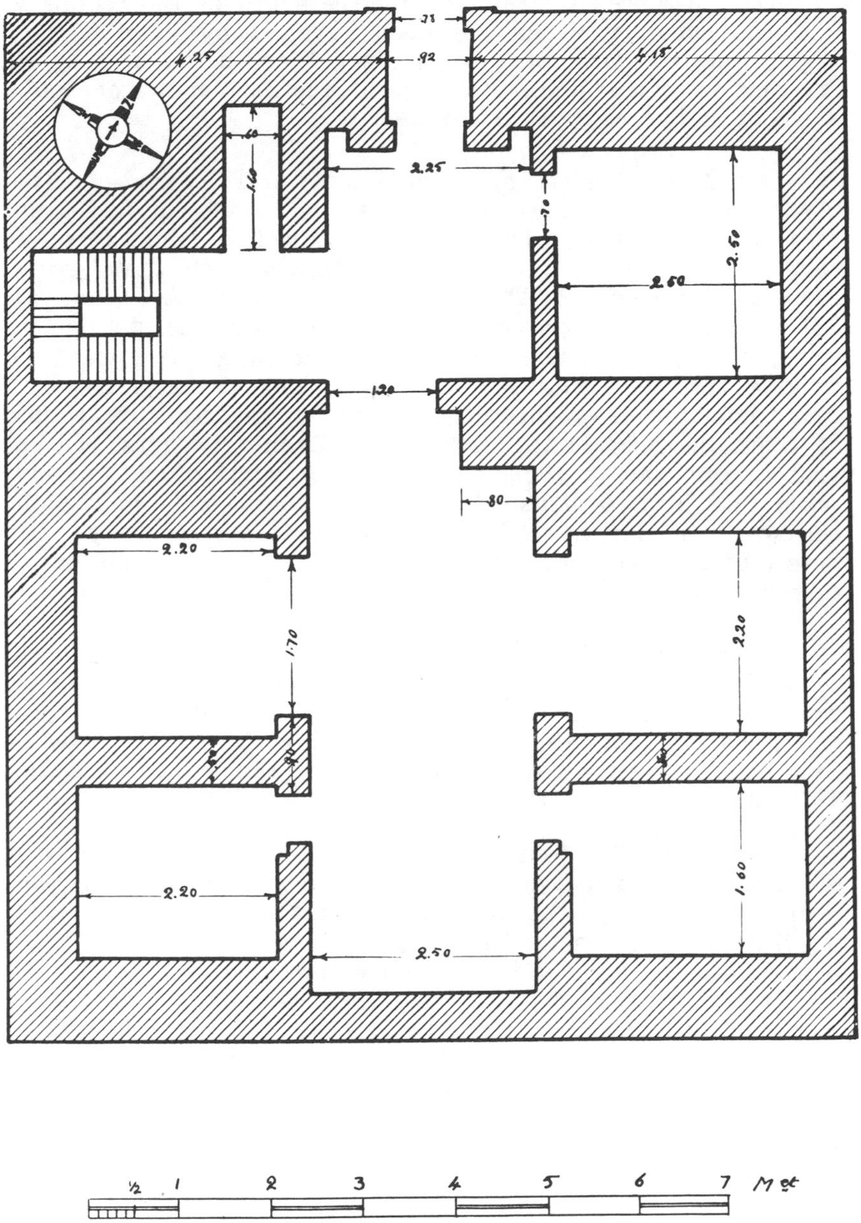

Fig. 32. The stone temple of Abū Shurūf.

At a distance of about 100 metres south of the temple we find the cemetery which has been ravaged by illicit diggers. Eighty metres south of the cemetery there is an ancient site in which we can still see the ruins of another small stone building, almost buried beneath the debris.

The Tomb-Chapels of Abul-ʿAwwāf : The site of Abul-ʿAwwāf is an ancient cemetery whose tombs are cut in the surface of a stone ridge; but some of the rich inhabitants of ancient times had built stone tomb-chapels over their graves. Four of these chapels still stand in a ruinous condition (Fig. 33). They date, apparently, from the Ptolemaic period, and were built by rich landowners who owned the gardens and fields irrigated by the spring of al-Zaytūn. None of the walls of the four tomb-chapels are inscribed, but a few graffiti appear, some of them in Cufic script, written by Arab travellers. On my visit to this site in 1969, I noticed that some of the standing walls had been demolished in recent years and their stones removed. I also noticed that the illicit diggers were active here. Figure 34 shows the plan of the largest one of the four chapels.

When Steindorff visited Siwa in 1900, he excavated in this cemetery for a few days and found in the tombs a number of small objects and painted sarcophagae. He dated the objects as being from about the time of the birth of Christ, but I believe they can be dated to the second half of the Ptolemaic period. This site deserves to be excavated.

Al-Zaytūn: The fourth important site is that of al-Zaytūn, the last inhabited **ḥaṭīyah** on the eastern side of the depression. Here are the famous gardens, the richest in all Siwa, given by the Siwans in the last century as a present to the head of the Sanūsī order; they continued as the personal property of the family until the end of the First World War. This rich **ḥaṭīyah** was operated by officials of the Ministry of Agriculture until some years after the end of the Second World War, and then sold to one of the most energetic and intelligent Siwans, ʿAlī Ḥaydah, who made plenty of money during the occupation of Siwa by the Allied troops, and later on by the Italian troops during the war years. ʿAlī Ḥaydah began to dig drains and canals in the gardens but the land-reform law of 1952 forced him to keep only the land alloted to him under that law. When the Sanūsī family operated this rich **ḥaṭīyah,** they engaged for its cultivation a number of negro families who had formerly been their slaves, but who were then working with them as labourers, receiving their share of the crops. In the midst of the village built for the workers by the Sanūsī family stands a small ancient stone temple. The village houses are deserted now, but in 1940 they were still occupied by about sixty persons.

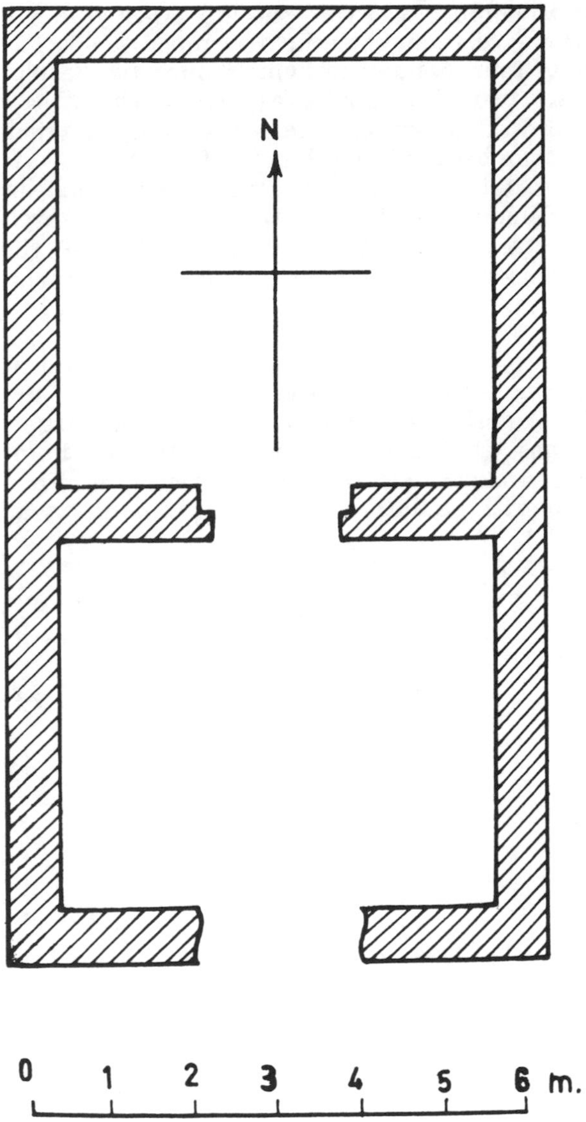

Fig. 33. One of the four tomb chapels at Abul'Awwāf.

The stone temple of al-Zaytūn is located about two kilometres southeast of the spring (Fig. 35). Most of its chambers are still buried under the houses of the deserted recent village; the accessible part consists of only two chambers; the entrance to the second is decorated in the Egyptian cavetto style, but the winged sun-disk is unfinished. Many decorated stones re-used in the construction of the walls, were taken either from this temple or from another monument in the district.

The Italians used to bomb Siwa from the air. Al-Zaytūn village was the target of one of their raids in November, 1940. The aircraft dropped twenty-four bombs, of which only two exploded; fortunately, these two fell far away from the village houses. Whenever an aircraft appeared, the few families hurried, terrified, to the two chambers of the temple for refuge. At least six of the bombs fell on houses; while they failed to explode, their weight demolished the straw roofs of the dwellings. Two bombs destroyed the house built on top of the temple, but the stone blocks of the temple ceiling were unharmed.

Of several cemeteries in this district, a relatively insignificant one lies about 200 metres west of the temple. About 400 metres northwest of the spring there is another much larger, with many sizable tombs, sometimes consisting of two chambers; this cemetery was ransacked by illicit diggers. Another cemetery with tomb-chapels similar to those at Abul-ʿAwwāf

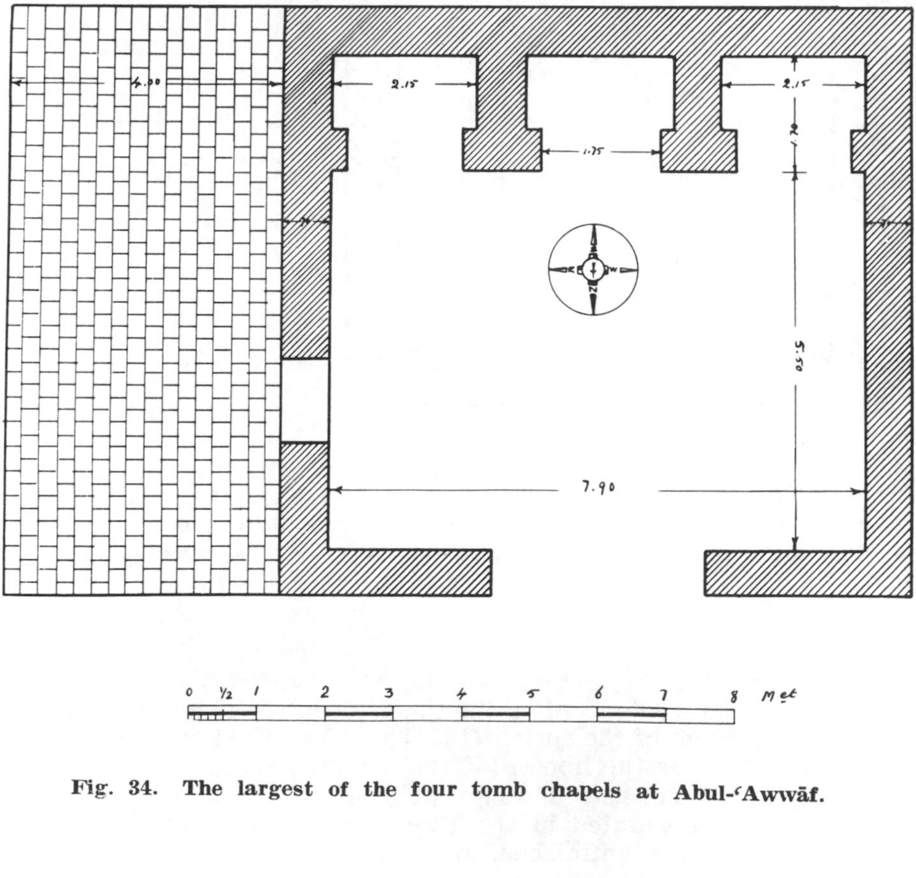

Fig. 34. The largest of the four tomb chapels at Abul-ʿAwwāf.

lies two kilometres south of the spring. The ruins of two of these chapels still exist; they were in good condition in 1819, when Cailliaud saw them. Of larger dimensions than those of Abul-'Awwāf, one had six small chambers; the entrances of the chapels were decorated as shown in the drawing made by Letorzec, Cailliaud's companion; the drawings were later published by Jomard. There are two other sites in this district; one is the ruin of a stone building, two kilometres west of 'Ayn Zuhrah; the inhabitants call it Qaṣr Fūnas. The other — the ruins of a stone building called "Belief" — stands to the north of the small spring of 'Ayn Ṣāfī.

Qāret Umm al-Ṣughayyar: This is a small oasis at the edge of Qaṭṭārah Depression, 130 kilometres from Siwa. Its water is brackish and its inhabitants live in extreme proverty; their crops are poor and of inferior quality. The census of 1966 gives the number of its population as 142. This disproves the old story that as a result of a curse they could never increase to more than 120 persons. The inhabitants have believed that whenever a child is born, one of the older people must die. More than once in recent history, when a child was born at the same time that some person fell ill, one of the relatives hurriedly left the oasis, to save the life of the stricken relation. The inhabitants speak the Siwan language and keep the same customs. Despite their extreme poverty, they refused to leave their homes when the government offered one day, out of pity, to give them the rich district of al-Zaytūn in exchange for their oasis (Fig. 36).

On the map of Ptolemy the geographer, this place was called "Camp of Alexander", probably because Alexander the Great visited it on his return journey from Siwa to Memphis. There are a few small rock tombs cut in a ridge near the spring, but all are uninscribed; I could find no remains of ancient stone buildings there.

Uninhabited Oases between Siwa and Baḥrīyah

This chapter will be incomplete if I do not mention or at least refer to a number of ancient sites which exist in the small oases of al-'Areg, Nuwamīsah, and al-Baḥrayn, on the route between Siwa and Baḥrīyah. Like the nearby oasis of Sitra, all these three oases are uninhabited now, although their springs continue to flow and make useful watering stations for the caravans, but the low parts of their small depressions have become salt marshes. Wild palm trees produce dates of very inferior quality, for nobody takes care of them. No Bedouin in this century takes the trouble to gather the crop. Moreover, the mosquitoes which breed in these depressions turn any overnight stay into a torture-session for humans and animals. Those who visit the place do their best to leave long before sunset; if they have to spend

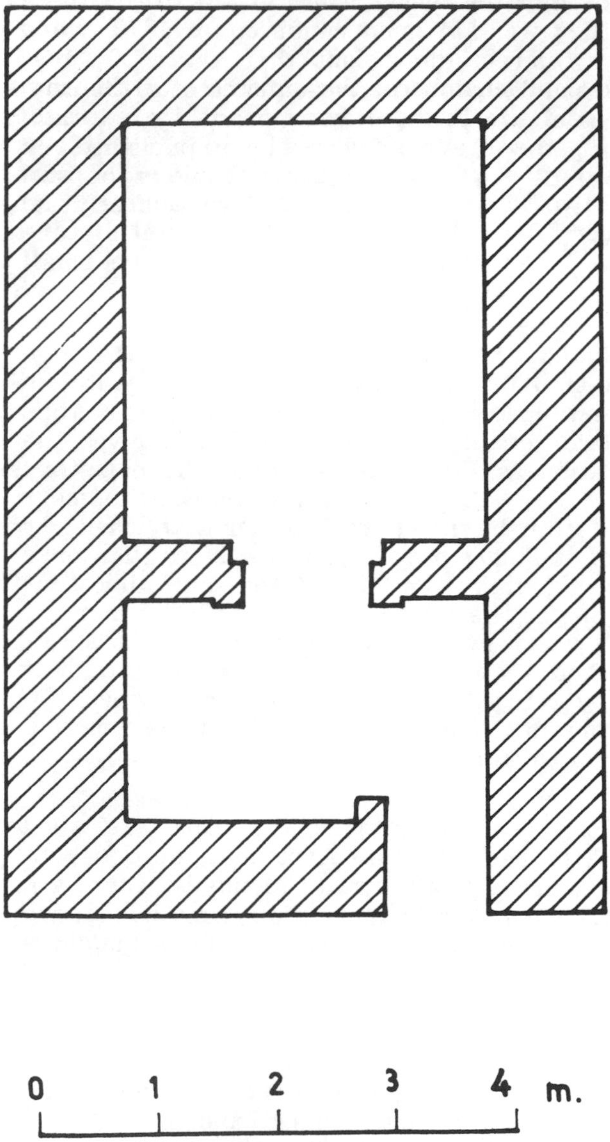

Fig. 35. The two accessible chambers of the stone temple of al-Zaytūn.

the night there, they climb the escarpment and camp in the desert as far as possible from the reach of the mosquitoes.

There are tombs cut in the rock of the hills at all three sites, proof that these small oases were once inhabited for a long time. In my opinion, this keen interest in the desert took place between the 1st century B.C. and the 2nd century A.D., when many projects were started in all the oases of the Western Desert.

Al-Baḥrayn and Nuwamīsah: The rock tombs of al-Baḥrayn and Nuwamīsah are small and have no decorations. A great number of them were opened by illicit diggers, who robbed whatever was there.(1) However, we cannot expect the dwellers of such places to put any valuables in the tombs of their dead. But al-'Areg is different.

Fig. 36. Qāret Umm al-Ṣughayyar in 1820 (After Von Minutoli, Atlas, Pl. XI, 6).

(1) De Cosson visited al-Baḥrayn and Nuwamisah and published his notes in **J.E.A.** (1937), pp. 226 - 9. He published in the same year the notes and some drawings made by J. Bramley in 1896. The paper is entitled: «Notes on the Bahrein, Nuwamiseh and El 'Areg Oases in the Libyan Desert.» In 1970, a well was drilled at al-Baḥrayn in the search for oil. The drillers struck a strata which produced very good and abundant water.

Al-'Areg Oasis : Nearest of these oases to Siwa is al-'Areg, fifty-five kilometres from Ḥaṭīyat al-Zaytūn. There are two flowing springs, palm and other trees grow in many places, but nobody lives there. Near one of the springs are a number of tombs cut in the rock of the two sides of a picturesque valley; the total number of opened sepulchres was forty-two when I visited this place in August 1938, but there were many more still covered with sand.(1) (Fig. 37)

Fig. 37. A view of one of the two groups of rock tombs at al-'Areg Oasis.

---

(1) The tombs of al-'Areg Oasis were visited by Cailliaud in 1819 but he did not refer to any paintings or decorations. Pacho passed by this place in 1826 but does not refer to the tombs. The first traveller who mentioned the antiquities of this oasis and described them, was Rohlfs in 1874 (**Drei Monate...** p. 195); Jennings-Bramley visited al-'Areg in 1896; his notes and sketches were published by De Cosson, 41 years later. It was visited also by Steindorff in 1900 when he was on his way from Siwa to Baḥrīyah; he was aware of Rohlfs' publication, and we are indebted to him for the first photographs of these tombs and a brief description of the representations in two of them (Steindorff, **Amonsoase...**, pp. 135 - 6). The results of my visit, and a description of the accessible tombs, was published in my paper, «The tombs of El-'Areg Oasis in the Libyan Desert,» in **Annales du Service**, vol. 39 (1939) pp. 609 - 19.

Fig. 38. Some of the decorations inside the tomb.

Most of the tombs are undecorated, but some of the larger ones display painted scenes of such Egyptian deities as Osiris, Isis, Anubis, Nut (Fig. 38), and others. Many of the entrances are decorated in the Egyptian style with cornices of serpent heads.

Rohlfs mentioned that he saw, near the tombs, the foundations of a temple with columns, the floor of which was paved with slabs of marble. This temple must have been covered with sand after his visit because it was not seen by Steindorff, and I could find no indication which might help to locate its exact position. However, at the end of the valley, a large area is now filled with drift sand which has also covered the entrances to seven tombs; in all probability, the temple lies underneath this area (Fig. 39).

In Christian times, hermits lived in some of these tombs, and left in them souvenirs of their stay. In one of the tombs of the southern group are three scenes painted by someone who lived in it; these have no apparent connection with religion

Fig. 39. A view at al-ʿAreg Oasis where a temple could be located.

Fig. 40. A drawing in red color of a palm tree in one of the tombs of al-ʿAreg.

either Christian or Egyptian. One represents a palm tree, the second shows a fierce animal attacking a man, the third consists of a short text which might be Libyan (Fig. 40).

The tombs of al-'Areg are well known to the Bedouin, who are treasure hunters by profession. Some of them have specialized in bringing lovers of desert trips to this uninhabited oasis to spend a few days opening the tombs and carrying away their finds. In 1965 one such enthusiast brought back with him from al-'Areg a mummy in perfect condition and succeeded in hiding it in his car until he could carry it into his apartment in Alexandria. It happened, to his misfortune, that his maid-servant was not at home when he arrived. He left in a hurry to visit one of the antiquity dealers, and while he was away the maid-servant entered the apartment. On seeing the feet of the mummy projecting from the blanket in which it was wrapped, she was horror-stricken, thinking it was the body of a murdered person. In her fright, she rushed downstairs and told her story to others. The police arrived and the enquiry disclosed that there was still another mummy, the share of a friend who accompanied the first to al-'Areg. The two mummies and the other objects found during their illicit digging are now in the Alexandria museum. In spite of such diggings, the tombs of this uninhabited oasis are worth excavating because the site is still full of undiscovered tombs which contain undisturbed graves.

We now leave al-'Areg and the scattered ancient sites in the depression, and go back to the town of Siwa to visit the Temple of the Oracle, the most important monument in this oasis and the other temple of Amun.

6

The Temples of Amun at Siwa

There are two temples of the god Amun at Siwa, both at Aghūrmī, four kilometres from the center of the town of Siwa. The first is built over the large rock which stands in the midst of the crumbling walls of the houses of the old village, which was completely deserted less than forty-five years ago after exceptionally heavy rainfalls. This is the famous temple of the Oracle

The other temple, also built for the worship of the god Amun, stands in the midst of the palm groves, not far from the first. It is now in ruins, its stones have been taken away, and only one wall stands in its place surrounded by many stone blocks.

The Temple of the Oracle

Before beginning to describe the remains of this temple, I give as an introduction some details of Alexander's journey to Siwa in the 4th century B.C. and his visit to consult its oracle. This was undoubtedly the most important episode in the history of the oasis. It was a subject for comment in many books by classical authors; it is still discussed with enthusiasm in recent works on ancient history. The visit of Alexander has immortalized the name of this small oasis among the sands of the Libyan Desert, and made its name well known to everyone interested in history or archeology and to all students of mysticism and the history of oracles (Fig. 41).

I have already discussed certain aspects of Alexander's childhood and the early years of his youth in the chapter on the history of Siwa (see above, p. 84) ; I now continue the story and discuss his visit to the seat of the Oracle of Jupiter-Amun in Libya, as it was called in ancient times.

Fig. 41. Aghūrmī in 1820 (After Von Minutoli, Atlas, Pl. XI).

Alexander on his Way to Siwa

The journey of Alexander from Paraetonium to the Oasis of Amun began in winter, between the end of January and the middle of February in 331 B.C. He was accompanied by a large party of friends and a number of his soldiers. Among his companions was Callisthenes, the court historian, who left us an excellent description of this journey which has survived through later writers. They took the famous caravan route called on the maps, nowadays, Masrab al-Isṭabl. The Bedouin know it as Darb al-Maḥaṣḥaṣ or sometimes call it Sikkit al-Sulṭān. It is about 300 kilometres in length and requires seven to eight days' travel by camel.(1)

Plutarch wrote that the divine assistance which Alexander experienced in this march received more credit than the oracles delivered at the temple, although this extraordinary assistance in some measure confirmed the oracles.

According to Callisthenes, after a few days' march, the supply of water carried in skins on camels' backs gave out and the whole caravan was terrified. But divine protection intervened and a sudden fall of rain enabled them to refill their waterskins. On a later day, a southern sandstorm blew violently, and the guides announced that they had lost the track, but suddenly two crows were sighted and Alexander gave orders to follow their flight. According to the same author, when they marched briskly on, the crows flew with equal alacrity; when they lagged behind or halted the crows also slowed down. What is still more strange, he says, at night when the party took the wrong route, these birds called them by their croaking and put them right again.

Whether these two incidents really occurred as they are told or were subject to exaggeration by the ancient historian, they suggest the belief of his followers and contemporaries that supernatural powers were protecting Alexander and miracles were apt to happen at any moment to save his life.

After an exhausting and dangerous march in the desert, they reached the oasis and were astonished at the pleasant shade provided by the groves of palms and olive trees and the abundant running water of the springs.

---

(1) For the texts of classical authors who mentioned the routes leading to this oasis, see Jean Leclant, «Témoignages des sources classiques sur les pistes menant à l'oasis d'Ammon,» **Bulletin de l'Institut Francais d'Arch. Orien., T. XLIX** (Cairo, 1950), pp. 193 - 253.

Alexander in Siwa

It seems that Alexander did not send messengers to announce his visit. We can imagine the excitement of the priests and the inhabitants when they learnt that the caravan was that of none less than the King of Egypt himself, the renowned conqueror, the greatest and most famous man of his time. Callisthenes describes the oasis and refers to two temples. One among the groves of palm trees was the Temple of Umm 'Ubaydah whose ruins still exist; the other, the seat of the oracle, was built on a rock which he called the "acropolis", the "Temple of Aghūrmī"; as it is called now.

Alexander was eager to visit the Oracle as quickly as possible and proceeded to its temple. On his approach some priests were sent to receive the king and his followers outside the gate, in all probability at the foot of the rock. When Alexander reached the temple, the high-priest of Amun of Siwa greeted him (most probably in Greek), "Son of Zeus-Amun, the master of all countries, unconquered until he is united with the gods." Thus he might address any living king of Egypt, since every Pharaoh, including Alexander after his conquest of Egypt, had among his titles that of "Son of Re" the sun-god and other appellations of distinction descriptive of his divine origin and supernatural powers.(1)

Alexander and a small number of his followers stood in the temple court where the procession of the god took place. The image of Amun was in the shape of an **omphalos** (umbilicus) decorated with emerald stones; it was placed in a boat and carried on the shoulders of the priests. Female musicians, young and old, dressed in white garments were singing and dancing, and the whole procession marched round and round the temple courtyard in the presence of Alexander and his followers till the high priest announced that the heart of the god was satisfied.

The Macedonian followers were permitted to ask any questions of the oracle. One inquired whether they might give their king divine honours; the answer was that this would please Amun.

---

(1) Plutarch relates a rather interesting and curious story about this greeting. He says : «Some say, Ammon's prophet being desirous to address him in an obliging manner in Greek, intended to say, «O Paidion», which signifies «My Son». But in his barbarous pronunciation, he made the word end with an «s» instead of an «n» and so said: «O Pai Dios», which signifies «O Son of Jupiter». Alexander, they add, «was delighted with the mistake and from that error was circulated a report that the god Jupiter himself had called him his son». These statements can be considered as later additions and literary embellishments.

In the Sanctuary

Reluctant to ask questions in the presence of the others, Alexander requested to be alone with the god. He was conducted to the **cella** (sanctuary) of the temple where his sacred boat was placed. After some time, he returned to his friends who asked him what had happened and what the Oracle had told him; he said only that he heard what was according to his wish. He kept secret his audience with the Oracle; and when he wrote to his mother Olympias afterward he told her that he received certain private answers from the Oracle, which he would communicate to her only, on his return to Macedonia. Eventually, Alexander pushed forward his conquests in Asia, but he did not live to see his mother. He died eight years later in Babylon in the year 323 B.C. at the age of thirty-three, and took his secret with him to the grave.

Although these events were recorded in most of his biographies, we read in many books written about Alexander in ancient or modern times, a few reports of his questions and the answers he received.

Plutarch, for example, mentions that when Alexander enquired "whether any of the assassins of his father had escaped him, the priest declared he would not express himself in that manner, for his father was not a mortal. Then he asked whether all the murderers of Philip were punished, and whether it was given the proponent to be the conqueror of the world. Jupiter-Amun answered that he granted him that high distinction and that the death of Philip was sufficiently avenged." Later writers seized upon these statements and some historians still believe them, even in modern times, as a historical fact.

Alexander sacrificed to Amun and gave the priests many presents. His stay in the oasis was apparently for a few days only. For his return journey he took another desert route via Qāret Umm al-Ṣughayyar and al-Mughrah in Qaṭṭārah depression, thence directly to Memphis without going to the coast. The trip can be made in a fortnight.

Alexander was, from his early youth, an ardent believer in supernatural powers and in oracles.(1) His mother inspired him to believe that he was not like other men but was of divine origin, counting among his divine ancestors Perseus, Hercules and Achilles. Some modern biographers state that his pretence or claim to divinity was merely a matter of policy, because a man of Alexander's intelligence could not really believe it himself. But in my opinion it is unfair to judge, on the basis of modern

---

(1) Arrian, **Exped. Alex.** 14 : 23,6 ; Pausanias, 9; 16,1 - related several stories on this subject. A good summary is given in Parthey, **Das Orakel**, pp. 167 - 9.

customs, religion and mentality, occurrences of the past among people of traditions and beliefs quite different from our own. We can say with confidence that Alexander went to Siwa like any other visitor before him, believing in its oracle and in the truth of every word he heard from its priests, including his divine origin and his right to be worshipped by others

Nobody knows what happened in the sanctuary of Amun, what questions were asked or answers given, but it is an established fact that from that day, Alexander was a great believer in Amun, and was proud to consider himself his son.(1) In the remaining eight years of his life as he pursued his conquests in Asia, he frequently sent messengers bearing gifts to the priests of Siwa and was always keen to know the oracle's answers to the questions which disturbed his mind.

When his dearest and most devoted friend, Hephaeston, died, Alexander's grief was beyond all bounds of sanity; he made arrangements to build for him a prodigious sepulchral monument in Babylon and two cenotaphs in Alexandria in Egypt. In those days of distress, he sent messengers to Siwa to inquire of the oracle if Hephaeston could be raised to the rank of god or demi-god, but the answer was that his friend was permitted only to receive the worship of the cult of a hero according to the Greek religion.(2) Alexander had to concede.

---

(1) The divine origin of some humans, or the union between gods and some females, was accepted in more than one ancient civilization. From ancient Egyptian history, we know of several cases in which the god Amun himself was the physical father of certain monarchs after having intercourse with the queens. Queen Hatshpsut and Amenhotep III, both in the 18th Dynasty, are examples.

According to popular belief at the time, Cyrus, the founder of the Persian Empire and its first great conqueror was the son of a similar union. Zoroaster, the founder of the Persian religion, was miraculously conceived in the same manner. Perseus, whom Alexander reckoned as one of his ancestors, was the son of Zeus by a mortal princess named Danae, and Hercules, also one of his forefathers, was the son of Zeus by Alkemene, grand-daughter of Perseus. Achilles, another ancestor and whom he admired most was the grandson of the god Nereus. The philosopher Plato, the teacher of Aristotle, Alexander's tutor, was believed to have been born of the union of his virgin mother with a god. Even in the days after Alexander, Julius Caesar was stated by Askelepiades to have been the son of Apollo, and Apollonius of Tyana was said to have been born of the union of his mother with a god. Alexander, however, had the definite statement of his mother Olympias that Amun actually came to her bed in the form of a serpent. Since boyhood, he must have repeatedly heard word of his mysterious origin and that his father, Philip, having consulted the oracle of Delphi on the subject, had been told to pay particular respect to Amun.

(2) Arrian, **Exped. Alex.** 7 : 14.

Fig. 42. The entrance to the fortress — village of Aghūrmī.

As an illustration of his great devotion to Amun of Siwa, Alexander a short time before his death, gave orders to Aridaeus, one of his intimate friends, to bury him near his father Amun in the oasis. A great funeral procession set out from Babylon with the body of Alexander on a splendid funeral car. It was met in Palestine by Ptolemy, his satrap in Egypt, with a large escort on the way to Egypt for burial in the Temple of the Oracle as he had wished. But when the cortege reached Memphis, Ptolemy insisted that Alexander be buried in Alexandria, the city which he founded. He conciliated the priests of Amun with gifts and sent a stela to be erected in the temple there.(1)

Such was the love and devotion of Alexander to his father Amun and his oasis, that he thought not of Macedonia, Babylon or Alexandria as the eternal resting place of his body, but preferred to be interred in Siwa, that small oasis in the Western Desert of Egypt.

The Temple

When the visitor approaches Aghūrmī and views the remains of the fallen houses built over the rock, he cannot help recalling Alexander and his visit to this place (Fig. 42).

We ascend a small path among the falling rocks until we reach the entrance to the small fortified town which was inhabited until the first quarter of this century. Its gate, made of planks of palm tree trunks, still stands in place; on both sides are the mud seats on which the heads of the families were accustomed to sit during the day and talk of their problems in this cool, shady place. The mosque is built over the town gate, but it is disused now because a part of its floor has fallen down.(2) At the end of the winding passage we find to our right a small entrance leading to the top of the minaret where we can enjoy a beautiful view of this part of the oasis. The ruins of the temple of Umm 'Ubaydah are to be seen to the east, and in the distance the town of Siwa clearly appears with the old ruined fortress, the houses of the more recent town, and the minarets of the mosques. Jabal al-Mawtā, is visible in the distance; wherever we turn our eyes, we see the thick groves of trees, the large salt lakes glittering in the sunshine, the many hills and the surrounding desert sands.

---

(1) This stela of Ptolemy was seen by Pausanias who visited Siwa in the second half of the 2nd century A.D.

(2) The gate and the mosque were repaired by the Antiquities Department in January 1971, when I was excavating this temple.

In front of us we observe a large, open place. The rock is higher on the north side, but in front of us the ground is uneven and there are breaks in the rock; for this has always been a favourite site for treasure hunters who believe the local legends of great hoards of gold and precious stones hidden near the temple. To the left of the short winding passage, a path leads to the entrance of a mosque built of ancient stone blocks; in front of it is the ancient well.

In order to visit the Temple of the Oracle we must climb to the northwestern corner. Until recently, its facade was hidden by the walls of the village houses; the temple itself was inhabited by several families and many walls were built inside the temple and over it. In April 1970, during a fortnight's work at Siwa, most of these walls were pulled down and their debris removed from the place; the work was resumed for one month in January 1971.

It is important here to mention that the rock of Aghūrmī is cracking; from time to time parts of it, sometimes of large size, slide down. Fissures are seen on all sides; this continuous deterioration must have begun many years ago. The top surface of the rock was much larger in ancient times than it is now; a number of the huge separated blocks are scattered all round (Fig. 44).

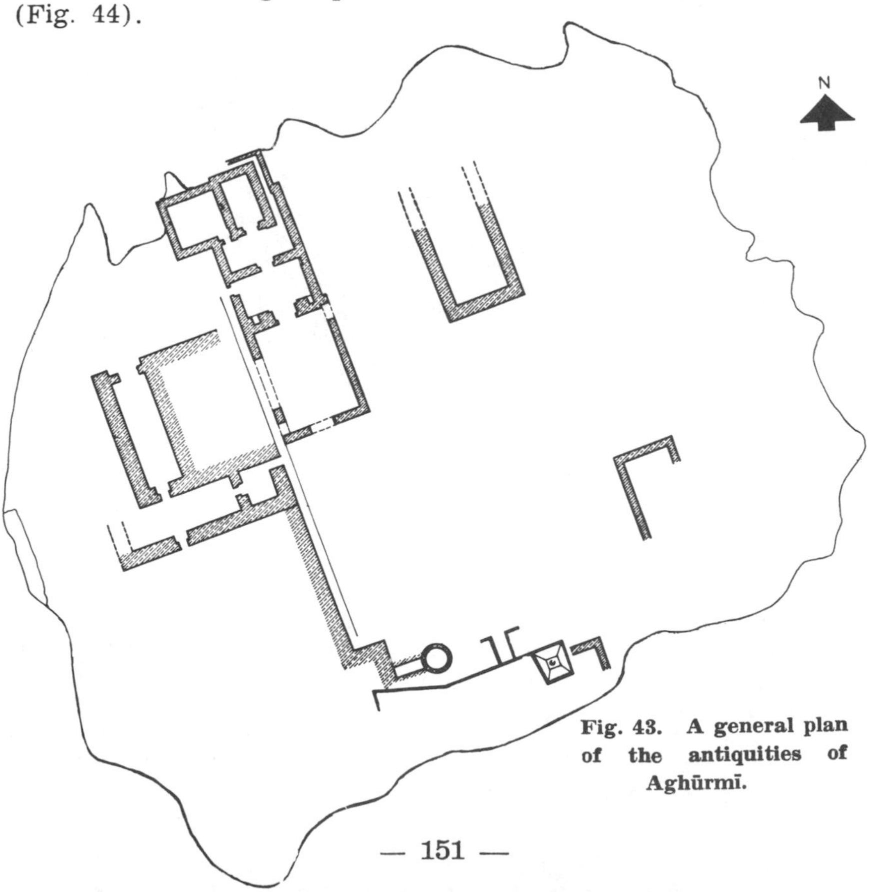

Fig. 43. A general plan of the antiquities of Aghūrmī.

Fig. 44. A view of the back wall of the Temple of the Oracle at the edge of the rock.

Clitarchus[1] flourished about 300 B.C. He was the author of the most famous book about Alexander, and from this we quote the following passage : "The inhabitants of the Oasis of Amun live in villages; in the middle of the oasis stands the Akropolis which is fortified with three enclosures. The first enclosure contains the palace of the ancient rulers, in the second one are the harem houses of the women, children and the other relatives as well as the guards, and lastly the chapel of the god and the sacred spring in which the offerings of the god are purified. The third one is the soldiers' barracks and the houses of the private guards of the ruler. A short distance from the Akropolis, a second temple of Amun stands in the shade of many large trees. Nearby, is a spring called 'Spring of the Sun' because of its nature."

The rear wall of the temple is now at the edge of the cracking rock and will fall down if any new slides occur ; I hope that

(1) Clitarchus (Kleitarchos in Greek), a Greek historian who lived in Alexandria, was the author of a great work in at least twelve books about Alexander the Great. In spite of all his defects, and because of his inclination to believe in the marvellous, his narrative was so interesting that he became the most popular of all the writers on Alexander. The Romans were very fond of his book, which was indeed the main authority for the narratives of Diodorus and Curtius Rufus about Alexander. His books have perished, and only parts are preserved in the works of the later writers.

the Egyptian Antiquities Department will consolidate it before this takes place (Fig. 45). If we examine the plan (Fig. 43), we can say that the second enclosure, in which was "the chapel of the god and the sacred spring", occupied the western part of the acropolis, while the other two must be at the eastern side; among the modern mud walls we can see a few stone walls. The "spring" is, in fact, a well.

As for the temple of Umm 'Ubaydah, the second temple of Amun, its ruins still exist. The Spring of the Sun, or 'Ayn al-Gūbah, is in the vicinity as I have already mentioned in the previous chapter.

Description of the Temple

The Temple of the Oracle is comparatively well-preserved, but it needs immediate consolidation in some places. The court in which the processions of the god took place stretches in front of the temple proper but only the foundations of its northern and eastern walls exist. According to the inscriptions in the sanctuary, the present building goes back to the reign of King Amasis of the 26th Dynasty, but some alterations and additions were made in later times (Fig. 46).

Opening to the south, the temple consists of two halls, after which we find the sanctuary whose entrance is in the main axis. As we see in the plan, there is a narrow corridor at the right, i.e. at the east side of the sanctuary, and continues behind the back wall. Another large chamber is on the west side (Fig. 47).

The open court preceding the temple is at a short distance from the edge of the sinking rock inside the acropolis. Consequently, we have to suppose either that this sinking was filled up in ancient times, or that visitors had to climb a staircase if, as we might expect, the entrance of the court was in the axis of the temple. It is possible also that the entrance to the court may have been on the east side, reached, as nowadays, by climbing the slope.

The original facade of the temple is about eight metres high, of the plain Egyptian type. Its entrance is of the cornice style, 2.22 metres wide, with no inscriptions. Later builders, apparently in the Ptolemaic period, tried to make it look to some extent like a Greek temple; they added a wall in front on which they built a half-column of the fluted Doric type, at each side of the entrance. The lower part of the eastern column has disappeared, but the western column is preserved ; it was finally discovered in April, 1970. The first court is 7.74 metres in length and 4.95 metres in breadth. Its entrance is not exactly in the middle of the wall, the western side being slightly longer.

Fig. 45. The northwest corner of the Temple of the Oracle showing its dangerous condition.

There are two niches in the southern wall, one in each of the two corners; the western niche measures 60 cms. in breadth by 1.8 metres deep. The niche in the eastern side is smaller in dimensions. (See Fig. 48). At floor level in the west wall, there is an entrance to a crypt. The second court is a little higher, and its dimensions are almost identical to the first. According to Ricke,[1] there were two stages in the building; the older part was plain; the later builders added the decorated entrances and modified the plan. But in the light of recent work, it seems more probable that there were three stages in the building rather than two

Fig. 46. The Temple of the Oracle before excavations.

(1) Herbert Ricke, «Die Baureste des Burgtempels von Aghurme,» **Z.A.S.**, 69 : 4 - 13.

There are three entrances in the north wall of the second court; the middle one, larger than the other two, leads to the sanctuary, or **cella** entered by Alexander alone to hear the answers of the Oracle of Amun. The small entrance to the right, only 80 cms. wide, leads to a narrow corridor which might have been used as a crypt for storing the precious utensils of the temple and/or to assist in delivering the oracles. In the left wall, which separates the corridor from the **cella,** there are three niches, 66 cms. higher than the floor, each measuring 52 by 52 cms. by 33 cms. deep; near the ceiling there are two apertures for light. The three niches and the apertures are not mentioned in Ricke's report, nor do they appear in his published plan. Did this corridor which goes around the sanctuary have any part in the answering voices which were heard when visitors consulted the god ? In other words, were the answers uttered by a priest, secreted in that corridor ?

In the temple of Khonsu at Karnak built in the Ramesside period, there is a crypt near the ceiling between two accessible chapels; Maspero suggested that it was built to serve as the hiding place for the priest who pronounced the oracles. Under the floor of the two sanctuaries in the temple of Kom Ombo, there are crypts which served the same purpose.

Description of the Sanctuary

The sanctuary, or **cella,** is the only place in this Temple of the Oracle whose walls are inscribed; it measures 3.3 metres in breadth by 6.1 metres deep. It was roofed over like the other rooms of the temple ; near the top of the east and west walls we find stone projections on which the rafters rested. The walls have been rather badly damaged by seekers after the lengendary treasure, who hammered or drove holes. The Siwans believe that a king called "Khuraybīsh" was the last ruler of Siwa, and that this temple is called "al-Khazīnah", i.e. "the safe", because the king was buried in it, with him were interred all his treasures, including his arms and his sword.(1)

The inscriptions begin at the two sides of the entrance and continue on the side walls. It seems, however, that the back wall was not inscribed. It is true that it is very badly damaged, but no remains of any figures or texts can be detected. On the right-hand side of the entrance was the figure of the king in whose reign the temple was built and decorated. His head and body

(1) This story is still related by the Siwans to their visitors. We read also in the Siwan Manuscript that the palace of King Khuraybīsh stood between the temple of Umm 'Ubaydah and Aghūrmī. He built a high, suspended road which connected his palace with both temples. Whenever he wanted to visit one of them, he used the upper road, while his soldiers walked beneath.

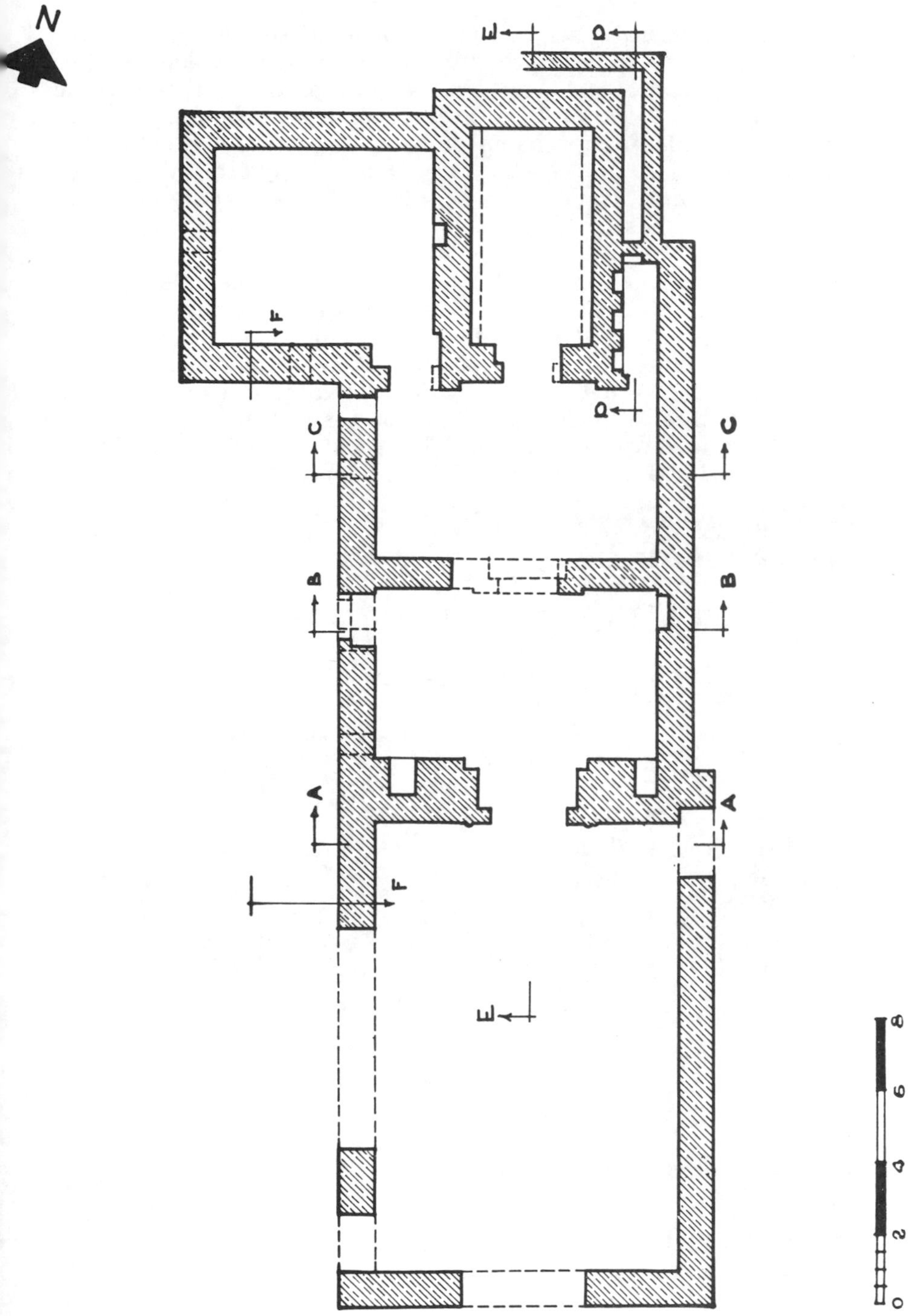

Fig. 47. Plan of the Temple of the Oracle.

have been chiselled out, but the crown of the North (Lower Egypt) remains. He offers rounded vases of wine to eight deities represented on the east wall. The king's name is written inside a cartouche in front of him. Steindorff read this fragmentary cartouche in 1900 as the name of King Akoris who ruled Egypt between 392 - 380 B.C. in the 29th Dynasty; but on his second visit in 1932 he was not sure of his previous reading but still thought it the most probable.[1]

In 1938 when I examined this text I became completely convinced that it was the name of King Amasis of the 26th Dynasty. The eight deities stand in a row facing him ; they are preceded by the god Amun (Fig. 49) and include Amenre', his consort Mut, and a ram-headed god with a two-feathered crown on his head. Here, the text is badly damaged and corrupt, but it very probably refers to Amun who had a special prominence in this oasis, or perhaps to Harsaphis, the god of Heracleopolis. The fourth deity

Fig. 48. The entrance to the second hall of the temple before removing the mud walls.

(1) Steindorf, **Amonsoase...**, p. 9.

Fig. 49. A part of one of the inscribed walls of the sanctuary.

is Khonsu, but the fifth and sixth are impossible to identify because the wall is severely damaged. The seventh deity is the god Mahesa, and his accompanying text reads: "I give life to the Chief of the desert-dwellers, Sutekh-irdes" The last deity is a female who wears the double crown, but her inscription is completely destroyed.

To the left of the entrance of the sanctuary stands the is completely destroyed except for the feather which was stuck in his hair and denotes his Libyan origin. He was apparently a descendant of one of the powerful families of the Mashwish tribes who settled in the oases before moving to the Nile Valley to become the kings of the 22nd Dynasty. The family which settled in Siwa continued to rule it. They were more or less independent, although they recognised the supremacy of the Pharoahs of the land. These families became Egyptianized, and after a short time, they accepted the Egyptian religion, and the Egyptian language became their mother tongue. There was a rich and powerful family in Baḥrīyah whose chiefs flourished greatly in the reigns of Apries and Amasis. They were represented on the walls of the chapels behind King Amasis.(1) But since Siwa lies at a considerable distance further west, apparently its governors enjoyed more independence. We know from Herodotus that they were called "kings".(2)

Here on Siwa's temple walls the governor does not walk behind the king and offer to the same gods as at Baḥrīyah. He is represented on the opposite side of the chamber, of the same position as the king ; like him, he offers to eight deities. From the inscriptions written in front of him and the other inscriptions accompanying the deities, his name was "Sutekh-irdes" ; his title was "Chief of the Desert-dwellers"; his father held the same post and was called "Rerwatneb".

Among the eight deities to whom he offers are : Amenre', Mut, god Dedun-Amun(3) and goddess Tefnut. Behind the goddess Tefnut, part of the wall is uninscribed, because in the original plan of the temple there was at this point a door leading to the adjacent chamber ; this was walled up at a later date. The fifth of these deities is the god Harsaphis(4) with human body and ram's head ; he wears a two-feathered crown. The sixth deity was the goddess Nut; the seventh is the god Thoth represented with the head of an ibis ; the eighth is the consort of Thoth, the goddess "Ḥebenu of the Two Lands", Neḥem'awa (Fig. 49).

There were one or more chambers on the roof of the temple; the staircase which led to them was at the west side, in the corner which fell down when this part of the rock slid off.

Without excavating this site completely, we can never determine whether other parts are still hidden under the debris. Remains of walls southwest of the court are visible, and we can distinguish the outlines of some chambers built in stone,

---

(1) Fakhry, **Baḥria Oasis,** pp. 21, 28 and Pl. XLIV - LII.

(2) See above, p. 79 in this book.

(3) The worship of the god Dedun had a prominent place in Nubia, and is generally called «the honoured one in the western lands.» For the relationship of this god with the desert, see Sethe, **Urkunden** IV, 333; Scharff, **Z.A.S.** 61 : 27, and Fakhry, **Baḥria Oasis,** 1 : 152,

(4) Harsaphis was the chief deity of Ehnasia, the town which had become the center of power of the Libyan family before they were kings of the whole land.

but we cannot say with any certainty whether they are connected with this temple or are the remains of another construction at its side. The same can be said of the stone walls among the remains of the falling houses at the east side of the temple.

The Well

In front of the mosque, the visitor finds a well built of stone blocks. In use throughout the ages, it was mentioned by writers who recorded the visit of Alexander the Great. The mosque was in use until ten years ago, and many of the people who came to perform their prayers fetched from it the water necessary for their ablutions. It is constructed of carefully dressed stone blocks, and the water was drawn from the top of the shaft in the conventional manner, but the well itself could also be reached by descending steps. These are in two flights; at the end of the top flight was a door. The entrance to this passage is now blocked with debris; it will be impossible to reach the steps and study their architecture until the rubble is cleared away.

However, as we look down from the mouth of the shaft we can see that, near the bottom, and above the level of the water, two small entrances are cut in the north and south sides of the masonry (Fig. 50). Perhaps these led to side chambers for storing the vessels used in drawing the water from the well or for some similar purpose ; or possibly they served as entrances to a small staircase which goes round the inner wall of the well as in the case of the nilometre of Idfū. This was suggested by Borchardt to Aubin who studied this well in 1932 and 1933.[1] In the south wall, slightly above the water level, there is probably an aperture, perhaps to admit light into the inner part to which the two entrances led. In any event, we must wait until the staircase is cleaned out before the place can be thoroughly studied.

In 1874, Rohlfs expressed the hope that the Egyptian Government might financially assist an excavator to buy the houses of Aghūrmī from their inhabitants so that they might be demolished and the site excavated. The houses have been deserted since 1926, but neither the Egyptian Government nor any foreign institution has shown any real interest in excavating this very important site. Only in April 1970, almost a century after Rohlfs'

---

(1) Hermann Aubin, «Bericht uber die Untersuchungen von Aghurmi in Januar 1933,» **Z.A.S.** 69: 13 ff; for the construction of the nilometres which resemble this well in construction see L. Borchardt, «Nilmesser und Nilstandmarken,» **Z.A.S.** 61 : 27, Fig. 17; see also Wreszinski, «Der Gott Uh,» **Orient. Litt. Zeit.** (O.L.Z.) 35 : 521 ff.

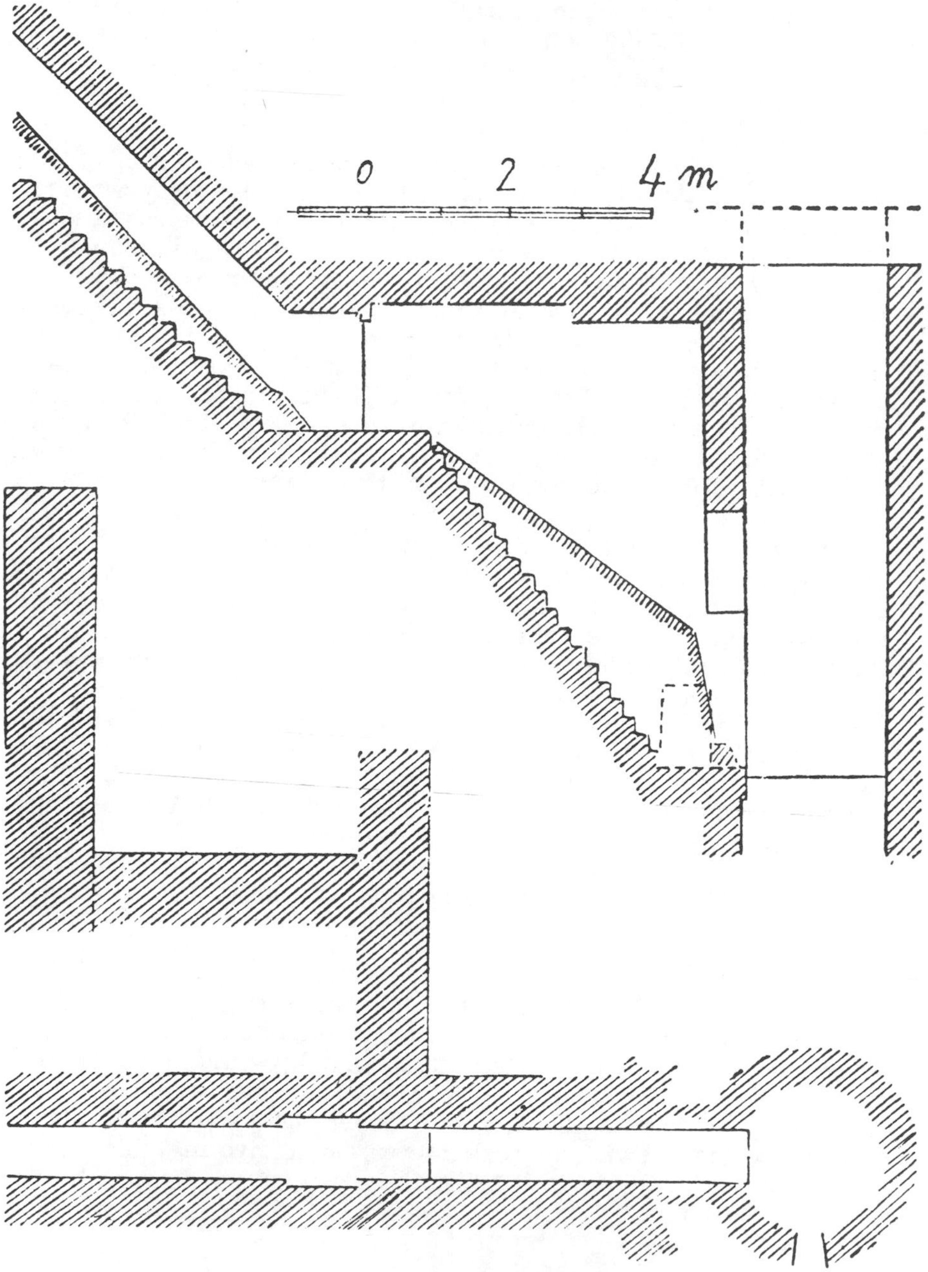

Fig. 50. Plan and section of the ancient well at Aghūrmī (Adapted from Aubin, Z.A.S., 69, p. 15).

visit, I succeeded in persuading the Antiquities Department to begin, at least, to clean out the debris inside the temple so that visitors might enter it. The preliminary work, which was of only a fortnight's duration, brought very pleasant results ; the facade of the temple is visible now, and more recent walls built inside the temple and on top of its walls were pulled down (Fig. 51).

Two of the stones used in the foundations of the recent walls were inscribed with Greek texts. One of these is part of a limestone stela dating from the 2nd century B.C.; the other is a very small fragment of an alabaster stela of a much later date, probably from the 2nd century A.D. This was a very encouraging start[1] (Fig. 52).

On the last day of the excavations, I climbed to the top of the minaret of the mosque of Aghūrmī to take some photographs and have a look at the whole site. As I stood there thinking of future steps in the excavations, I could not help recalling the story of Alexander and his visit. As I looked down upon the court, I could easily imagine the procession with the barque of Amun carried on the shoulders of the priests accompanied by white-robed female musicians. I thought of Alexander and his visit to the **cella**, but all these scenes faded from my mind when I remembered the passages written by Pausanias and his mention of the many stelae he saw in the temple court in the 2nd century A.D. Is it possible that some of them are still there ? I thought also of Clitarchus and his description, and asked myself if some of the other buildings near the temple or at least their foundations could be discovered under the modern walls now standing there. Who can tell ?

The voice of the oracle stopped many centuries ago, and the walls of the temple of Aghūrmī echo no more to the sound of music, or of singers repeating their hymns to the god Amun, but his spell still remains. I felt as if tens of voices were crying out from all the corners of Aghūrmī, declaring that it is time to help these ruins to tell their own story ; and I hope sincerely that this will be realized in the very near future.

---

(1) My assistant 'Abdul-Fattāḥ Maḥmūd, one of the inspectors of the Antiquities Department had the work at Aghūrmī under his supervision ; he helped me also in the work done there during January 1971. The architect, Ḥasan Shiḥātah, made a new plan of the site, and a detailed plan and elevations of the temple. My preliminary report on this work is published in the Festschrift of Herbert Ricke, **Beitrage zur Aegyptischen Bauforschung**... etc. Heft 12 (Wiesbaden, 1971), under the title «Recent Excavations at the Temple of the Oracle at Siwa Oasis,» pp. 17 - 33, and Pls. 10 - 13.

Fig. 51. The facade of the Temple of the Oracle after the excavations of April, 1970.

Fig. 52. A Greek inscription dating from 2nd century B.C. discovered in April, 1970. It was reused in the foundations of one of the modern walls inside the temple.

The Temple of Umm 'Ubaydah

The second temple of Amun is called now Umm 'Ubaydah, which might be a corruption of the name Umm Ma'bad.(1) It is a short distance from the rock of Aghūrmī, and its ruins lie now, as the temple did in the days of Alexander, amidst groves of trees. The site is marked by a large area of whitish ground in which blocks of stones are scattered about ; only one wall stands among these ruins, and near it is a number of huge stone blocks. The wall and blocks are inscribed, and in many places the blue colours are still visible. Here stood a temple of Amun which was built in the 30th Dynasty, and which was mentioned in the story of Alexander's visit to this oasis (Fig. 53).

Until the beginning of the 19th century a great part of the temple was preserved, but in 1811 an earthquake damaged part of it. Visitors between the years 1819 - 1821 (Cailliaud, Drovetti and Von Minutoli) found that some of the blocks from the ceiling had fallen down and that one of the temple walls was leaning. But despite this damage, much still remained, as we see in the drawings published in their books. The surviving wall is a side of an inscribed chamber which stood on the site, like other remains of the temple, until 1897 when one of the Ma'mūrs of Siwa (Maḥmūd 'Azmī) placed gunpowder in the foundations of this chamber and blew it up to obtain stones for the staircase of the police station at Qaṣr Ḥassūnah and for the construction of his own house. What the severe hand of time could not do, was accomplished by an ignorant government official in a few minutes. From the plans, sketches and drawings of Von Minutoli and Cailliaud, and the descriptions published by them and by Rohlfs in 1874 we can say that the original temple faced north, and the temple itself was surrounded by two girdle walls.

The enclosure wall was square in plan; and at the time of the visits, many parts of the temple had already fallen down. But the **pronaos** and the sanctuary existed (Fig. 54); and in front of these there was a pillared hall. Inside the enclosure wall, and in front of the temple was an elevated construction built of alabaster blocks. One of these, either an altar or a pedestal for a statue of the god Amun, was decorated on its four sides with a representation of a large human head with ram's horns, the head of the god Amun in whose honour the temple was built.

From the sketches of Von Minutoli we can get some idea of the arrangement of the scenes on the wall of the sanctuary and the gods represented on it, before the place was demolished

---

(1) It was called in the last century Umm Ma'bad which means «the mother of temple,» or «the place which has a temple». This is its name in the Siwan Manuscript.

Fig. 53. The Temple of Umm ʿUbaydah in 1820 (After Von Minutoli, Atlas, Pl. VII, 2).

Fig. 54. The same ruins from another angle (After Von Minutoli, Atlas, Pl. VII).

by the Ma'mūr. It resembles, to a certain degree, the one which stood opposite in the same chamber and which still stands. The large stone blocks which are still lying near the standing wall are the remains of the ceiling.(1) We are grateful for the sketches of Von Minutoli identifying the builder of this temple. On one of the blocks there are two cartouches, which despite certain inaccuracies in the heiroglyphics, are undoubtedly those of King Nectanebo II, the energetic ruler of the 30th Dynasty and one of the most active builders in the late period of the Egyptian history. He constructed and restored many monuments in the Nile Valley and extended his activities to the oases. He restored and added to the Temple of Kharga, and built this temple at Siwa.

Fig. 55. The remaining wall of the Temple of Umm ʿUbaydah.

(1) The complete text of the description of Cailliaud, and the important parts in the descriptions of Browne, Hornemann, Von Minutoli and Rohlfs are published in Fakhry, **Siwa Oasis: Its History and Antiquities,** pp. 97-100.

The site of the temple of Umm 'Ubaydah was for many years a favourite place of the illicit diggers who found in it a few bronze statuettes and other objects. In spite of its sad story, I must say that if this temple is properly excavated it will repay all the effort and will certainly add to our knowledge of the history of this oasis.

The Inscriptions

The wall still standing has a long text at the top consisting of fifty-one lines and three registers of representations of deities. In 1820, the same wall was in a better state of preservation, and if we compare its photograph now (Fig. 55), with the drawing of Von Minutoli (Fig. 56), we find that above the text there was a decoration which served as an upper frieze. At the top was a repetition of the king's cartouche protected by the vulture goddess Nekhbeyt; under it a number of figures perform some of the ceremonies of the rite of Opening the Mouth. It was in sunken relief, and is the beginning of the text of the same rite.

Under the inscriptions there are three rows of figures, all in high relief. At the top, we see the builder of the temple, the Ruler of Siwa at that time, kneeling in front of the god Amun who sits inside a shrine. Behind the ruler are seven deities. On the middle register nine deities appear; in the middle row we can now distinguish eight, while on the bottom one there are now only three. In 1820 more figures of the deities were preserved. Each deity has his name written at his side. We cannot mention here all details, the identity of every deity and the translation of his text; these already appear in my book "Siwa Oasis". It is enough to mention here that behind Amenre', who sits in his shrine at the top row, stands the goddess Mut; the other deities are either Amenre' or Mut.

The deities in the middle row are (from right to left) Atum, Shu, Tefnut, Seth, Geb, Nut; the name of the last one is destroyed. Those in the bottom register look to the left. The first is a male deity whose name is not preserved, but in all probability this was the god Horus; the second is a female whose name is destroyed; the third is the goddess Nekhbeyt.

Two important points need to be discussed in some detail. The first concerns the builder of this temple ; the second is the significance of the presence of the text of the rite of Opening of the Mouth, on this monument.

The Builder of the Temple

According to the texts on this wall, the builder of the temple seen kneeling in front of the shrine of the god Amenre' was called "Wenamun"; his principal title was "The Great Chief of the Desert". His father's name was Nakht-tit; he held

Fig. 56. A drawing of the scenes which were on the other wall of the temple destroyed in 1895 (After Von Minutoli, Atlas, Pl. VIII, 1820).

the same title and must have preceded his son as ruler of this oasis. His mother was called "Nefer-renpet". Wenamun wears an ostrich feather in his hair which shows that he was a descendant of a Libyan family, perhaps the same family which continued to rule the oasis for several centuries. The temple was built in the reign of Nektanebo II.

The Text of the Rite of Opening the Mouth

It is very rare to find this text written on temple walls; we are more likely to find it on papyri, on coffins or sometimes on the walls of tombs, since it is connected with the burial ceremonies.(1) However, this text does appear on temple or chapel walls which served as funerary monuments — as, for example, the Chapel of Amenirdes at Madinat Habu.(2) Consequently, I believe that Wenamun was buried not far from this temple.

But we cannot leave the Temple of Umm 'Ubaydah without saying a few words about the inscriptions on the other walls which were demolished in 1897. Our main source is in the drawings of Von Minutoli. In Pl. VIII of his Atlas we find a drawing of the scenes on the other wall. As shown in Fig. 56, these were arranged in the same way and the texts of the rite of Opening the Mouth were continued on the upper frieze. There were also three registers of deities, and on the left side of the top register Wenamun kneels before Amenre' in his shrine opposite the same scene on the other wall. The deities represented in the three registers vary and many of them are not represented on the opposite wall. An interesting one preserves the upper part of Wenamun with a feather in his hair, standing in front of a deity inside a shrine. The deity also wears a feather in his hair — which might suggest Libyan origin or at least Libyan appearance. This can lead us to think that this is probably the ancient god who was worshipped in Siwa before the supremacy of Amun in this oasis.(3) His name is not preserved; and a similar scene does not appear anywhere else on the monuments of Siwa (Fig. 56).

---

(1) The ceremonies of the Opening of the Mouth were supposed to be performed on the mummy by a lector-priest before placing it in the tomb. This makes it possible for the deceased to speak again after his death and enjoy his future life. A concise survey of this rite and its ceremonies is found in A. Blackman, «The Rite of Opening the Mouth,» **J.E.A.** 10 : 47ff; and J.C. Baly, «Notes on the Ritual of Opening the Mouth,» **J.E.A.** 16 : 137ff.

(2) U. Hölscher, **Medinet Habu,** p. 55.

(3) For the question of the Libyan gods known to the Egyptians, and the different references to the works on this subject, see Scharff, «Vorgeschichtliches zur Libyerfrage,» **Z.A.S.,** 61: 16ff; and Wreszinski, «Der Gott Uh,» p 521 ff.

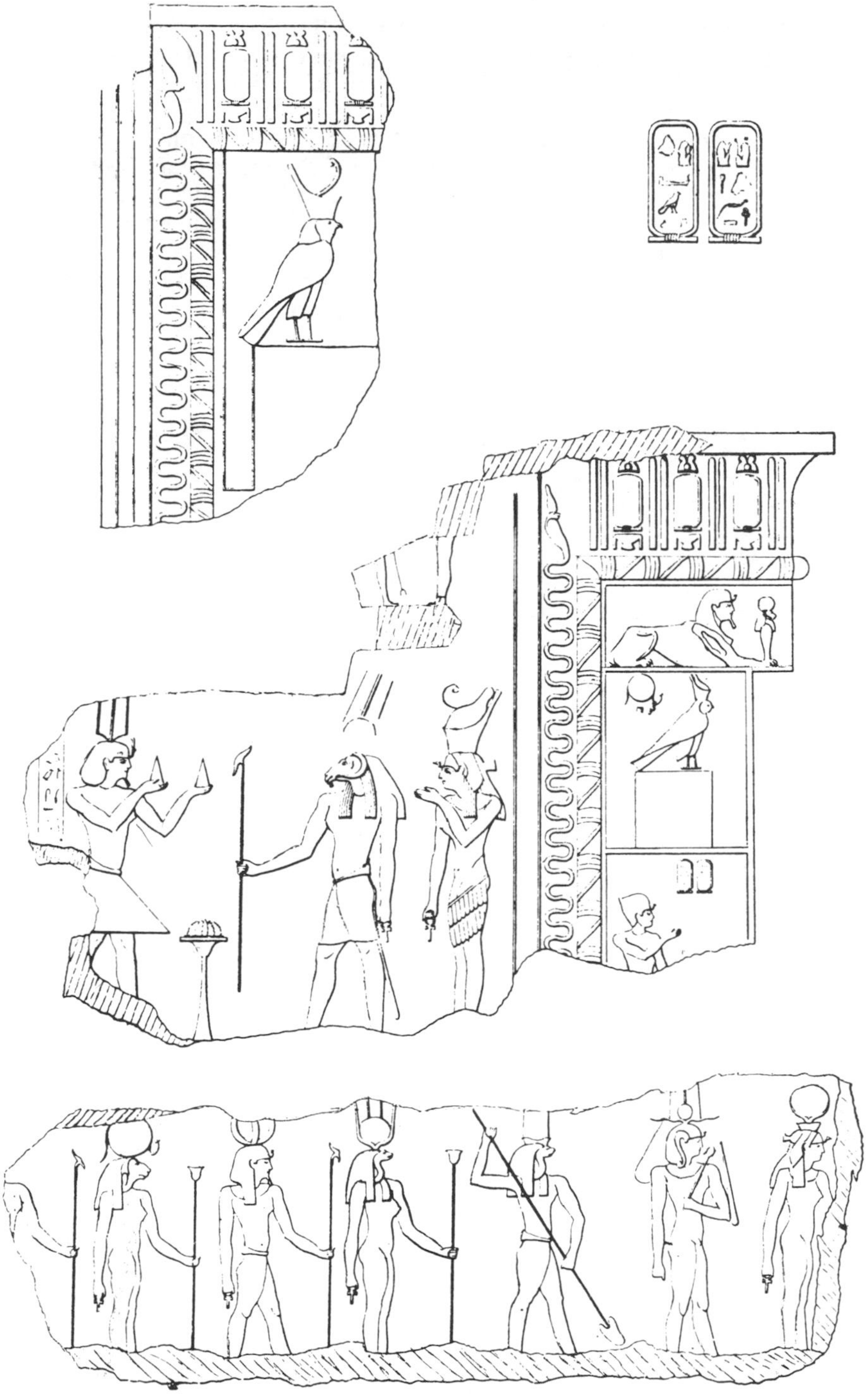

Fig. 57. Sketches of different parts of Umm 'Ubaydah and some inscribed stones including the name of Nectanebo II of the 30th Dynasty (After Von Minutoli, Atlas, Pl. X).

We find in the drawings of Minutoli other blocks decorated with figures of deities, as well as scenes of other parts of the temple which were still standing in his day (Fig. 57).

Apparently Minutoli's draughtsman was concerned only with the figures of the deities, for he filled the place occupied by hieroglyphics with small signs or lines of his own which made no sense. But we are grateful to him nevertheless, because this is the only document of its kind that we have. We must not forget that the hieroglyphs were not deciphered at that time; and he was only doing an artistic work.

7

The Tombs of Jabal al-Mawta

Jabal al-Mawtā (lit., The Hill of the Dead), or Qāret al-Miṣṣabbarīn (lit., The Ridge of the Mummified) as it is sometimes called, is a conical ridge at a distance of about one and one-half kilometres from the center of the town of Siwa. It is honey combed with rock tombs cut at its foot, in the terrace and in all sides of the conical part at the top (Fig. 58). Many of its tombs are small and consist of one or two chambers, but there are larger ones which have several chambers and columns (Fig. 59). No systematic excavations were ever made at this site, but wherever we go we find the results of the destructive work of illicit diggers whose work has continued for many centuries. We see fragments of mummies, bones and shrouds scattered around everywhere. This was the scene which drew the attention of all the travellers who have described it in some detail since the visit of Browne in 1792. The Siwans used to open tombs, take away whatever they found in them and cut the mummies to pieces in search of amulets. Later they would sell their finds to the antiquity dealers in Alexandria. This is what they were doing in October-November, 1940 when they left their houses in the town and sought security in the rock tombs of this hill.

The older tombs in this necropolis date from the 26th Dynasty and the Ptolemaic Period; they were robbed in Roman times and were reused for burying the dead over many centuries during the Roman period. Side recesses **(loculli)** were cut in the walls for family burial places, without regard for the paintings thereon. The mummies found in these burial rooms in recent times date from the Roman period. They are poorly mummified and are prepared in more or less the same way as in the Nile Valley, the coffins and amulets also being the same. In other words, the inhabitants of Siwa were completely Egyptianized in the Ptolemaic and Roman Periods, had the same beliefs and used the same burial customs as the people in the Nile Valley. But to what race did they belong ? Many of the skulls and other bones found in the ravaged tombs of Siwa were brought to Cairo in the 1920's and carefully studied by Professor D. Derry. From his measurements and comparisons, he concluded that the Siwans in Ptolemaic and Roman times were not exactly like the Egyptians but were in many respects closer to the European stock than to the African.(1) These physical differences between the Siwans and the Egyptians of the Nile Valley, the inhabitants of the other oases and the Bedouin still exist.

It is noteworthy that so far, nothing has been found in Jabal al-Mawtā which in any way proves that Christians were buried here in the same cemetery not far from their pagan relatives, as in the Oasis of Kharga.(2) The Muslims however preferred to bury their dead near their town and avoided the place where the pagans were buried.

There is a reference to this cemetery in the Siwan Manuscript. Although without historical value, it is nevertheless interesting to read. Here is the literal translation :

Qāret al-Miṣṣabbarīn is one of the best hills of Siwa. When it was time that the will of God should take place and Islam should conquer, the chiefs of the priests and the magicians knew it because it was recorded in their books and they consequently informed their king. He asked them where the principal center of Islam would be and they told him it would be at a place to the west of the Temple of Amun. They agreed among themselves to make Jabal al-Miṣṣabbarīn a burial ground for their dead in order to spoil the water and other things of this hill. In one of the tombs which is at its northern side there is a passage which leads downwards and then turns eastwards until it reaches the treasury of King Khuraybīsh at Aghūrmī.(3)

Early Travellers

There is no doubt that the tombs of Jabal al-Mawtā have witnessed many robberies since ancient times. A number of its rock tombs were open for years and their contents scattered inside and near the entrance. This necropolis was one of the chief interests of the early visitors to Siwa. Browne, who was permitted to visit it in 1792, stated that the tombs contained

---

(1) Douglas E. Derry, «A Study of Crania from the Oasis of Siwa,» Varia Africana IV, **Harvard African Studies, VIII**, 1927.

(2) The necropolis of Bagawāt at Kharga was used by Christians and pagans at the same time.

(3) According to the same document, the treasury of King Khuraybīsh, the last king of Siwa, is buried in the Temple of the Oracle at Aghūrmī.

Fig. 58. A view of Jabal al-Mawtā.

Fig. 59. A rock cut tomb at the foot of the hill.

neither inscriptions nor paintings, "yet there are many parts of human skulls, and other bones, with fragments of skin, and even of hair, attached to them."(1) Hornemann, the second visitor to Siwa in the 18th century (1798), was also interested in the mummies, but he mentioned that the Siwans found gold inside the tombs, and that they were ravaging the ancient burials in search of it.(2)

The first traveller to mention the drawings and paintings in the tombs was Cailliaud, who visited this site on December 12, 1819.(3) His description follows:

"One of the most remarkable tombs contains three rooms, one after the other, whose total length is 11 metres. At right and left sides there are five chambers. On the walls of subterranean grottoes one finds the remains of hieroglyphs and Egyptian figures painted on the stucco; at the end there are two mutilated statues of a man and a woman cut in the rock, as it is generally seen in the Nile Valley."

This large tomb with the two statues at the end and paintings on the walls must have been buried after Cailliaud's visit because it was not observed by any other traveller after him. He writes further, "In general, these tombs are very small and are connected together. The hieroglyphs are very rare. Those which I saw with the greatest interest are hieroglyphic subjects which were only traced in red lines on white plaster."

The troops of Muḥammad 'Alī conquered Siwa in 1820. The French Consul in Cairo and other distinguished friends accompanied the troops and were able to go wherever they wanted. They visited Jabal al-Mawtā, but the notes of Drovetti add nothing of importance to what Cailliaud had written. In the same year, the German Consul in Egypt, Von Minutoli, visited Siwa. He referred to the tombs, stating that some of them were painted with green, red, yellow and blue colours and contained hieroglyphs.(4) He mentioned also that Siwans lived in some of the tombs,(5) and that during his stay a few hundred Bedouin of the Majābir tribe from Tripolis were living in the tombs.(6)

In the following years of the 19th century, Siwa attracted many travellers, but only nine among them published books on

---

(1) Browne, **Travels...**, p. 21.

(2) Hornemann, **Tagebuch...** p. 51.

(3) Cailliaud, **Voyage à Meroé**, pp. 68-69.

(4) Minutoli, **Reise...**, p. 171. In Pl. XII of his Atlas, we find small drawings of a view of the hill, an entrance to a tomb and a scene of the interior of another tomb.

(5) These must be at the foot of the hill near the cultivated gardens some of the tombs in that area were inhabited in the year 1938.

(6) **Ibid.**, p. 172.

their visits. Seven of them mentioned Jabal al-Mawtā, but we do not find in their works any new information which we can add to what we already know from the works of Cailliaud and Von Minutoli.[1]

In 1897, A. Silva White visited Siwa, entered the tombs of Jabal al-Mawtā and published in his book photographs of the entrances to some of them and the mummies inside. He also visited the tomb of Niperpathot, described some of its scenes and published a photograph of part of it. He acquired a coin of Ptolemy I, which he presented to the Museum of Alexandria, and two heavy metal ornaments "which were found in the tombs and brought for sale by a native." These ornaments are a bracelet and an unbent bar made of an alloy of gold, silver and copper. He also brought from the same cemetery "a fairly large piece of painted wrapping", which was described by Professor Sayce as follows :

"A mummy shroud, not incased in a coffin, but buried in the sand with bitumen. At the upper end is a picture of the deceased on his bier, with Anubis standing beside him and pouring the waters of life over the body, while a worshipper is standing on either side in the attitude of prayer. Below, on either side of the shroud, are figures of the four genii of the dead: Amost (Amesti), Duau-Mutef, Hapi and Qebehsenouf. The genii are placed one above the other two on each side and between them are bands of rosettes.[2]" This shroud was presented to the Ashmolean Museum at Oxford and was dated as Roman. Although the author did not publish a photograph, we can easily understand from the note of Sayce that the scene shows Osiris on his bier with the goddess Isis at his feet and Nephthys at his head, while Anubis is embalming the body. The four canopic jars representing the four sons of Horus are depicted below the scene.

In 1900, Siwa was visited by Brichetti-Robecchi[3] and by Hohler[4] but they did not add anything new. Steindorff visited

---

(1) Those travellers are Bayle St. John (1847 — **Adventures in the Libyan Desert and Oasis of Jupiter Amon**, Hamilton (1856 — **Wanderings in North Africa**), Rohlfs (1869 — **Von Tripolis nach Alexandrich**), Zittel (1867 — **Beitrage zur Geologie und Palaontologie der Libyschen Wuste**), Borchardt, (1893 — "Uber den Besuch der Oase Siwa in Februar 1893," in **Verhandl. der Gesellsch, fur Erdkunde zu Berlin, Band 20**), Mustafa Maher (1892 — "L'Oasis de Siouah," in **Bulletin Soc. Sult. de Geographie IX**, 1919, p. 55), and Jennings-Bramley (1896 — "A Journey to Siwa," in **Geographical Journal**, 1897, vol. 10).

(2) White, **From Sphinx to Oracle**, pp. 232 - 7.

(3) Brichetti-Robecchi, **All'oasi die Giove Ammone.**

(4) G. Hohler, **Report on the Oasis of Siwa** (Cairo, 1900).

Siwa in the same year and entered the tombs of Jabal al-Mawtā, including that of Niperpathot, and gave a brief description of some of its scenes.[1] He published a photograph of the walls, noting that the tomb betrayed no foreign influence. He read the name of the tomb owner as "Pa-Thoth." In his brief description of the other tombs, he mentioned seeing Egyptian and Greek art side by side in some of their paintings. In others he saw paintings of pure Greek style which he compared with those in Cyrene and Alexandria. He also referred to the mummies lying about, together with fragments of wall paintings.

Among those who visited Siwa and this cemetery in this century are Falls, who was in the company or Khedive ʿAbbās II in his visit in 1904,[2] Stanley,[3] and Quibell, who was an official of the Antiquities Department of Egypt and went to Siwa in a military car in 1917.[4] But the descriptions of these three visitors, as well as the booklet of Breccia, who accompanied King Fu'ād in his visit in 1928,[5] referred only to the tombs and mentioned the mummies, but nothing was added to what we already knew.

Since the end of the First World War, cars have been used in the Western Desert, and all who want to go to Siwa can make the trip easily. A number of visitors have left good accounts of the place, but none of them cared to make any researches in this cemetery.[6] In my visits to Siwa in 1938 and 1939, I photographed the tombs and copied the inscriptions on the walls of the tomb of Niperpathot. As mentioned in some detail in the chapter on history, the Siwans left their houses in the town in October-November, 1940 and went to Jabal al-Mawtā to live in its tombs. It was only at that time that new inscribed tombs came to light. The results of my work at Siwa are published in a few articles and two books. The principal one was published in 1944; the other book is abridged and written in a more popular style. It was published in 1950.[7]

---

(1) Steindorff, **Amonsoase...**, pp. 123-4, and Figs. 75-77.

(2) Falls, **Siwah...**, p. 15 ff.

(3) Stanley, A Report on the Oasis of Siwa (Public Health Department, Egyptian Government, 1911).

(4) Quibell, «A Visit to Siwa,» pp. 78-112.

(5) Breccia, «With King Fuad to the Oasis of Ammon.» Breccia expressed his pessimism towards any future excavations.

(6) The only work of importance is the article of Steindroff, «Ein Aegyptisches Grab in Siwa,» **Z.A.S.**, 61 (1926), pp. 94-98, based on his notes and photographs taken when he visited Siwa in 1900.

(7) **Siwa Oasis : Its History and Antiquities** (Cairo, 1944) and the **Oasis of Siwa : Its Customs, History and Monuments** (Cairo, 1950).

The hill of Jabal al-Mawtā has many tombs cut in it, most of which are now buried. A good number of them are open although choked with debris, but those which have paintings on their walls will be briefly described in this chapter.[1] These are the tombs of Niperpathot, which were already known before 1940, and the three discovered by the Siwans in that year and where I cleared off debris in January, 1941. These are the tombs of the Crocodile, Mesu-Isis and of Si-Amun — the most important one in this oasis. All four are cut in the rock of the conical part of the hill.

The Tomb of Niperpathot

This is one of the largest in the cemetery. As we see in its plan (Fig. 60), it has a court, now badly ruined, and six small chambers, three on either side. It ends with the burial chamber, which faces the entrance. Walls of the six side chambers were left uninscribed. The very small burial chamber, however, is covered with inscriptions and drawings in red colour on the rock. The owner's mummy was placed in a sarcophagus cut in the floor ; the lid, which no longer exists, was a stone slab resting on a ledge around the top of the sarcophagus.

The tomb owner was a man named Niperpathot (lit., He who belongs to the house of Thot), whose chief title was "Prophet of Osiris." This shows that a temple for the god Osiris existed in this oasis at the time. The "prophet" was also a "Scribe of the Divine documents", a "Wa'b-priest" and, among his other distinctions, "The great one in his town", "The follower of his god", "The excellent man", and "The straightforward one ".

The breadth of the burial chamber is 1.75 metres and its length is less than two metres. On the righthand wall stands the tomb owner with upraised arms, holding a sceptre in one hand. In front of him are, one above the other, the famous four boxes of the Sons of Horus, called **meret**-boxes, inside which there were garments (Fig. 61). From the texts we know that the father of Niperpathot was named Nes-Thot, who held the same titles as his son. The mother of Niperpathot was Nastit.

---

(1) Another inscribed tomb was discovered in 1940 at the foot of the hill, but I could not copy its texts or take photographs owing to its use as a storeroom by Shaykh 'Alī Ḥaydah. It was filled completely with sacks of wheat and rice at that time.

Near the conical summit of the hill, three tombs contain remains of paintings in Hellenistic style, and a fragmentary Greek graffito is still preserved on one of the walls.

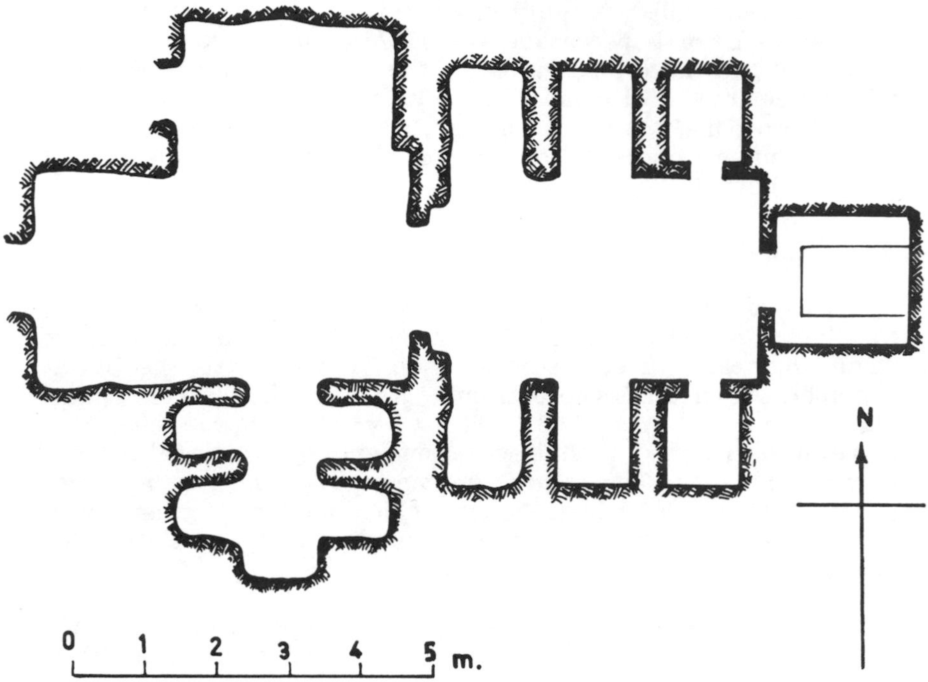

Fig. 60 Plan of the Tomb of Niperpathot.

On the wall facing the entrance, Niperpathot adores Osiris who sits on a stool, the goddess Hathor stands behind him. In front of Osiris is an offering table opposite which stands the tomb owner in worship. His head is shaved and he wears a necklace, a long apron with a panther's skin over it, and sandals. The stand of the offering table is in the shape of a lotus flower. Above the table appear six loaves of bread, a gazelle, two geese and a cucumber. Two vases of wine hang from the table edge; two others stand beneath. The goddess Hathor has a human body and a cow's head; her diadem is the sun-disk between the two horns, surmounted by two feathers.

On the wall at the left side of the entrance we find, to the right behind Hathor, in a long inscription, a hymn addressed to the god Thot. At the left of the wall stands Niperpathot, holding in one hand the ropes to the ends of which are fastened four calves, and in the other a whip (Fig. 62).

This well-known ceremony of the "dragging of the four calves" is depicted on the walls of the tombs beginning in the 18th Dynasty and had been represented in temples since the Old Kingdom. The four calves must be of different colours : one red, the second white, the third black and the fourth

Fig. 61 Inscriptions on one of the walls of the tomb.

spotted. Dating in all probability from the 26th Dynasty, this tomb is older than any other so far discovered in Siwa. The god Amun is not mentioned at all, although we know he was the principal deity in this oasis in the 26th Dynasty. The inscriptions on the walls of the Temple of the Oracle mention the name of King Amasis. In the light of our limited knowledge of this period of Siwa's history, we can only say that the worship of Osiris in Siwa was in all probability established before the time when the worship of Amun came to prominence, and that there was a temple for Osiris in Siwa with its own priests.

Fig. 62. Niperpathot holding the ropes of the four calves.

The Tomb of the Crocodile

In the northeastern corner of the terrace there is an inscribed tomb which opens east. It consists of three rooms, each coated with a layer of white plaster. Only the first (Plan, Fig. 63), was painted, the other two left undecorated. This tomb was found in October, 1940. The family which occupied it cleared the burial chamber and the side chamber only because they reached them through a break in the rock from a neighbouring tomb. The decorated chamber, which is nearest to the entrance was full of debris, the floor being four steps lower than the threshold. It was thoroughly excavated in January, 1941.

The Decorated Walls : The walls are coated with a layer of a poor quality of plaster; the paintings were made by an unskilled hand. At the two thicknesses of the entrance, the headless bodies of three figures of deities are represented holding knives in their hands, to protect the body of the tomb owner. Originally there were four such figures, in all probability the four sons of Horus. At our righthand side, at the corner of the north wall, the goddess Hathor is seated, holding three springs of a plant in her right hand while she pours water from a vase held in her left. Another vase hangs from her wrist.

There is a niche in the middle of the wall. To its right the tomb owner is represented seated on a chair, and behind him stands the ram-headed god, Amun, holding a knife in each hand. The body of the god is coloured blue while the body of the tomb owner is light red. Beneath these is a mat decorated with stepped pyramidal designs painted blue or red, bordered with two yellow lines. Below this, a crocodile appears painted in yellow; the intersecting lines representing its scales are red (Fig. 64). Under the niche is a stylized grape tree; a fox at each side eats a bunch of grapes (Fig. 65). To the left of the niche we find scenes in two registers, the upper one showing the tomb owner worshipping Osiris, the lower depicting two female deities protecting with their wings the sun-god, who is represented seated on a flower. The last painting on this wall shows the tomb owner worshipping Osiris, who sits on a chair, Isis standing behind him. On the right-hand side of the thickness of the door leading to the burial chamber there is a much damaged figure of the tomb owner, a bearded man with thick, curly hair. On the south wall, other fragments of figures remain from a scene of the god Thoth in the presence of Osiris.

The entrance to the burial chamber, which contained religious scenes, was blocked in antiquity; most of it was destroyed when the tomb was robbed in ancient times. The south wall is badly damaged, only a part being preserved. The god Osiris

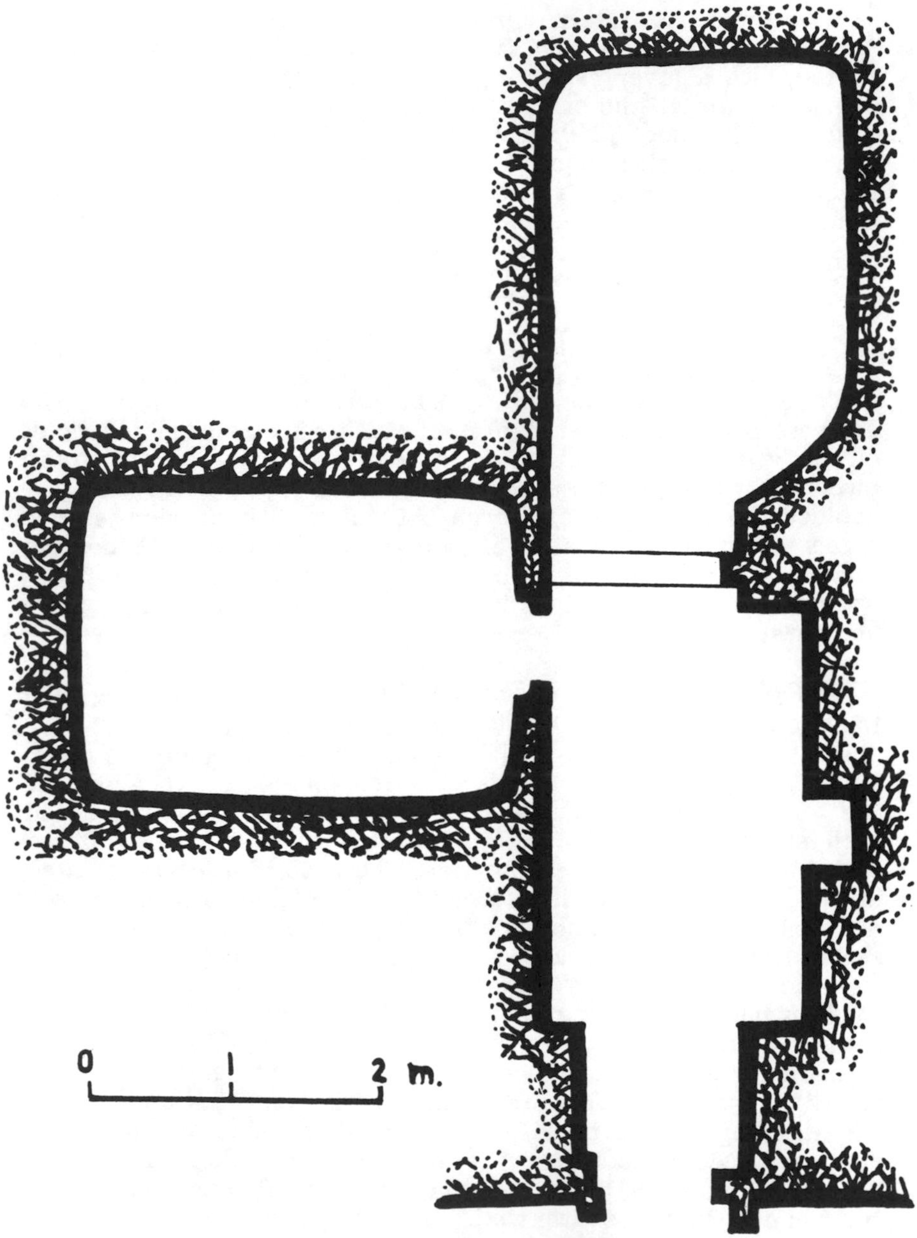

Fig. 63. Plan of the Tomb of the Crocodile.

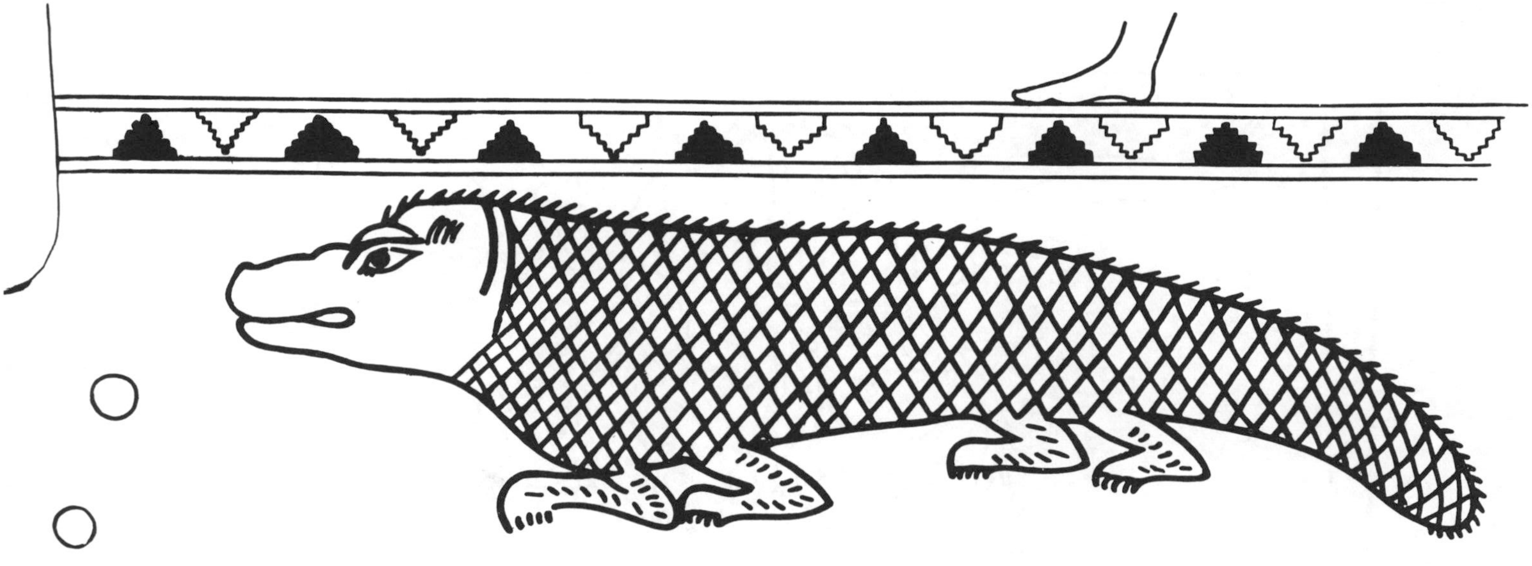

Fig. 64. The crocodile.

Fig. 65. A painting in the tomb of the Crocodile showing Hellenistic influence.

sits inside a shrine with an offering table in front of him. On the other side of the table stands the god Thoth, with an ibis head on a human body, writing on a palette. His body is coloured yellow, his apron is richly decorated in red and blue (Fig. 66).

The Date of the Tomb : Late Ptolemaic or early Roman is the probable date. Some of the details of its scenes, especially the offering tables, can be compared with those painted in the tomb of Si-Amun, in the same necropolis. The name of the owner is not preserved. I prefer to call it the Tomb of the Crocodile, because the Siwans gave it this name when it was freed from debris and the paintings became visible.

It is probable that during this period at Siwa, some cult of the crocodile-god, Sobek, was thus represented in this tomb. We should bear in mind that Siwa at all periods of its history had regular relations with the Fayyūm in which the crocodile god had the most prominent place.

The crocodile painting caused a great sensation among the inhabitants who flocked to see it when the tomb was cleaned, and to hear stories told by their compatriots who claimed to know all about crocodiles from their visits to the Cairo zoo. I was much amused by their descriptions. All agreed that one could swallow a man or a woman, but one character assured his listeners that it could swallow a loaded camel. As for length, their estimates varied from ten to a hundred metres! Some of them wanted to know the truth from me, but I refrained from saying anything which might spoil their fun.

The Tomb of Mesu-Isis

In the middle terrace, about twenty metres to the east of the tomb of Si-Amun, this tomb opens north with a slight deviation to the east. It was unfinished — the walls were neither coated with plaster nor decorated and the burial chamber was not completely cut out of the rock, although it might have been used for burial (Fig. 67). Only the wall facing the entrance, (i.e. where the burial chamber entrance is cut) was partly painted. The entrance to the tomb itself is built of seven courses of stone blocks in the cornice style. The floor of the first longitudinal chamber is lower than the threshold and is reached by a flight of steps cut in the rock.

This tomb was opened in the Roman period and several **loculli** were cut in its side walls and used for burials. Several of these were intact when the tomb was discovered in October, 1940. I was told that amulets and beads were found with the mummies. Two mummies had been placed in gilded plaster coffins.

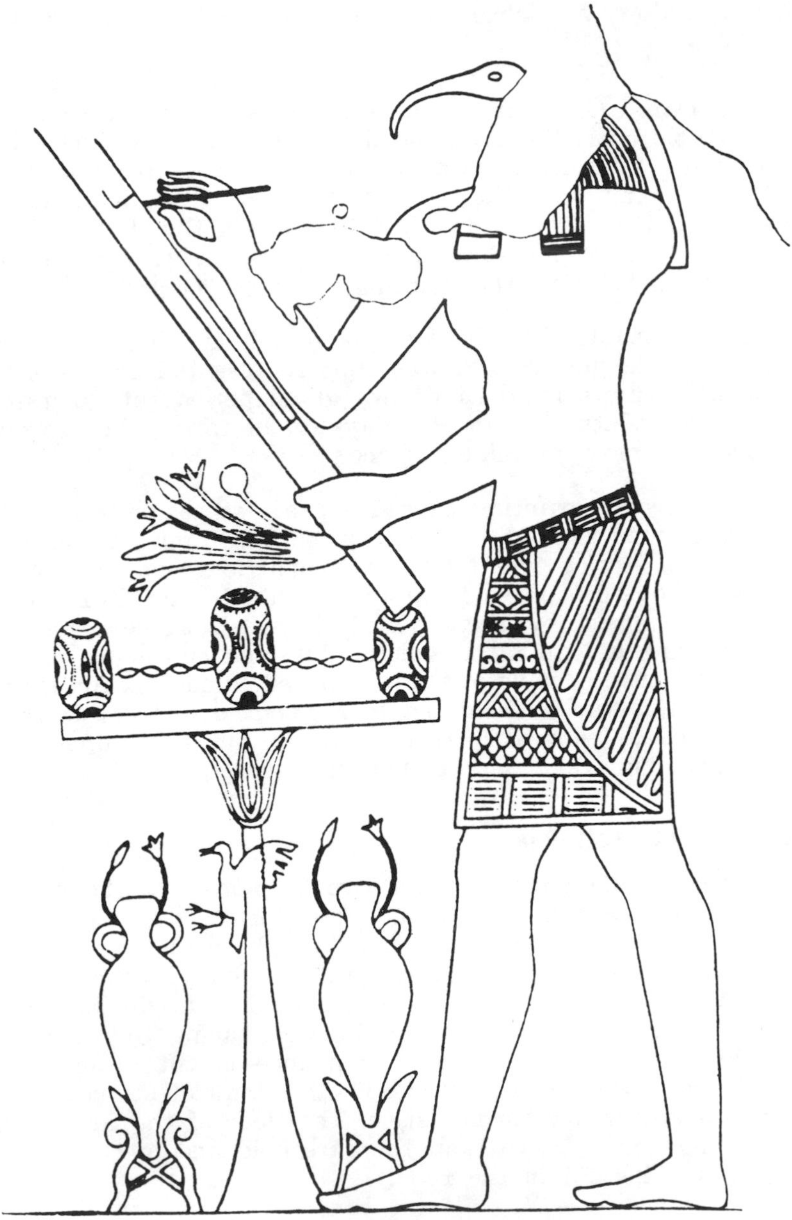

Fig. 66. The god Thoth, with an ibis head, writing on a palette (Tomb of the Crocodile).

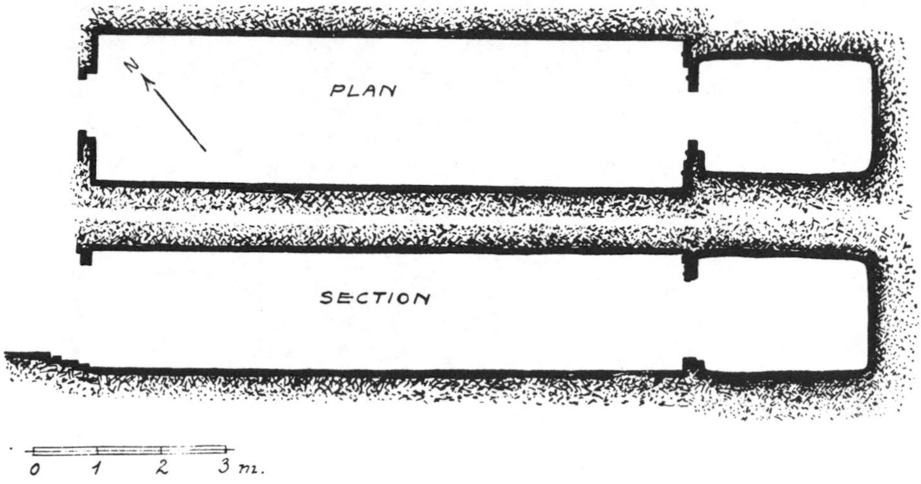

Fig. 67. Plan and section of the Tomb of Mesu-Isis.

Over the cornice of the decorated entrance are twenty-one **uraei (uraeus** — sacred asp, symbol of sovereignty) painted in relief, each with a sun-disk over its head. The bodies of the **uraei** are red and blue. There are two painted winged sun-disks (Fig. 68), and hieroglyphic texts at both sides of the **uraei** and at the two sides of the entrance. To the right of the entrance, Osiris sits on his stool, Isis sitting opposite. The colours are preserved, but the hieroglyphic inscriptions are partly damaged. There was a metal disk over the place of the sun in the winged sun-disk above the entrance. Either of gold or of bronze, such disks were covered with gold leaf and fixed in the stone by means of a metal nail.

From a study of the inscriptions we know that the wife of the tomb owner was named Mesu-Isis, but the name of her husband is partly damaged and cannot be read with certainty. In front of the good Osiris, two lines of inscriptions describe him as "The foremost of the Westerners, (i.e. the dead), Osiris, the great god, who is honoured in 'Tha-t'." This must be the ancient name of Siwa or one of its localities. It appears in this tomb, on the wall of the Temple of Umm 'Ubaydah and in the Tomb of Si-Amun.

Fig. 68. The entrance to the burial chamber.

The tomb dates from the period between the 4th and 2nd centuries B.C. and is more or less contemporaneous with the tomb of Si-Amun.

The Tomb of Si-Amun

The most important tomb at Jabal al-Mawtā, Si-Amun's, is no doubt the most beautiful in all the oases of the Western Desert. It is visited by all who come to this oasis. and for this reason I describe it in some detail.

Lying only a short distance west of the tomb of Mesu-Isis it opens north. It was discovered in October, 1940, and its once well-preserved scenes have suffered greatly at the hands of the soldiers in Siwa at that time, who cut away parts of the painted plaster.

Its plan is like that of the tomb of Mesu-Isis. A flight of steps leads to the entrance of a longitudinal chamber at whose far end is the burial chamber. This tomb, as the others, was robbed in the Roman period (Fig. 69). At that time ten recesses, used for family burials, were cut in the main chamber, five in each of the eastern and western walls. Many mummies were found in these recesses when they were discovered in 1940, but they were very badly mummified, and very few objects were found with them. These were sold to the troops.

The hewing out of these later burials demolished not less than one-fourth of the original painted scenes, but in spite of this and the disfiguration of many of the scenes after the tomb's discovery, it still preserves much of its ancient painting, both on the walls and on the ceiling.

The rock is good, the plaster used to coat the rock walls is of very good quality, and the artists who drew and painted the figures were exceptionally skilled, in all probability brought from the Nile Valley.

The Owner of the Tomb : The owner of this tomb was a man called "Si-Amun", represented on the walls in several scenes with a beard and thick, black, curly hair and fair complexion. No titles appear; in other words, he neither held a religious post in one of the temples, nor was connected with the oasis administration. His tomb, however, shows that he was a very important person whose financial means were such as to enable him to prepare such an elaborate place of burial. He must have been a great landowner or a rich merchant. His name means literally "the man of Amun", a common Egyptian name, but his father was called Periytu,(1) which is by no means Egyptian. His mother was Nefer-hert, meaning "the lady with the beautiful face".(2) The preserved scenes do not contain representations of either. Other relatives represented are Si-Amun's wife and his two sons. Of reddish brown complexion, his wife was named Re'-t. The older son was fair-skinned like his father, the younger brown like his mother. He was the favourite child of his father and was dressed like a Greek boy of his age during that period.

---

(1) This name does not exist in Ranke, **Personennamen,** and is most probably of foreign origin.

(2) Literally «it is beautiful, the face», with the feminine ending.

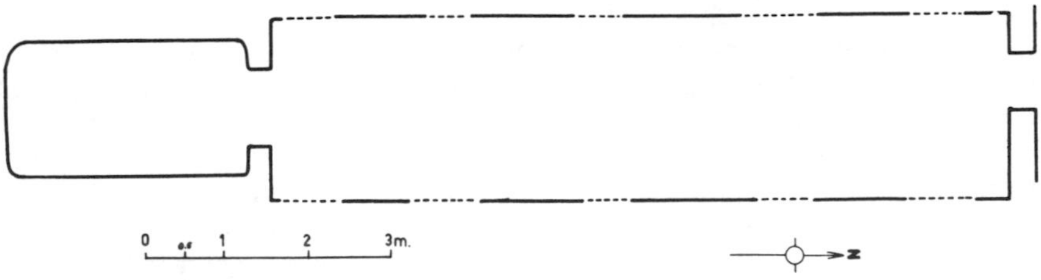

Fig. 69. **Plan of the Tomb of Si-Amun.**

In my opinion, Si-Amun's father, was a Greek who immigrated to Egypt, from Greece or more likely Cyrene, married an Egyptian lady and adopted the Egyptian religion. Although Si-Amun married an Egyptian, his pride in his Greek origin caused him to grow a beard and thick, black, curly hair in the Greek manner, and dress his son like a Greek child.

When Si-Amun lived at Siwa, this had been a very important caravan station between Cyrene on the coast, and the Sudan. Since its founding about 630 B.C., it was a very important commercial center. But we cannot say whether his father lived at Siwa before him or not. The tomb dates from the 3rd century B.C.

Description of the Wall Scenes : The tomb opens north; it was preceded by a courtyard in which two other tombs were cut, one to the east, the other to the west. A flight of steps leads down to the entrance, which is decorated in the cornice style. The facade, bears no inscription, and no trace of colours are preserved on it. Since it is impossible to describe all the scenes in detail in this book, I refer to only some of them.

The West Wall : The scenes are in two registers. The northern half of the upper register represented the Judgement Hall. Osiris was seated in his shrine, in front of him the scene of the weighing of the heart, and the forty-two deities. To the right of the scale were the monster 'Amm and the tomb owner, protected by the goddess Ma't. Unfortunately three recesses had been cut in this scene, demolishing most of it,

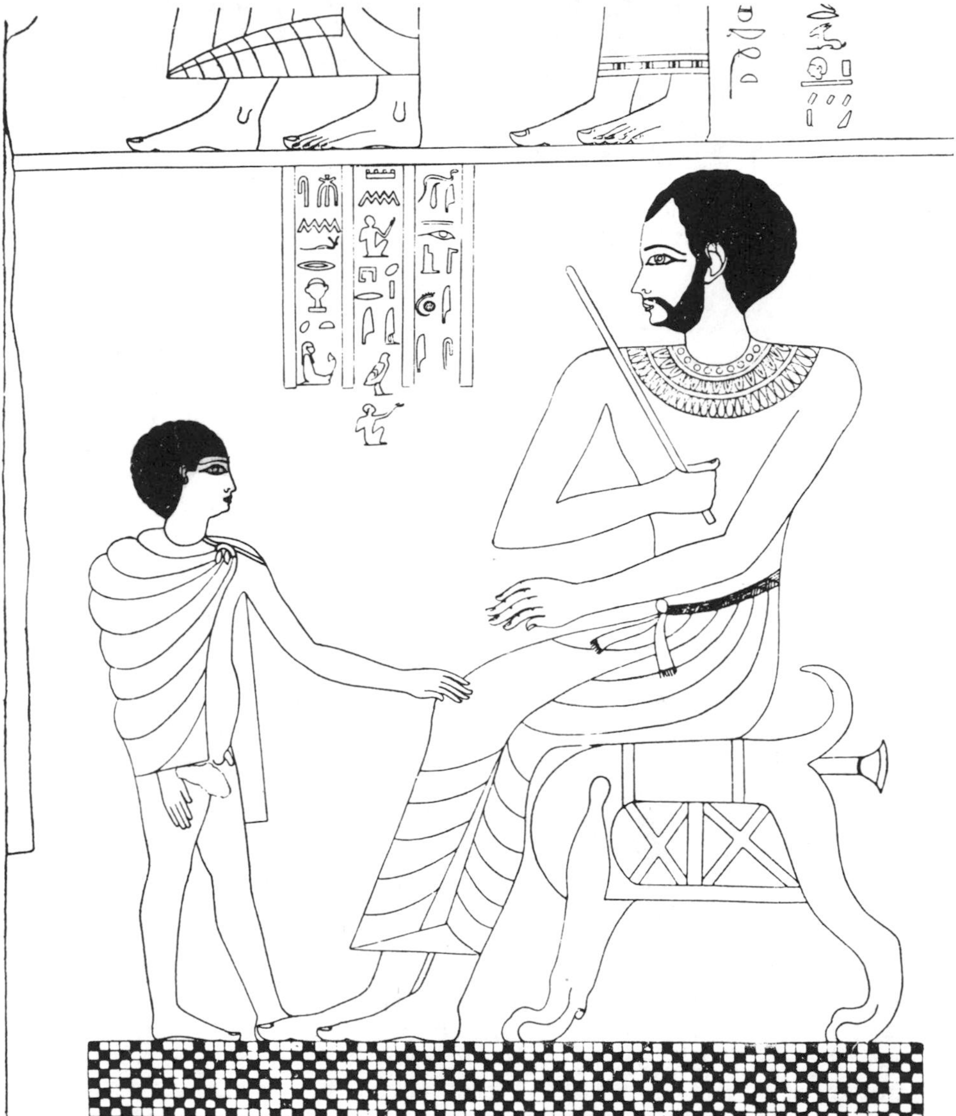

Fig. 70. Si-Amun and his younger son.

but parts are preserved, as for instance the god Osiris and the monster 'Amm who was supposed to devour the guilty. A large part of the text which accompanied this scene remains.

In the bottom register, near the entrance, Si-Amun sits on a chair and his younger son, with thick, black, curly hair, and wearing a short Greek cloak, stands in front of him (Fig. 70). Nearby stands the goddess Nut beside a sycamore tree. In her right hand she holds a tray with offerings of bread and incense; with her left she pours water from a vase into a pond. Between the two streams of water is a chain of the "signs of life,"(1) (Fig. 71). To the left of this scene, Si-Amun was represented praying to several deities; the goddes Isis and the **bennu**-bird are preserved.

The scenes continue on the southern half of the wall. In the upper register a false door was painted; at its left Si-Amun, holding a long staff of eb ıy worked with gold, sits on a chair of an uncommon type. To the right of the false door stood six deities; two — Re'Horus and Nephthys — are preserved (Fig. 72). In the bottom register is the embalming scene, the mummy lying on the bed of Osiris. Anubis takes care of the body while Isis stands at the head and Nephthys at the feet. Behind Nephthys stand the Four Sons of Horus, Amesti, Hapi, Doua-mutef and Qebehsenouf. The last scene in the bottom register represents Si-Amun seated on a chair, holding the symbol of life in one hand and the symbol of breath in the other (Fig. 73). In front of him there is a box above which appeared the instruments used in the rite of Opening the Mouth. At the other side stood the deceased's older son, wearing a leopard skin and holding in both hands instruments used in performing this rite. Si-Amun's wife is shown standing behind him. Unfortunately, some time after 1965, someone succeeded in cutting away the whole figure of Si-Amun. The wall facing the tomb entrance, in which the burial chamber was cut, was also decorated, but nothing now remains.

The East Wall : I give now a brief description of the east wall beginning from the entrance to the tomb. To our left as we enter, i.e. in the north corner, the wall was divided into two registers, the bot om one showing the mummy inside the canopy of a boat on a wheeled cart (Fig. 74) drawn by two people. To the left of the canopy appears the **ba**-bird with its

(1) The Siwans explain this scene as a tree of olives, noting that olive oil was abundant in Siwa in ancient times. This erroneous explanation was taken from one of the Arabic books written about Siwa in recent years by an official of the Ministry of Agriculture.

Fig. 71. The goddess Nut standing beside a sycamore tree.

Fig. 72. Osiris inside his shrine. It was complete when the tomb was found in 1940.

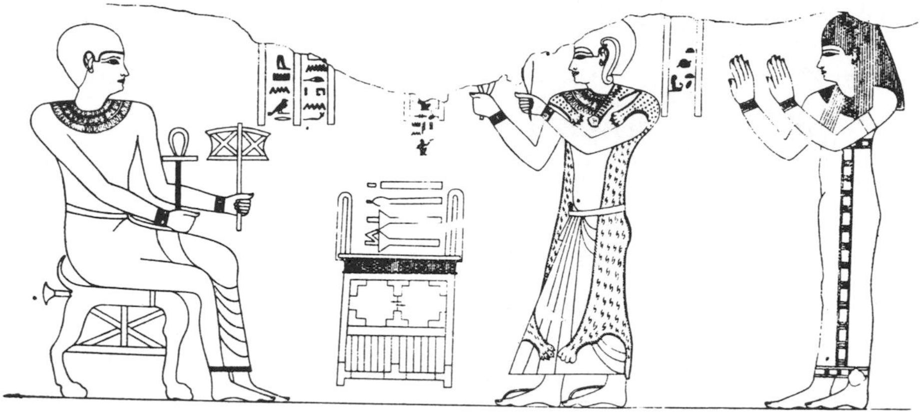

Fig. 73. Si-Amun, in front of whom stands his son followed by Si-Amun's wife.

human head; to its left is the jackal god, Wepwawet. The canopy is preceded by the standards of the gods Horus, Thot and Anubis. The prow of the boat is in the shape of a lotus flower; its stern has been destroyed. At the north end of the eastern wall there is a representation of a false door, at the right of which we see Si-Amun with the vulture goddess Nekhbeyt hovering over his head. Behind him is the box of instruments for the rite of Opening the Mouth, and his son, who wears the leopard skin and holds in his left hand the **Wer-Hekau** used in this rite (Fig. 75). The vulture goddess was drawn by a very skillful hand and very carefully and tastefully painted. It was complete when the tomb was discovered.

Si-Amun is praying to a number of deities. A rich table of offerings probably was destroyed when one of the recesses was cut in this wall. The deities are headed by Amun who is followed by a female goddess, most probably his consort, Mut. Behind Mut stands Hathor, looking to the right and holding the god Douamutef in her hands (Fig. 76).

On the other side of the recess are two deities looking to the right. The first is the lion-headed god, Mahesa; the other is a female, holding in her right hand the **sistrum** of Hathor. The last preserved scene on this wall shows Si-Amun in a standing position praying to Osiris and Isis. The paintings in this tomb are incomplete; in the above and the previous scenes

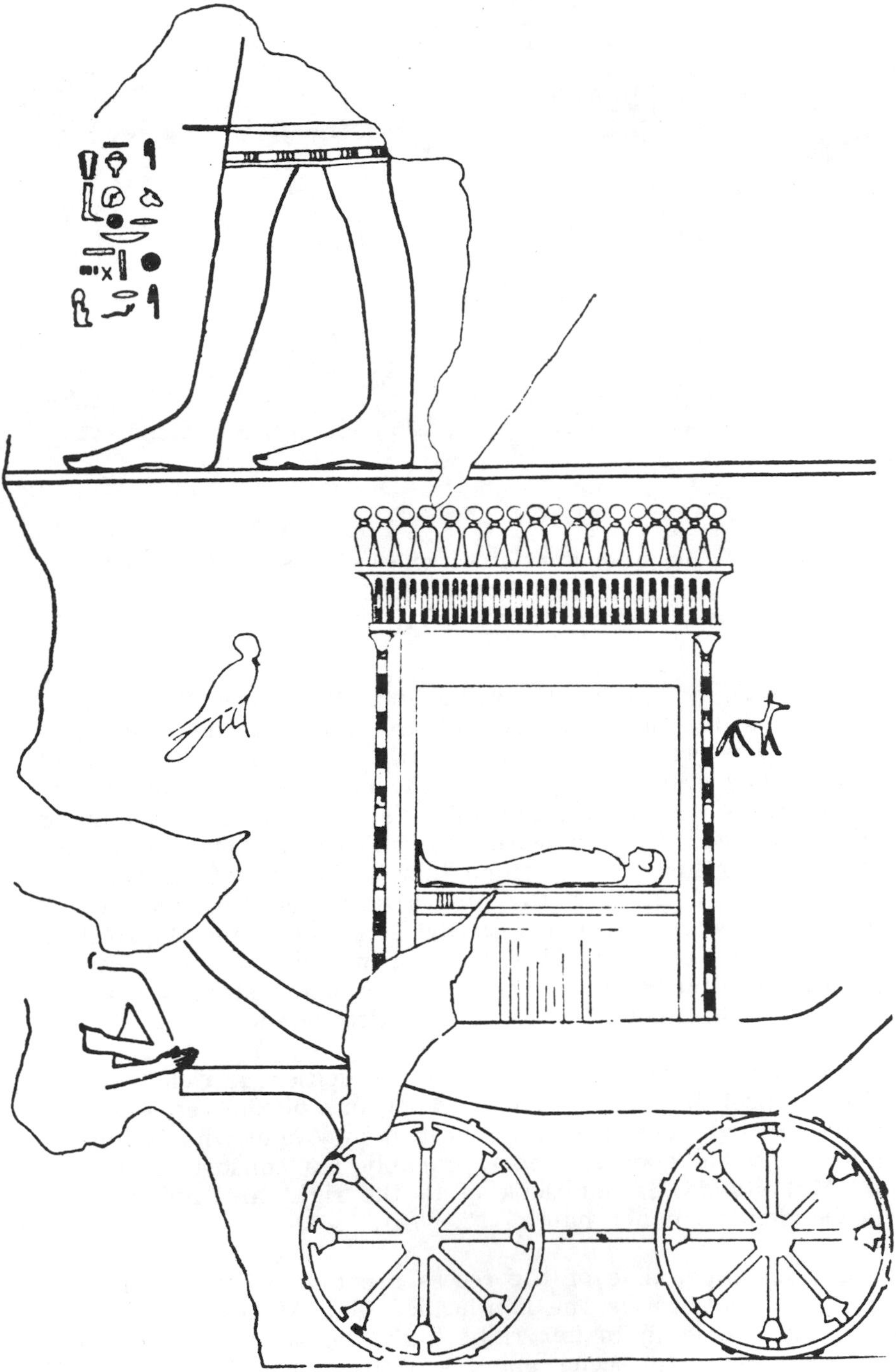

Fig. 74. The mummy of Si-Amun on a wheeled cart.

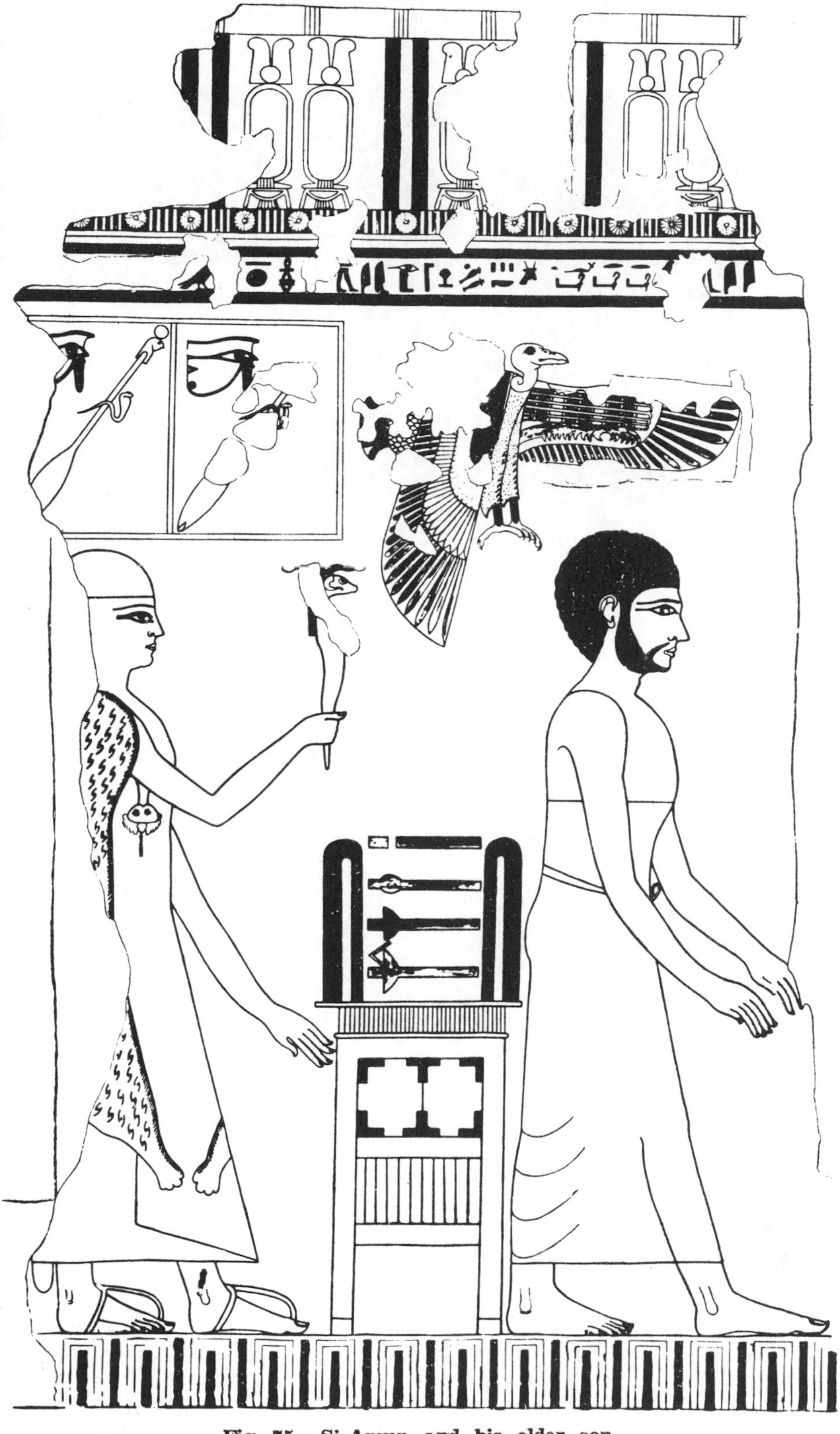

Fig. 75. Si-Amun and his older son.

Fig. 76. A part of the east wall of the tomb showing the goddess Mut behind Amenreʿ. Behind her stands Hathor holding the image of a falcon-headed deity.

we can see the guiding squares drawn by. the artist prior to what was to be the final work in all its colours (Fig. 77). The details of the clothes of the deities are very carefully executed: they are among the best examples of Egyptian art from this late period.

The Top Frieze: The top frieze on the walls of this tomb has two designs. The one nearer to the entrance consists of uninscribed cartouches above which appears a line, four centimetres broad, divided into small squares. Below the cartouches there is a line of rosettes (see Fig. 75). The second design, consists of a broad line of inscription at the top, with a band of small squares of geometric designs. Beneath the above inscription there is a fairly long representation of the sign of the sky. Uninscribed, the cartouches repeat in groups of two blue followed by two yellow, each group being separated from the next by three broad lines rounded at the top. Each rosette appears inside a small square, with eight petals and a point in the center.

The Ceiling: The ceiling is beautifully decorated and better preserved. When the tomb was newly discovered, attempts were made to remove pieces of the painting; but the debris which had accumulated inside the tomb had been cleaned out in the meantime, and thus the ceiling was out of reach. It is divided into three parts. Above the center of the room, five broad, horizontal lines, each of a different design, connect the two walls. The first contains an inscription written in yellow characters on blue ground; the second is painted blue; the third is a good imitation of wood; the fourth is composed of a double row of yellow stars on blue ground; and the fifth is painted yellow (Fig. 78). From these inscriptions to the back of the tomb, the painted ceiling decoration consists of a line of hieroglyphics in the center and on each side, alternate rows of falcons and vultures with outstretched wings, holding feathers in their claws (Fig. 79). The falcon represents Lower Egypt, the vulture Upper Egypt. Each has two stars on each side. On each side of the above divisions, two different kinds of rosettes appear in a painted band.

Near the entrance to the tomb the ceiling is decorated as follows : In the front, is a horizontal line of inscriptions. In the center, Nut, the godness of the sky, is represented (Fig. 80). Her body is coloured light brown ; her face was damaged when the tomb was discovered. Over her head, which is turned toward the tomb entrance, the sign of the sky is filled with stars. Under her feat is the symbol of earth, coloured yellow to represent sand with black dots representing pebbles. The winged sun emerges from the middle part of her body. To her right and left, the blue sky is filled with yellow stars, and at each side there are three boats, a representation of water under each.

Fig. 77. Si-Amun praying to Osiris. The tomb was not completely finished, and we see here the squares drawn by the artist to help him in his work.

Fig. 78. A part of the beautifully decorated ceiling.

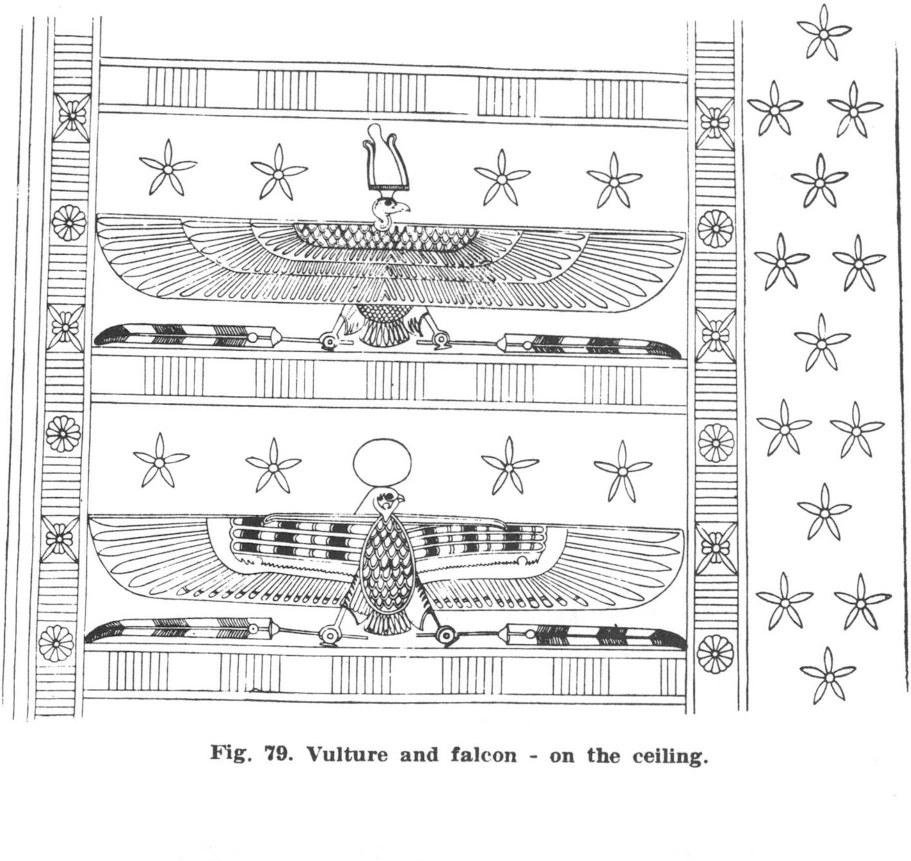

Fig. 79. Vulture and falcon - on the ceiling.

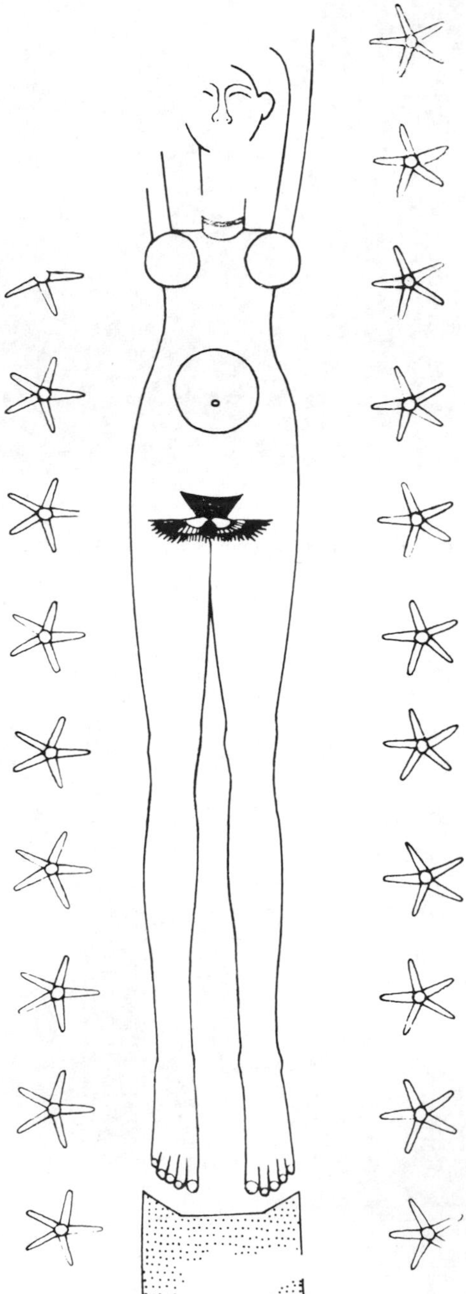

Fig. 80. Nut, the goddess of the sky.

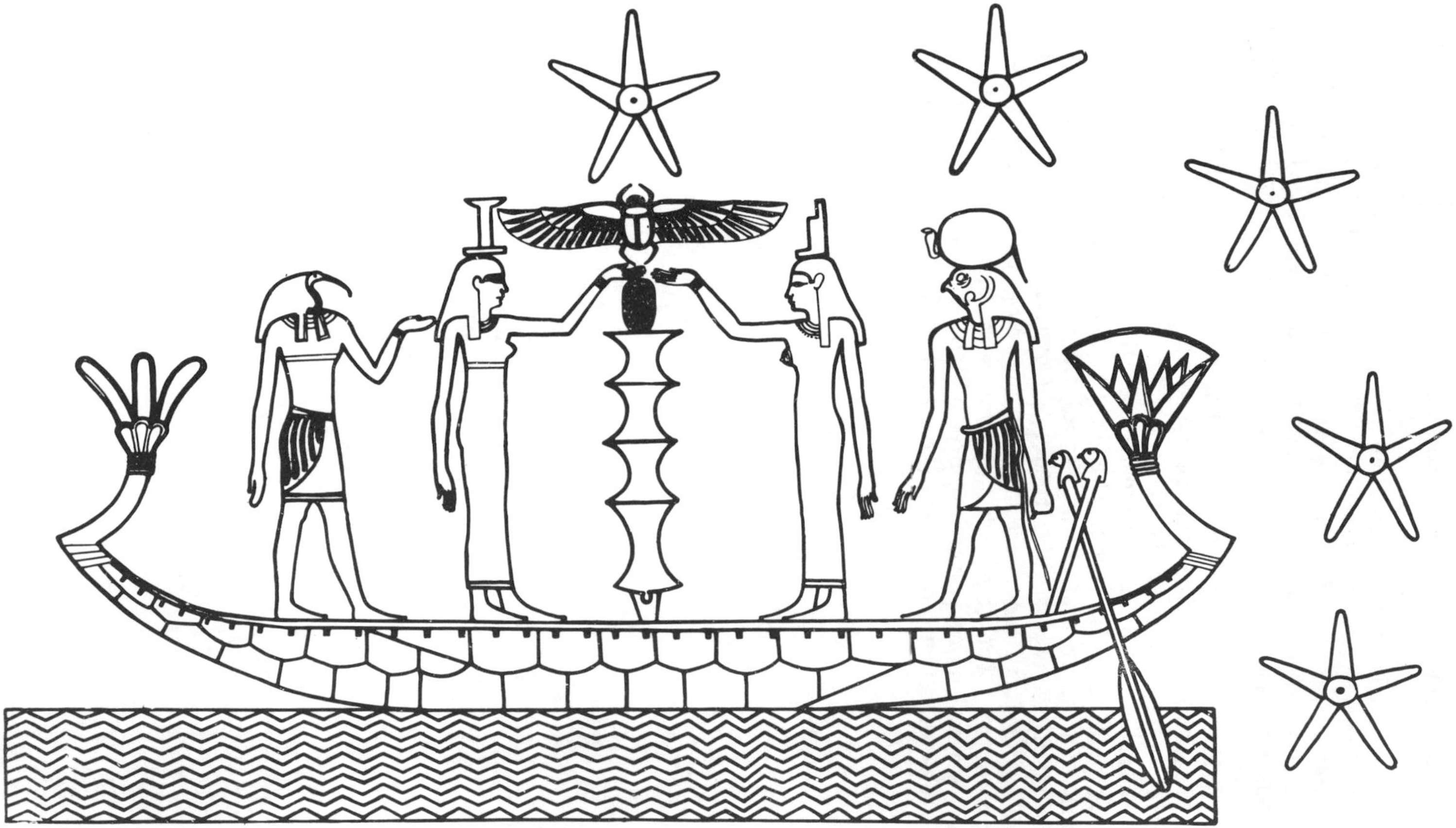

Fig. 81. One of the boats of the journey of the sun.

These are the six boats of the sun's journey by day and by night. They all have the same general shape, with sterns and prows shaped like flowers, but their interior details differ, as do the deities shown in each. The boat which I chose as an example (Fig. 81), depicts the first hour of the sun when the god Kheper comes out of his egg. Isis and Nephthys help, Horus stands near the steering oars and Thot stands behind Nephthys.

When E. Breccia visited Jabal al-Mawtā in 1928 he was very pessimistic about the result of any potential excavations there; it was hopeless, he thought. The work of the inhabitants in October, 1940, unsystematic as it was, showed that this judgement was far from the truth. Even now, after all the work of digging and cutting in all sides of the hill, I have not the slightest doubt that future excavations in this cemetery will bring forth new data, possibly leading to the discovery of new tombs. The tomb of Si-Amun is an example. Let us hope that several more painted tombs will be discovered in this hill, to help us better understand the ancient history of Siwa.

Index

(B)

(C)

(D)

(E)

(F)

(G)

(H)

Ḥaddādīn (family) 29
Hadrian (Roman Emperor) 89
Hairdressing 45
Hamilton, James (traveller) 107 ff.
Hamitic tribes 76
Ḥamrāyah (the desert) 3
Hannibal 88
Hapi (Son of Horus) 177, 194
Harsaphis (god) 158, 160
Ḥasan Bey al Shamāshirgī (governer of Biḥīrah) 104 ff.
Ḥassānah, al- 8
Hathor (goddess) 180, 183, 197
Ḥaṭīyah 33
Ḥaṭīyat Arsanīn 130
Hephaeston 148
Heracleopolis 158
Hercules 87, 147
Hermes 94
Herodotus 25, 79, 80, 81, 124, 160
Hierakonpolis 74
Ḥinnā 52, 53
Hölscher, Wilhelm 74
Hornemann, Frederick (German traveller) 101, 176
Horus (god) 73, 168, 197, 206
Hurghādah 9
Ḥusayn, al- 67
Ḥusayn Dughghār (Bedouin chieftain) 109

(I)

Ibn Duqmāq 93
Ibn Khaldūn 71
Ibn al-Wardī 93, 94
Ibn Wāṣif Shāh (Arab author) 93, 94, 95
Ibrāhīm Bāghī (head of al-Zanāyin) 97, 104
Idfū 2, nilometer of — 161, temple of — 70
Idrīsī, al- 93, 94
Iraq 7, 67
Isaac 64
Ishmael 64
Isis (goddess) 140, 177, 183, 194, 206
Islam, introduction of — 93 ff.,
Issus 84
'Izzāwī (date) 27

(J)

Jabal Amilāl 126
Jabal al-Dakrūr 17, 103, 127, rock tombs of — 124
Jabal Ḥamāṭah 9
Jabal Idrār 34
Jabal al-Mawtā 71, 88, 99, 103, 105, 107, 112, 120, 123, 124, 125, 150 tombs of — 173 ff.
Jabal al-Shāyib 9
Jaghbūb (oasis) 15, 37, 97, 110, 111, 112, 115, 121
Jallātī 127
Jami' al-Durrah (place) 65
Jird (sheet of wool) 55
Jupiter-Amun (god) 147, oasis of — 70, 100, oracle of — 87, 143

(K)

Karbalā' 67
Karshīf 18, 19, 21, 24
Karussah (cart) 47
Khalīj Tanṣar (place) 65
Khamīsah 17, 23, 27, 33, 36, 103, 126, 127, ḥaṭīyah — 33, 125, 126, salt lake of — 99, 129
Khamīsah (Queen) 126
Kharga 2, 8, 9, 11, 12, 13, 71, 76, 81, 82, 96, 174
Kharīdat al-'Ajā'ib 93
Khazīnah, al- 156
Kheper (god) 206
Khnumḥotep, tomb of — 76
Khonsu (god) 159, — temple at Karnak 159
Khuit-iotes 74
Khuraybīsh (King) 156, 174
Kirdāsah (village) 15, 47, 101
Kleobolus (Greek philosopher) 87

Kleombrotus 89
Kom Ombo, temple of — 156
Kuḥl 47, 62 (v. ornaments)
Kuḥl-pot 57

(L)

Labgī 27, 65, 67
Lafāyah (v. Westerners) 21, 29
Lakedaemonia 89
Lawāṭah (tribe) 71
Letorzec (French painter) 103
Libya 15, 37, 47, 74, 75, 76, 77, 79, 97
Libyans 76
Libyan Desert (v. Western Desert) 8, 33, 35
Libyssa 88
Lindos (Greek town) 87
Lūgīyāt 52 (v. ornaments)
Lysander (Spartan general) 83, 84

(M)

Macedonia 84, 147
Madanīyah (religious order) 113, 117
Maghārah, al- 8
Mahesa 159, 197
Mahr (dowry) 55 (v. Marriage)
Majābir, Bedouin of — 176
Makhmakh (kind of food) 65
Manaqyūsh 94, 95
Maqrīzī, al- (Arab historian) 24, 70, 93, 94 ff., 127, 129
Marāqī, al- 17, 23, 24, 127 ff.
Marāqīyah (land of al-Marāqī) 127, 129
Mareotis 36 (v. Maryūt)
Margūnah 27, 61
Marriage 55 ff.
Marsā Maṭrūḥ 14, 15, 37, 82, 87, 114, 116, 119
Maryūṭ 36, 73, 113, lake of — 74
Ma'ṣarah, al- 126
Mashwish (Libyan tribes) 79, 159
Maspero 156
Masrab Diqnāsh 15
Masrab al-Isṭabl 14, 15, 145
Ma't (goddess) 192
Mawlid (yearly festival) 65, 67
Mazaces (Persian Satrap) 84
Mecca (also Makkah) 29, 64, 96
Memphis 15, 85, 86, 135, 147, 150
Mesu-Isis, tomb of — 71, 187 ff., 191
Middle Ages 29, 70
Middle Egypt 73
Middle Kingdom 73, 76 ff.
Milāyah 21, 47 (v. clothes)
Milesia 80
Miletus (Greek town) 87
Miltiades (father of Cimon) 82
Mirkidah, Spring of — 129
Mishandid 126
Morals 43
Minyā, al- 10, 12, 13
Morocco 71
Mubārak, al- 34
Mughrah, al- (Spring) 15, 147
Moḥammad 'Alī 19, 34, 103, 104 ff., 176
Moḥammad Ṣāliḥ Ḥarb (Egyptian officer) 116 ff.
Muḥarram (month) 65, 67
Mūsā Būbash (head of the oasis of Siwa) 19
Mūsā ibn Nuṣayr (Arab general) 93
Muṣṭafā Māhir Bey (governer of Biḥīrah) 111
Mut (goddess) 160, 168, 197

(N)

Nakht-tit (father of Wenamun) 168
Naqb, al- 36
Nastit (mother of Niperpathot) 179
Necklace bead 45 (v. ornaments)
Nectanebo II (King) 167
Nefer-renpet (mother of Wenamun) 170
Nefer-ḥert (mother of Si-Amun) 191
Neḥem'awa (goddess) 160
Neith (goddess) 73
Nekhbeyt (goddess) 168, 197
Neolithic time 71, 72
Nephthys (goddess) 194
Nes-Thot (father of Niperpathot) 179

(O)

(P)

(Q)

(T)

(U)

(V)

(W)

(Y)

(Z)